THE CONTENT OF THE FORM

Le fait n'a jamais qu'une existence linguistique.
BARTHES

Hayden White

The Content of the Form

Narrative Discourse and Historical Representation

THE JOHNS HOPKINS UNIVERSITY PRESS   BALTIMORE AND LONDON

The Johns Hopkins University Press
701 West 40th Street
Baltimore, Maryland 21211
The Johns Hopkins Press Ltd., London

*The paper used in this publication meets the minimum requirements
of American National Standard for Information Sciences — Permanence
of Paper for Printed Library Materials, ANSI Z39.48–1984.*

LIBRARY OF CONGRESS CATALOGING-IN-PUBLICATION DATA
White, Hayden V., 1928–
  The content of the form.
  Bibliography: p.
  Includes index.
  1. Historiography.   2. History—Philosophy.   I. Title.
D13.W564   1987   901   86-21404
ISBN 0-8018-2937-2 (alk. paper)

FOR MARGARET . . . *perché nascesse una margherita.*

Contents

Preface

The essays in this volume represent some of the work I have done over the last seven years in historiography and theory of narrative and on the problem of representation in the human sciences. I have entitled the collection *The Content of the Form* because all of the essays deal, in one way or another, with the problem of the relation between narrative discourse and historical representation.

This relation becomes a problem for historical theory with the realization that narrative is not merely a neutral discursive form that may or may not be used to represent real events in their aspect as developmental processes but rather entails ontological and epistemic choices with distinct ideological and even specifically political implications. Many modern historians hold that narrative discourse, far from being a neutral medium for the representation of historical events and processes, is the very stuff of a mythical view of reality, a conceptual or pseudoconceptual "content" which, when used to represent real events, endows them with an illusory coherence and charges them with the kinds of meanings more characteristic of oneiric than of waking thought.

This critique of narrative discourse by recent proponents of scientific historiography is of a piece with the rejection of narrativity in literary modernism and with the perception, general in our time, that real life can never be truthfully represented as having the kind of formal coherency met with in the conventional, well-made or fabulistic story. Since its invention by Herodotus, traditional historiography has featured predominantly the belief that history itself consists of a congeries of lived stories, individual and collective, and that the principal task of historians is to uncover these stories and to retell them in a narrative, the truth of which would reside in the correspondence of the story told to the story lived by real people in the past. Thus conceived, the literary aspect of the historical narrative was supposed to inhere solely in certain stylistic embellishments that renderd the account vivid and interesting to the reader rather than in the kind of poetic inventiveness presumed to be characteristic of the writer of fictional narratives.

According to this view, it was possible to believe that whereas writers of fictions invented everything in their narratives—characters, events, plots, motifs, themes, atmosphere, and so on—historians invented nothing but certain rhetorical flourishes or poetic effects to the end of engaging their readers' attention and sustaining their interest in the true story they had to tell. Recent theories of discourse, however, dissolve the distinction between realistic and fictional discourses based on the presumption of an ontological difference between their respective referents, real and imaginary, in favor of stressing their common aspect as semiological apparatuses that produce meanings by the systematic substitution of signifieds (conceptual contents) for the extra-discursive entities that serve as their referents. In these semiological theories of discourse, narrative is revealed to be a particularly effective system of discursive meaning production by which individuals can be taught to live a distinctively "imaginary relation to their real conditions of existence," that is to say, an unreal but meaningful relation to the social formations in which they are indentured to live out their lives and realize their destinies as social subjects.

To conceive of narrative discourse in this way permits us to account for its universality as a cultural fact and for the interest that dominant social groups have not only in controlling what will pass for the authoritative myths of a given cultural formation but also in assuring the belief that social reality itself can be both lived and realistically comprehended as a story. Myths and the ideologies based on them presuppose the adequacy of stories to the representation of the reality whose meaning they purport to reveal. When belief in this adequacy begins to wane, the entire cultural edifice of a society enters into crisis, because not only is a specific system of beliefs undermined but the very condition of possibility of socially significant belief is eroded. This is why, I think, we have witnessed across the whole spectrum of the human sciences over the course of the last two decades a pervasive interest in the nature of narrative, its epistemic authority, its cultural function, and its general social significance.

Lately, many historians have called for a return to narrative representation in historiography. Philosophers have sought to justify narrative as a mode of explanation different from, but not less important than, the nomological-deductive mode favored in the physical sciences. Theologians and moralists have recognized the relation between a specifically narrativistic view of reality and the social vitality of any ethical system. Anthropologists, sociologists, psychologists, and psychoanalysts have begun to reexamine the function of narrative representation in the preliminary description of their objects of study. And cultural critics, Marxist and non-Marxist alike, have commented on the death of the great "master narratives" that formerly provided precognitive bases of belief in the higher civilizations and sustained, even in the early phases of industrial society, utopistic impulses to social transformation. And indeed, a whole cultural movement in the arts, generally gathered under the name post-modernism, is informed by a programmatic, if ironic, commitment to the return to narrative as one of its enabling presuppositions.

All of this can be taken as evidence of the recognition that narrative, far from being merely a form of discourse that can be filled with different contents, real or imaginary as the case may be, already possesses a content prior to any given actualization of it in speech or writing. It is this "content of the form" of narrative discourse in historical thought that is examined in the essays in this volume.

I have considerably revised the essays on Foucault, Jameson, and Ricoeur in order to take into account new work by these authors that appeared after their original publication. I have also changed the last essay so that it can be read without reference to the volume in which it originally appeared.

Acknowledgments

The essays included in this volume are revisions of pieces that appeared originally in the following places:

"The Value of Narrativity in the Representation of Reality," *Critical Inquiry* 7, no. 1 (1980).

"The Question of Narrative in Contemporary Historical Theory," *History and Theory* 23, no. 1 (1984).

"The Politics of Historical Interpretation: Discipline and De-Sublimation," *Critical Inquiry* 9, no. 1 (1982).

"Droysen's *Historik:* Historical Writing as a Bourgeois Science," *History and Theory* 19, no. 1 (1980).

"Foucault's Discourse," in *Structuralism and Since: From Lévi-Strauss to Derrida,* ed. John Sturrock (Oxford: Oxford University Press, 1979).

"Getting Out of History: Jameson's Redemption of Narrative," *Diacritics* 12 (Fall 1982).

"The Rule of Narrativity: Symbolic Discourse and the Experiences of Time in Ricoeur's Thought," in *A la recherche du sens/In Search of Meaning,* ed. Théodore F. Geraets (Ottawa: University of Ottawa Press, 1985).

"The Context in the Text: Method and Ideology in Intellectual History," in *Modern European Intellectual History: Reappraisals and New Perspectives,* ed. Dominick LaCapra and Steven L. Kaplan (Ithaca: Cornell University Press, 1982).

THE CONTENT OF THE FORM

1. The Value of Narrativity in the Representation of Reality

To raise the question of the nature of narrative is to invite reflection on the very nature of culture and, possibly, even on the nature of humanity itself. So natural is the impulse to narrate, so inevitable is the form of narrative for any report on the way things really happened, that narrativity could appear problematical only in a culture in which it was absent—or, as in some domains of contemporary Western intellectual and artistic culture, programmatically refused. Considered as panglobal facts of culture, narrative and narration are less problems than simply data. As the late (and profoundly missed) Roland Barthes remarked, narrative "is simply there like life itself . . . international, transhistorical, transcultural."[1] Far from being a problem, then, narrative might well be considered a solution to a problem of general human concern, namely, the problem of how to translate knowing into telling,[2] the problem of fashioning human experience into a form assimilable to structures of meaning that are generally human rather than culture-specific. We may not be able fully to comprehend specific thought patterns of another culture, but we have relatively less difficulty understanding a story coming from another culture, however exotic that culture may appear to us. As Barthes says, narrative is *translatable* without fundamental damage," in a way that a lyric poem or a philosophical discourse is not.

This suggests that far from being one code among many that a culture may utilize for endowing experience with meaning, narrative is a meta-code, a human universal on the basis of which transcultural messages about the nature of a shared reality can be transmitted. Arising, as Barthes says, between our experience of the world and our efforts to describe that experience in language, narrative "ceaselessly substitutes meaning for the straightforward copy of the events recounted." And it would follow that the absence of narrative capacity or a refusal of narrative indicates an absence or refusal of meaning itself.

But what kind of meaning is absent or refused? The fortunes of narrative in the history of historical writing give us some insight into this question. Historians do not have to report their truths about the real world in narrative form. They may choose other, nonnarrative, even antinarrative modes of representation, such as the meditation, the anatomy, or the epitome. Tocqueville, Burckhardt, Huizinga, and Braudel, to mention only the most notable masters of modern historiography, refused narrative in certain of their historiographical works, presumably on the assumption that the meaning of the events with which they wished to deal did not lend itself to representation in the narrative mode.[3] They refused to tell a story about the past, or rather, they did not tell a story with well-marked beginning, middle, and end phases; they did not impose upon the processes that interested them the form that we normally associate with storytelling. While they certainly narrated their accounts of the reality that they perceived, or thought they perceived, to exist within or behind the evidence they had examined, they did not narrativize that reality, did not impose upon it the form of a story. And their example permits us to distinguish between a historical discourse that narrates and a discourse that narrativizes, between a discourse that openly adopts a perspective that looks out on the world and reports it and a discourse that feigns to make the world speak itself and speak itself as a story.

The idea that narrative should be considered less as a form of representation than as a manner of speaking about events, whether real or imaginary, has been recently elaborated within a discussion of the relationship between discourse and narrative that has arisen in the wake of Structuralism and is associated with the work of Jakobson, Benveniste, Genette, Todorov, and Barthes. Here narrative is regarded as a manner of speaking characterized, as Genette expresses it, "by a certain number of exclusions and restrictive conditions" that the more "open" form of discourse does not impose upon the speaker.[4] According to Genette, Benveniste showed that

> certain grammatical forms like the pronoun "I" (and its implicit reference "thou"), the pronominal "indicators" (certain demonstrative pronouns), the adverbial indicators (like "here," "now,"

"yesterday," "today," "tomorrow," etc.) and, at least in French, certain verb tenses like the present, the present perfect, and the future, find themselves limited to discourse, while narrative in the strictest sense is distinguished by the exclusive use of the third person and of such forms as the preterite and the pluperfect.[5]

This distinction between discourse and narrative is, of course, based solely on an analysis of the grammatical features of two modes of discourse in which the "objectivity" of the one and the "subjectivity" of the other are definable primarily by a "linguistic order of criteria." The "subjectivity" of the discourse is given by the presence, explicit or implicit, of an "ego" who can be defined "only as the person who maintains the discourse." By contrast, the "objectivity of narrative is defined by the absence of all reference to the narrator." In the narrativizing discourse, then, we can say, with Benveniste, that "truly there is no longer a 'narrator.' The events are chronologically recorded as they appear on the horizon of the story. No one speaks. The events seem to tell themselves."[6]

What is involved in the production of a discourse in which "events seem to tell themselves," especially when it is a matter of events that are explicitly identified as real rather than imaginary, as in the case of historical representations?[7] In a discourse having to do with manifestly imaginary events, which are the "contents" of fictional discourses, the question poses few problems. For why should not imaginary events be represented as "speaking themselves"? Why should not, in the domain of the imaginary, even the stones themselves speak—like Memnon's column when touched by the rays of the sun? But real events should not speak, should not tell themselves. Real events should simply be; they can perfectly well serve as the referents of a discourse, can be spoken about, but they should not pose as the subjects of a narrative. The lateness of the invention of historical discourse in human history and the difficulty of sustaining it in times of cultural breakdown (as in the early Middle Ages) suggest the artificiality of the notion that real events could "speak themselves" or be represented as "telling their own story." Such a fiction would have posed no problems before the distinction between real and imaginary events was imposed upon the storyteller; storytelling becomes a problem only after two orders of events dispose themselves before the storyteller as possible components of stories and storytelling is compelled to exfoliate under the injunction to keep the two orders unmixed in discourse. What we wish to call mythic narrative is under no obligation to keep the two orders of events, real and imaginary, distinct from one another. Narrative becomes a problem only when we wish to give to real events the form of story. It is because real events do not offer themselves as stories that their narrativization is so difficult.

What is involved, then, in that finding of the "true story," that discovery of the "real story" within or behind the events that come to us in the chaotic form of "historical records"? What wish is enacted, what desire is gratified, by the fantasy that real events are properly represented when they can be shown to display the formal coherency of a story? In the enigma of this wish, this desire, we catch a glimpse of the cultural function of narrativizing discourse in general, an intimation of the psychological impulse behind the apparently universal need not only to narrate but to give to events an aspect of narrativity.

Historiography is an especially good ground on which to consider the nature of narration and narrativity because it is here that our desire for the imaginary, the possible, must contest with the imperatives of the real, the actual. If we view narration and narrativity as the instruments with which the conflicting claims of the imaginary and the real are mediated, arbitrated, or resolved in a discourse, we begin to comprehend both the appeal of narrative and the grounds for refusing it. If putatively real events are represented in a nonnarrative form, what kind of reality is it that offers itself, or is conceived to offer itself, to perception in this form? What would a nonnarrative representation of historical reality look like? In answering this question, we do not necessarily arrive at a solution to the problem of the nature of narrative, but we do begin to catch a glimpse of the basis for the appeal of narrativity as a form for the representation of events construed to be real rather than imaginary.

Fortunately, we have examples aplenty of representations of historical reality that are nonnarrative in form. Indeed, the *doxa* of the modern historiographical establishment has it that there are three basic kinds of historical representation—the annals, the chronicle, and the history proper—the imperfect "historicality" of two of which is evidenced in their failure to attain to full narrativity of the events of which they treat.[8] Needless to say, narrativity alone does not permit the distinction of the three kinds. In order for an account of events, even of past events or of past real events, to count as a proper history, it is not enough that it display all of the features of narrativity. In addition, the account must manifest a proper concern for the judicious handling of evidence, and it must honor the chronological order of the original occurrence of the events of which it treats as a baseline not to be transgressed in the classification of any given event as either a cause or an effect. But by common consent, it is not enough that an historical account deal in real, rather than merely imaginary, events; and it is not enough that the account represents events in its order of discourse according to the chronological sequence in which they originally occurred. The events must be not only registered within the chronological framework of their original occurrence but narrated as well, that is to say, revealed as possessing a structure, an order of meaning, that they do not possess as mere sequence.

Needless to say, also, the annals form lacks completely this narrative component, since it consists only of a list of events ordered in chronological sequence. The chronicle, by contrast, often seems to wish to tell a story, aspires to narrativity, but typically fails to achieve it. More specifically, the chronicle usually is marked by a failure to achieve narrative closure. It does not so much conclude as simply terminate. It starts out to tell a story but breaks off *in medias res,* in the chronicler's own present; it leaves things unresolved, or rather, it leaves them unresolved in a storylike way.

While annals represent historical reality as if real events did not display the form of story, the chronicler represents it as if real events appeared to human consciousness in the form of unfinished stories. And the official wisdom has it that however objective a historian might be in his reporting of events, however judicious he has been in his assessment of evidence, however punctilious he has been in his dating of *res gestae,* his account remains something less than a proper history if he has failed to give to reality the form of a story. Where there is no narrative, Croce said, there is no history.[9] And Peter Gay, writing from a perspective directly opposed to the relativism of Croce, puts it just as starkly: "Historical narration without analysis is trivial, historical analysis without narration is incomplete."[10] Gay's formulation calls up the Kantian bias of the demand for narration in historical representation, for it suggests, to paraphrase Kant, that historical narratives without analysis are empty, while historical analyses without narrative are blind. Thus we may ask, What kind of insight does narrative give into the nature of real events? What kind of blindness with respect to reality does narrativity dispell?

In what follows I treat the annals and chronicle forms of historical representation, not as the imperfect histories they are conventionally conceived to be, but rather as particular products of possible conceptions of historical reality, conceptions that are alternatives to, rather than failed anticipations of, the fully realized historical discourse that the modern history form is supposed to embody. This procedure will throw light on the problems of both historiography and narration alike and will illuminate what I conceive to be the purely conventional nature of the relationship between them. What will be revealed, I think, is that the very distinction between real and imaginary events that is basic to modern discussions of both history and fiction presupposes a notion of reality in which "the true" is identified with "the real" only insofar as it can be shown to possess the character of narrativity.

When we moderns look at an example of a medieval annals, we cannot but be struck by the apparent naîveté of the annalist; and we are inclined to ascribe this naîveté to the annalist's apparent refusal, inability, or unwillingness to transform the set of events ordered vertically as a file of annual markers into the elements of a linear/horizontal process. In other words, we are likely to be put off by the annalist's apparent failure to see that historical events dispose themselves to the percipient eye as stories waiting to be told, waiting to be narrated. But surely a genuinely historical interest would require that we ask not how or why the annalist failed to write a "narrative" but rather what kind of notion of reality led him to represent in the annals form what, after all, he took to be real events. If we could answer this question, we might be able to understand why, in our own time and cultural condition, we could conceive of narrativity itself as a problem.

Volume 1 of the *Monumenta Germaniae Historica,* in the *Scriptores* series, contains the text of the *Annals of Saint Gall,* a list of events that occurred in Gaul during the eighth, ninth, and tenth centuries of our era.[11] Although this text is "referential" and contains a representation of temporality[12]—Ducrot and Todorov's definition of what can count as a narrative—it possesses none of the characteristics that we normally attribute to a story: no central subject, no well-marked beginning, middle, and end, no peripeteia, and no identifiable narrative voice. In what are, for us, the theoretically most interesting segments of the text, there is no suggestion of any necessary connection between one event and another. Thus, for the period 709–34, we have the following entries:

709. Hard winter. Duke Gottfried died.
710. Hard year and deficient in crops.
711.

712. Flood everywhere.
713.
714. Pippin, mayor of the palace, died.
715. 716. 717.
718. Charles devastated the Saxon with great destruction.
719.
720. Charles fought against the Saxons.
721. Theudo drove the Saracens out of Aquitaine.
722. Great crops.
723.
724.
725. Saracens came for the first time.
726.
727.
728.
729.
730.
731. Blessed Bede, the presbyter, died.
732. Charles fought against the Saracens at Poitiers on Saturday.
733.
734.

This list immediately locates us in a culture hovering on the brink of
dissolution, a society of radical scarcity, a world of human groups
threatened by death, devastation, flood, and famine. All of the events
are extreme, and the implicit criterion for selecting them for remembrance is their liminal nature. Basic need—food, security from external
enemies, political and military leadership—and the threat of their not
being provided are the subjects of concern; but the connection between
basic needs and the conditions for their possible satisfaction is not explicitly commented on. Why "Charles fought against the Saxons"
remains as unexplained as why one year yielded "great crops" and
another produced "flood everywhere." Social events are apparently as
incomprehensible as natural events. They seem to have the same order
of importance or unimportance. They seem merely to have occurred,
and their importance seems to be indistinguishable from the fact that
they were recorded. In fact, it seems that their importance consists in
nothing other than their having been recorded.

And by whom they were recorded we have no idea; nor do we have
any idea of when they were recorded. The entry for 725—"Saracens

came for the *first* time"—suggests that this event at least was recorded after the Saracens had come a second time and set up what we might consider to be a genuine narrativist expectation; but the coming of the Saracens and their repulsion is not the subject of this account. Charles's fight "against the Saracens at Poitiers on Saturday" is recorded, but the outcome of the battle is not. And that "Saturday" is disturbing, because the month and day of the battle are not given. There are too many loose ends—no plot in the offing—and this is frustrating, if not disturbing, to the modern reader's story expectations as well as his desire for specific information.

We note further that this account is not really inaugurated. It simply begins with the "title" (is it a title?) *Anni domini,* which stands at the head of two columns, one of dates, the other of events. Visually, at least, this title links the file of dates in the left-hand column with the file of events in the right-hand column in a promise of signification that we might be inclined to take for mythical were it not for the fact that *Anni domini* refers us both to a cosmological story given in Scripture and to a calendrical convention that historians in the West still use to mark the units of their histories. We should not too quickly refer the meaning of the text to the mythic framework it invokes by designating the "years" as being "of the Lord," for these "years" have a regularity that the Christian mythos, with its clear hypotactical ordering of the events it comprises (Creation, Fall, Incarnation, Resurrection, Second Coming), does not possess. The regularity of the calendar signals the "realism" of the account, its intention to deal in real rather than imaginary events. The calendar locates events, not in the time of eternity, not in *kairotic* time, but in chronological time, in time as it is humanly experienced. This time has no high points or low points; it is, we might say, paratactical and endless. It has no gaps. The list of times is full even if the list of events is not.

Finally, the annals do not conclude; they simply terminate. The last entries are the following:

1045. 1046. 1047. 1048. 1049. 1050. 1051. 1052. 1053. 1054. 1055.
1056. The Emperor Henry died; and his son Henry succeeded to the rule.
1057. 1058. 1059. 1060. 1061. 1062. 1063. 1064. 1065. 1066. 1067. 1068. 1069. 1070. 1071. 1072.

The continuation of the list of years at the end of the account does, to be sure, suggest a continuation of the series ad infinitum, or rather, until the Second Coming. But there is no story conclusion. How could there be, since there is no central subject about which a story could be told?

Nonetheless, there must be a story, since there is surely a plot—if by plot we mean a structure of relationships by which the events contained in the account are endowed with a meaning by being identified as parts of an integrated whole. Here, however, I am referring, not to the myth of the Fall and Redemption (of the just parts of humankind) contained in the Bible, but to the list of dates of the years given in the left-hand file of the text, which confers coherence and fullness on the events by registering them under the years in which they occurred. To put it another way, the list of dates can be seen as the signified of which the events given in the right-hand column are the signifiers. The meaning of the events is their registration in this kind of list. This is why, I presume, the annalist would have felt little of the anxiety that the modern scholar feels when confronted with what appear to be gaps, discontinuities, and lack of causal connections between the events recorded in the text. The modern scholar seeks fullness and continuity in an order of events; the annalist has both in the sequence of the years. Which is the more "realistic" expectation?

Recall that we are dealing with neither oneiric nor infantile discourse. It may even be a mistake to call it discourse at all, but it has something discursive about it. The text summons up a "substance," operates in the domain of memory rather than in that of dream or fantasy, and unfolds under the sign of "the real" rather than that of "the imaginary." In fact, it seems eminently rational and, on the face of it, rather prudent in its manifest desire to record only those events about which there could be little doubt as to their occurrence and in its resolve not to interpellate facts on speculative grounds or to advance arguments about how the events are really connected to one another.

Modern commentators have remarked on the fact that the annalist recorded the Battle of Poitiers of 732 but failed to note the Battle of Tours which occurred in the same year and which, as every schoolboy knows, was one of "the ten great battles of world history."[13] But even if the annalist had known of Tours, what principle or rule of meaning would have required him to record it? It is only from our knowledge of the subsequent history of Western Europe that we can presume to rank events in terms of their world-historical significance, and even then that significance is less world historical than simply Western

European, representing a tendency of modern historians to rank events in the record hierarchically from within a perspective that is culture-specific, not universal at all.

It is this need or impulse to rank events with respect to their significance for the culture or group that is writing its own history that makes a narrative representation of real events possible. It is surely much more "universalistic" simply to record events as they come to notice. And at the minimal level on which the annals unfold, what gets put into the account is of much greater theoretical importance for the understanding of the nature of narrative than what gets left out. But this does raise the question of the function in this text of the recording of those years in which "nothing happened." Every narrative, however seemingly "full," is constructed on the basis of a set of events that might have been included but were left out; this is as true of imaginary narratives as it is of realistic ones. And this consideration permits us to ask what kind of notion of reality authorizes construction of a narrative account of reality in which continuity rather than discontinuity governs the articulation of the discourse.

If we grant that this discourse unfolds under a sign of a desire for the real, as we must do in order to justify the inclusion of the annals form among the types of historical representation, we must conclude that it is a product of an image of reality according to which the social system, which alone could provide the diacritical markers for ranking the importance of events, is only minimally present to the consciousness of the writer, or rather, is present as a factor in the composition of the discourse only by virtue of its absence. Everywhere it is the forces of disorder, natural and human, the forces of violence and destruction, that occupy the forefront of attention. The account deals in qualities rather than agents, figuring forth a world in which things happen to people rather than one in which people do things. It is the hardness of the winter of 709, the hardness of the year 710 and the deficiency of the crops of that year, the flooding of the waters in 712 and the imminent presence of death that recur with a frequency and regularity lacking in the representation of acts of human agency. Reality for this observer wears the face of adjectives that override the capacity of the nouns they modify to resist their determinacy. Charles does manage to devastate the Saxons, to fight against them, and Theudo even manages to drive the Saracens out of Aquitaine, but these actions appear to belong to the same order of existence as the natural events which bring either "great" crops or "deficient" harvests, and are as seemingly incomprehensible.

The absence of a principle for assigning importance or significance to events is signaled above all in the gaps in the list of events in
the right-hand file, for example in the year 711, in which, it seems,
"nothing happened." The overabundance of the waters noted for the
year 712 is preceded and followed by years in which also "nothing happened." Which puts one in mind of Hegel's remark that periods of
human happiness and security are blank pages in history. But the presence of these blank years in the annalist's account permits us to perceive, by way of contrast, the extent to which narrative strains for the
effect of having filled in all the gaps, of having put an image of continuity, coherency, and meaning in place of the fantasies of emptiness,
need, and frustrated desire that inhabit our nightmares about the destructive power of time. In fact, the annalist's account calls up a world
in which need is everywhere present, in which scarcity is the rule of existence, and in which all of the possible agencies of satisfaction are
lacking or absent or exist under imminent threat of death.

The notion of possible gratification is, however, implicitly present
in the list of dates that make up the left-hand column. The fullness of
this list attests to the fullness of time, or at least to the fullness of the
"years of the Lord." There is no scarcity of the years: they descend
regularly from their origin, the year of the Incarnation, and roll relentlessly on to their potential end, the Last Judgment. What is lacking in
the list of events to give it a similar regularity and fullness is a notion
of a social center by which to locate them with respect to one another
and to charge them with ethical or moral significance. It is the absence
of any consciousness of a social center that prohibits the annalist from
ranking the events he treats as elements of a historical field of occurrence. And it is the absence of such a center that precludes or undercuts
any impulse he might have had to work up his discourse into the form
of a narrative. Without such a center, Charles's campaigns against the
Saxons remain simply fights, the invasion of the Saracens simply a
coming, and the fact that the Battle of Poitiers was fought on a Saturday as important as the fact that the battle was even fought at all. All
this suggests to me that Hegel was right when he opined that a genuinely historical account had to display not only a certain form, namely,
the narrative, but also a certain content, namely, a politicosocial order.

In his introduction to his *Lectures on the Philosophy of History,*
Hegel wrote:

> In our language the term *History* unites the objective with the
> subjective side, and denotes quite as much the *historia rerum*

gestarum, as the *res gestae* themselves; on the other hand it comprehends not less what has *happened,* than the *narration* of what has happened. This union of the two meanings we must regard as of a higher order than mere outward accident; we must suppose historical narrations to have appeared contemporaneously with historical deeds and events. It is an internal vital principle common to both that produces them synchronously. Family memorials, patriarchal traditions, have an interest confined to the family and the clan. The *uniform course of events* [my italics] which such a condition implies, is no subject of serious remembrance; though distinct transactions or turns of fortune, may rouse Mnemosyne to form conceptions of them—in the same way as love and the religious emotions provoke imagination to give shape to a previously formless impulse. But it is only the state which first presents subject-matter that is not only *adapted* to the prose of History, but involves the production of such history in the very progress of its own being.[14]

Hegel goes on to distinguish between the kind of "profound sentiments," such as "love" and "religious intuition and its conceptions," and "that outward existence of a political constitution which is enshrined in . . . rational laws and customs." The latter, he says, "is an *imperfect* Present; and cannot be thoroughly understood without a knowledge of the past." This is why, he concludes, there are periods that, although filled with "revolutions, nomadic wanderings, and the strangest mutations," are destitute of any "*objective* history." And their destitution of an objective history is a function of the fact that they could produce "no *subjective* history, no annals."

We need not suppose, he remarks, "that the records of such periods have accidentally perished; rather, because they were not possible, do we find them wanting." And he insists that "only in a State cognizant of Laws, can distinct transactions take place, accompanied by such a clear consciousness of them as supplies the ability and suggests the necessity of an enduring record." When, in short, it is a matter of providing a narrative of real events, we must suppose that a subject of the sort that would provide the impulse to record its activities must exist.

Hegel insists that the proper subject of such a record is the state, but the state is to him an abstraction. The reality that lends itself to narrative representation is the conflict between desire and the law. Where there is no rule of law, there can be neither a subject nor the kind of event that lends itself to narrative representation. This is not a proposition that could be empirically verified or falsified, to be sure; it is in the nature of an enabling presupposition or hypothesis that permits us to imagine how both "historicity" and "narrativity" are possible. And it authorizes us to consider the proposition that neither is possible without some notion of the legal subject that can serve as the agent, agency, and subject of historical narrative in all of its manifestations, from the annals through the chronicle to the historical discourse as we know it in its modern realizations and failures.

The question of the law, legality, or legitimacy does not arise in those parts of the *Annals of Saint Gall* that we have been considering; at least, the question of human law does not arise. There is no suggestion that the coming of the Saracens represents a transgression of any limit, that it should not have been or might have been otherwise. Since everything that happened did so apparently in accordance with the divine will, it is sufficient simply to note its happening, to register it under the appropriate "year of the Lord" in which it occurred. The coming of the Saracens is of the same moral significance as Charles's fight against the Saxons. We have no way of knowing whether the annalist would have been impelled to flesh out his list of events and rise to the challenge of a narrative representation of those events if he had written in the consciousness of the threat to a specific social system and the possibility of falling into a condition of anarchy against which the legal system might have been erected.

But once we have been alerted to the intimate relationship that Hegel suggests exists between law, historicality, and narrativity, we cannot but be struck by the frequency with which narrativity, whether of the fictional or the factual sort, presupposes the existence of a legal system against which or on behalf of which the typical agents of a narrative account militate. And this raises the suspicion that narrative in general, from the folktale to the novel, from the annals to the fully realized "history," has to do with the topics of law, legality, legitimacy, or, more generally, authority. And indeed, when we look at what is supposed to be the next stage in the evolution of historical representation after the annals form, namely, the chronicle, this suspicion is borne out. The more historically self-conscious the writer of any form of historiography, the more the question of the social system and the law that sustains it, the authority of this law and its justification, and threats to the law occupy his attention. If, as Hegel suggests, historicality as a distinct mode of human existence is unthinkable without the presupposition of a system of law in relation to which a specifically legal subject could be constituted, then historical self-consciousness, the kind of consciousness capable of imagining the need to represent reality as a history, is conceivable only in terms of its interest in law, legality, and legitimacy, and so on.

Interest in the social system, which is nothing other than a system of human relationships governed by law, creates the possibility of conceiving the kinds of tensions, conflicts, struggles, and their various kinds of resolutions that we are accustomed to find in any representation of reality presenting itself to us as a history. This permits us to speculate that the growth and development of historical consciousness, which is attended by a concomitant growth and development of narrative capability (of the sort met with in the chronicle as against the annals form), has something to do with the extent to which the legal system functions as a subject of concern. If every fully realized story, however we define that familiar but conceptually elusive entity, is a kind of allegory, points to a moral, or endows events, whether real or imaginary, with a significance that they do not possess as a mere sequence, then it seems possible to conclude that every historical narrative has as its latent or manifest purpose the desire to moralize the events of which it treats. Where there is ambiguity or ambivalence regarding the status of the legal system, which is the form in which the subject encounters most immediately the social system in which he is enjoined to achieve a full humanity, the ground on which any closure of a story one might wish to tell about a past, whether it be a public or a private past, is lacking. And this suggests that narrativity, certainly in factual storytelling and probably in fictional storytelling as well, is intimately related to, if not a function of, the impulse to moralize reality, that is, to identify it with the social system that is the source of any morality that we can imagine.

The annalist of Saint Gall shows no concern about any system of merely human morality or law. The entry for 1056, "The Emperor Henry died; and his son Henry succeeded to the rule," contains in embryo the elements of a narrative. Indeed, it is a narrative, and its narrativity, in spite of the ambiguity of the connection between the first event (Henry's death) and the second (Henry's succession) suggested by the particle *and,* achieves closure by its tacit invocation of the legal system, the rule of genealogical succession, which the annalist takes for granted as a principle rightly governing the passing of authority from one generation to another. But this small narrative element, this "narreme," floats easily on the sea of dates that figures succession itself as a principle of cosmic organization. Those of us who know what was awaiting the younger Henry in his conflicts with his nobles and with the popes during the period of the Investiture Struggle, in which the issue of precisely where final authority on earth was located was fought out, may be irritated by the economy with which the annalist recorded an event so fraught with future moral and legal implications. The years 1057–72, which the annalist simply lists at the end of his record, provided more than enough "events" prefiguring the onset of this struggle, more than enough conflict to warrant a full narrative account of its inception. But the annalist simply ignored them. He apparently felt that he had done his duty solely by listing the dates of the years themselves. What is involved, we might ask, in this refusal to narrate?

To be sure, we can conclude — as Frank Kermode suggested — that the annalist of Saint Gall was not a very good diarist; and such a commonsensical judgment is manifestly justified. But the incapacity to keep a good diary is not theoretically different from the unwillingness to do so. And from the standpoint of an interest in narrative itself, a "bad" narrative can tell us more about narrativity than a good one. If it is true that the annalist of Saint Gall was an untidy or lazy narrator, we must ask what he lacked that would have made him a competent one. What is absent from his account that, if it had been present, would have permitted him to transform his chronology into a historical narrative?

The vertical ordering of events itself suggests that our annalist did not want in metaphoric or paradigmatic consciousness. He does not suffer from what Roman Jakobson calls "similarity disorder." Indeed, all of the events listed in the right-hand column appear to be considered as the same kind of event; they are all metonymies of the general condition of scarcity or overfullness of the "reality" the annalist is recording. *Difference,* significant variation within similitude, is figured only in the left-hand column, the list of dates. Each of these functions as a metaphor of the fullness and completion of the time of the Lord. The image of orderly succession that this column calls up has no counterpart in the events, natural and human, listed on the right-hand side. What the annalist lacked that would have led him to make a narrative out of the set of events he recorded was a capacity to endow events with the same kind of "propositionality" that is implicitly present in his representation of the sequence of dates. This lack resembles what Jakobson calls "contiguity disorder," a phenomenon represented in speech by "agrammatism" and in discourse by a dissolution of "the ties of grammatical coordination and subordination" by which

"word heaps" can be aggregated into meaningful sentences.[15] Our
annalist was not, of course, aphasic—as his capacity to contrive meaningful sentences amply shows—but he lacked the capacity to substitute
meanings for one another in chains of semantic metonymies that
would transform his list of events into a discourse about the events
considered as a totality evolving in time.

Now, the capacity to envision a set of events as belonging to the
same order of meaning requires some metaphysical principle by which
to translate difference into similarity. In other words, it requires a "subject" common to all of the referents of the various sentences that
register events as having occurred. If such a subject exists, it is the
"Lord" whose "years" are treated as manifestations of His power to
cause the events that occur in them. The subject of the account, then,
does not exist in time and could not therefore function as the subject
of a narrative. Does it follow that in order for there to be a narrative,
there must be some equivalent of the Lord, some sacral being endowed
with the authority and power of the Lord, existing in time? If so, what
could such an equivalent be?

The nature of such a being, capable of serving as the central
organizing principle of meaning of a discourse that is both realistic and
narrative in structure, is called up in the mode of historical representation known as the chronicle. By common consensus among historians
of historical writing, the chronicle is a "higher" form of historical
conceptualization and represents a mode of historiographical representation superior to the annals form.[16] Its superiority consists in its greater commprehensiveness, its organization of materials "by topics and
reigns," and its greater narrative coherency. The chronicle also has a
central subject—the life of an individual, town, or region; some great
undertaking, such as a war or crusade; or some institution, such as a
monarchy, episcopacy, or monastery. The link of the chronicle with the
annals is perceived in the perseverance of the chronology as the organizing principle of the discourse, and this is what makes the chronicle
something less than a fully realized "history." Moreover, the chronicle,
like the annals but unlike the history, does not so much conclude as
simply terminate; typically it lacks closure, that summing up of the
"meaning" of the chain of events with which it deals that we normally
expect from the well-made story. The chronicle typically promises
closure but does not provide it—which is one of the reasons why the
nineteenth-century editors of the medieval chronicles denied them the
status of genuine "histories."

Suppose that we look at the matter differently. Suppose we grant, not that the chronicle is a "higher" or more sophisticated representation of reality than the annals, but that it is merely a different kind of representation, marked by a desire for a kind of order and fullness in an account of reality that remains theoretically unjustified, a desire that is, until shown otherwise, purely gratuitous. What is involved in the imposition of this order and the provision of this fullness (of detail) which mark the differences between the annals and the chronicle?

I take as an example of the chronicle type of historical representation the *History of France* by one Richerus of Rheims, written on the eve of the year A.D. 1000 (ca. 998).[17] We have no difficulty recognizing this text as a narrative. It has a central subject ("the conflicts of the French"); a proper geographical center (Gaul) and a proper social center (the archepiscopal see of Rheims, beset by a dispute over which of two claimants to the office of archbishop is the legitimate occupant); and a proper beginning in time (given in a synoptic version of the history of the world from the Incarnation down to the time and place of Richerus's own writing of his account). But the work fails as a proper history, at least according to the opinion of later commentators, by virtue of two considerations. First, the order of the discourse follows the order of chronology; it presents events in the order of their occurrence and cannot, therefore, offer the kind of meaning that a narratologically governed account can be said to provide. Second, probably owing to the "annalistic" order of the discourse, the account does not so much conclude as simply terminate; it merely breaks off with the flight of one of the disputants for the office of archishop and throws onto the reader the burden for retrospectively reflecting on the linkages between the beginning of the account and its ending. The account comes down to the writer's own "yesterday," adds one more fact to the series that began with the Incarnation, and then simply ceases. As a result, all of the normal narratological expectations of the reader (this reader) remain unfulfilled. The work appears to be unfolding a plot but then belies its own appearance by merely stopping *in medias res,* with the cryptic notation "Pope Gregory authorizes Arnulfus to assume provisionally the episcopal functions, while awaiting the legal decision that would either confer these upon him or withdraw the right to them" (2:133).

And yet Richerus is a self-conscious narrator. He explicitly says at the outset of his account that he proposes "especially to preserve in writing [ad memoriam recuere scripto specialiter propositum est]" the "wars," "troubles," and "affairs" of the French and, moreover, to write them up in a manner superior to other accounts, especially that of one

Flodoard, an earlier scribe of Rheims who had written an annals on which Richerus has drawn for information. Richerus notes that he has drawn freely on Flodoard's work but that he has often "put other words" in the place of the original ones and "modified completely the style of the presentation [pro aliis longe diversissimo orationis scemate disposuisse]" (1:4). He also situates himself in a tradition of historical writing by citing such classics as Caesar, Orosius, Jerome, and Isidore as authorities for the early history of Gaul and suggests that his own personal observations gave him insight into the facts he is recounting that no one else could claim. All of this suggests a certain self-consciousness about his own discourse that is manifestly lacking in the writer of the *Annals of Saint Gall*. Richerus's discourse is a fashioned discourse, the narrativity of which, compared with that of the annalist, is a function of the self-consciousness with which this fashioning activity is entered upon.

Paradoxically, however, it is this self-conscious fashioning activity, an activity that gives to Richerus's work the aspect of a historical narrative, that decreases its "objectivity" as a historical account — or so the consensus of modern analysts of the text has it. For example, a modern editor of the text, Robert Latouche, indicts Richerus's pride in the originality of his style as the cause of his failure to write a proper history. "Ultimately," Latouche notes, "the *History* of Richerus is not, properly speaking [*proprement parler*], a history but a work of rhetoric composed by a monk . . . who sought to imitate the techniques of Salluste." And he adds, "What interested him was not the material [*matière*], which he molded to fit his fancy, but the form" (1:xi).

Latouche is certainly right in saying that Richerus fails as a historian supposedly interested in the "facts" of a certain period of history, but he is just as surely wrong in his suggestion that the work fails as a history because of the writer's interest in "form" rather than "matter." By *matière,* of course, Latouche means the referents of the discourse, the events taken individually as objects of representation. But Richerus is interested in "the conflicts of the French [Gallorum congressibus in volumine regerendis]" (1:2), especially the conflict in which his patron, Gerbert, archbishop of Rheims, was currently involved for control of the see. Far from being interested primarily in form rather than matter or content, Richerus was only interested in the latter, for this conflict was one in which his own future was entailed. Where authority lay for the direction of affairs in the see of Rheims was the question that Richerus hoped to help resolve by the composition of his narrative. And we can legitimately suppose that his impulse to write a narrative of this conflict was in some way connected with a desire on his part to represent (both in the sense of writing about and in the sense of acting as an agent of) an authority whose legitimacy hinged upon the establishment of "facts" of a specifically historical order.

Indeed, once we note the presence of the theme of authority in this text, we also perceive the extent to which the truth claims of the narrative and indeed the very right to narrate hinge upon a certain relationship to authority per se. The first authority invoked by the author is that of his patron, Gerbert; it is by his authority that the account is composed ("imperii tui, pater sanctissime G[erbert], auctoritas seminarium dedit" [1:2]). Then there are those "authorities" represented by the classic texts on which he draws for his construction of the early history of the French (Caesar, Orosius, Jerome, and so on). There is the "authority" of his predecessor as a historian of the see of Rheims, Flodoard, an authority with whom he contests as narrator and on whose style he professes to improve. It is on his own authority that Richerus effects this improvement, by putting "other words" in place of Flodoard's and modifying "completely the style of presentation." There is, finally, not only the authority of the Heavenly Father, who is invoked as the ultimate cause of everything that happens, but the authority of Richerus's own father (referred to throughout the manuscript as "p.m." [pater meus] [1:xiv]), who figures as a central subject of a segment of the work and as the witness on whose authority the account in this segment is based.

The problem of authority pervades the text written by Richerus in a way that cannot be ascribed to the text written by the annalist of Saint Gall. For the annalist there is no need to claim the authority to narrate events, since there is nothing problematical about their status as manifestations of a reality that is being contested. Since there is no "contest," there is nothing to narrativize, no need for them to "speak themselves" or be represented as if they could "tell their own story." It is necessary only to record them in the order that they come to notice, for since there is no contest, there is no story to tell. It is because there was a contest that there is something to narrativize for Richerus. But it is not because the contest was not resolved that the quasi narrative produced by Richerus has no closure; for in fact the contest *was* resolved—by the flight of Gerbert to the court of King Otto and the installation of Arnulfus as archbishop of Rheims by Pope Gregory.

What was lacking for a proper discursive resolution, a narrativizing resolution, was the moral principle in light of which Richerus might have judged the resolution as either just or unjust. Reality itself has judged the resolution by resolving it as it has done. To be sure, there is the suggestion that a kind of justice was provided for Gerbert by King Otto, who, "having recognized Gerbert's learning and genius, installs him as bishop of Ravenna." But that justice is located at another place and is disposed by another authority, another king. The end of the discourse does not cast its light back over the events originally recorded in order to redistribute the force of a meaning that was immanent in all of the events from the beginning. There is no justice, only force, or, rather, only an authority that presents itself as different kinds of forces.

I do not offer these reflections on the relation between historiography and narrative as aspiring to anything other than an attempt to illuminate the distinction between story elements and plot elements in the historical discourse. Common opinion has it that the plot of a narrative imposes a meaning on the events that make up its story level by revealing at the end a structure that was immanent in the events all along. What I am trying to establish is the nature of this immanence in any narrative account of real events, events that are offered as the proper content of historical discourse. These events are real not because they occurred but because, first, they were remembered and, second, they are capable of finding a place in a chronologically ordered sequence. In order, however, for an account of them to be considered a historical account, it is not enough that they be recorded in the order of their original occurrence. It is the fact that they can be recorded otherwise, in an order of narrative, that makes them, at one and the same time, questionable as to their authenticity and susceptible to being considered as tokens of reality. In order to qualify as historical, an event must be susceptible to at least two narrations of its occurrence. Unless at least two versions of the same set of events can be imagined, there is no reason for the historian to take upon himself the authority of giving the true account of what really happened. The authority of the historical narrative is the authority of reality itself; the historical account endows this reality with form and thereby makes it desirable by the imposition upon its processes of the formal coherency that only stories possess.

The history, then, belongs to the category of what might be called "the discourse of the real," as against the "discourse of the imaginary" or "the discourse of desire." The formulation is Lacanian, obviously, but I do not wish to push its Lacanian aspects too far. I merely wish to suggest that we can comprehend the appeal of historical discourse by recognizing the extent to which it makes the real desirable, makes the real into an object of desire, and does so by its imposition, upon events that are represented as real, of the formal coherency that stories possess. Unlike that of the annals, the reality represented in the historical narrative, in "speaking itself," speaks to us, summons us from afar (this "afar" is the land of forms), and displays to us a formal coherency to which we ourselves aspire. The historical narrative, as against the chronicle, reveals to us a world that is putatively "finished," done with, over, and yet not dissolved, not falling apart. In this world, reality wears the mask of a meaning, the completeness and fullness of which we can only imagine, never experience. Insofar as historical stories can be completed, can be given narrative closure, can be shown to have had a plot all along, they give to reality the odor of the ideal. This is why the plot of a historical narrative is always an embarrassment and has to be presented as "found" in the events rather than put there by narrative techniques.

The embarrassment of plot to historical narrative is reflected in the all but universal disdain with which modern historians regard the "philosophy of history," of which Hegel is the modern paradigmatic example. This (fourth) form of historical representation is condemned becauses it consists of nothing but plot; its story elements exist only as manifestations, epiphenomena of the plot structure, in the service of which its discourse is disposed. Here reality wears a face of such regularity, order, and coherence that it leaves no room for human agency, presenting an aspect of such wholeness and completeness that it intimidates rather than invites imaginative identification. But in the plot of the philosophy of history, the various plots of the various histories that tell us of merely regional happenings in the past are revealed for what they really are: images of that authority that summons us to participation in a moral universe that but for its story form, would have no appeal at all.

This puts us close to a possible characterization of the demand for closure in the history, for the want of which the chronicle form is adjudged to be deficient as a narrative. The demand for closure in the historical story is a demand, I suggest, for moral meaning, a demand that sequences of real events be assessed as to their significance as elements of a moral drama. Has any historical narrative ever been written that was not informed not only by moral awareness but specifically by the moral authority of the narrator? It is difficult to think of any historical work produced during the nineteenth century, the classic age of historical narrative, that was not given the force of a moral judgment on the events it related.

But we do not have to prejudge the matter by looking at historical texts composed in the nineteenth century. We can perceive the operations of moral consciousness in the achievement of narrative fullness in an example of late medieval historiography, the *Cronica* of Dino Compagni, written between 1310 and 1312 and generally recognized as a proper historical narrative.[18] Dino's work not only "fills in the gaps" that might have been left in an annalistic handling of its subject matter (the struggles between the Black and White factions of the dominant Guelf Party in Florence between 1280 and 1312) and organizes its story according to a well-marked ternary plot structure but achieves narrative fullness by explicitly invoking the idea of a social system to serve as a fixed reference point by which the flow of ephemeral events can be endowed with specifically moral meaning. In this respect, the *Cronica* clearly displays the extent to which the chronicle must approach the form of an allegory, moral or anagogical as the case may be, in order to achieve both narrativity and historicality.

It is interesting to observe that as the chronicle form is displaced by the proper history, certain of the features of the former disappear. First of all, no explicit patron is invoked. Dino's narrative does not unfold under the authority of a specific patron as Richerus's does. He simply asserts his right to recount notable events (*cose notevoli*) that he has "seen and heard" on the basis of a superior capacity of foresight. "No one saw these events in their beginnings [*principi*] more certainly than I," he says. His prospective audience is not, then, a specific ideal reader, as Gerbert was for Richerus, but rather a group that is conceived to share his perspective on the true nature of all events: those citizens of Florence capable, as he puts it, of recognizing "the benefits of God, who rules and governs for all time." At the same time, he speaks to another group, the depraved citizens of Florence, those responsible for the "conflicts" (*discordie*) that had wracked the city for some three decades. To the former, his narrative is intended to hold out the hope of deliverance from these conflicts; to the latter, it is intended as an admonition and a threat of retribution. The chaos of the last ten years is contrasted with more "prosperous" years to come, after the emperor Henry VII has descended on Florence in order to punish a people whose "evil customs and false profits" have "corrupted and spoiled the whole world."[19] What Kermode calls "the weight of meaning" of the events recounted is "thrown forward" onto a future just beyond the immediate present, a future fraught with moral judgment and punishment for the wicked.[20]

The jeremiad with which Dino's work closes marks it as belonging to a period before which a genuine historical "objectivity," which is to say, a secularist ideology, had been established—so the commentators tell us. But it is difficult to see how the kind of narrative fullness for which Dino Compagni is praised could have been attained without the implicit invocation of the moral standard that he uses to distinguish between those real events worthy of being recorded and those unworthy of it. The events that are actually recorded in the narrative appear to be real precisely insofar as they belong to an order of moral existence, just as they derive their meaning from their placement in this order. It is because the events described conduce to the establishment of social order or fail to do so that they find a place in the narrative attesting to their reality. Only the contrast between the governance and rule of God, on the one side, and the anarchy of the current social situation in Florence, on the other, could justify the apocalyptical tone and narrative function of the final paragraph, with its image of the emperor who will come to chasten those "who brought evil into the world through [their] bad habits." And only a moral authority could justify the turn in the narrative that permits it to come to an end. Dino explicitly identifies the end of his narrative with a "turn" in the moral order of the world: "The world is beginning now to turn over once more [*Ora vi si ricomincia il mondo a revolgere adosso*] . . .: the emperor is coming to take you and despoil you, by land and by sea."[21]

It is this moralistic ending that keeps Dino's *Cronica* from meeting the standard of a modern, "objective" historical account. Yet it is this moralism that alone permits the work to end, or rather to conclude, in a way different from the way the annals and the chronicle forms do. But on what other grounds could a narrative of real events possibly conclude? When it is a matter of recounting the concourse of real events, what other "ending" could a given sequence of such events have than a "moralizing" ending? What else could narrative closure consist of than the passage from one moral order to another? I confess that I cannot think of any other way of "concluding" an account of real events, for we cannot say, surely, that any sequence of real events actually comes to an end, that reality itself disappears, that events of the order of the real have ceased to happen. Such events could only seem to have ceased to happen when meaning is shifted, and shifted by narrative means, from one physical or social space to another. Where moral sensitivity is lacking, as it seems to be in an annalistic account of reality, or is only potentially present, as it appears to be in a chronicle, not only meaning but the means to track such shifts of meaning, that is, narrativity, appears to be lacking also. Where, in any account of reality, narrativity is present, we can be sure that morality or a moralizing impulse is present too. There is no other way that reality can be endowed with the kind of meaning that both displays itself in its consummation and withholds itself by its displacement to another story "waiting to be told" just beyond the confines of "the end."

What I have been working around to is the question of the value attached to narrativity itself, especially in representations of reality of the sort embodied in historical discourse. It may be thought that I have stacked the cards in favor of my thesis — that narrativizing discourse serves the purpose of moralizing judgments — by my use of exclusively medieval materials. And perhaps I have, but it is the modern historiographical community that has distinguished between the annals, chronicle, and history forms of discourse on the basis of their attainment of narrative fullness or failure to attain it. And this same scholarly community has yet to account for the fact that just when, by its own account, historiography was transformed into an "objective" discipline, it was the narrativity of the historical discourse that was celebrated as one of the signs of its maturation as a fully "objective" discipline — a science of a special sort but a science nonetheless. It is historians themselves who have transformed narrativity from a manner of speaking into a paradigm of the form that reality itself displays to a "realistic" consciousness. It is they who have made narrativity into a value, the presence of which in a discourse having to do with "real" events signals at once its objectivity, its seriousness, and its realism.

What I have sought to suggest is that this value attached to narrativity in the representation of real events arises out of a desire to have real events display the coherence, integrity, fullness, and closure of an image of life that is and can only be imaginary. The notion that sequences of real events possess the formal attributes of the stories we tell about imaginary events could only have its origin in wishes, daydreams, reveries. Does the world really present itself to perception in the form of well-made stories, with central subjects, proper beginnings, middles, and ends, and a coherence that permits us to see "the end" in every beginning? Or does it present itself more in the forms that the annals and chronicle suggest, either as mere sequence without beginning or end or as sequences of beginnings that only terminate and never conclude? And does the world, even the social world, ever really come to us as already narrativized, already "speaking itself" from beyond the horizon of our capacity to make scientific sense of it? Or is the fiction of such a world, capable of speaking itself and of displaying itself as a form of a story, necessary for the establishment of that moral authority without which the notion of a specifically social reality would be unthinkable? If it were only a matter of realism in representation, one could make a pretty good case for both the annals and chronicle forms as paradigms of ways that reality offers itself to perception. Is it possible that their supposed want of objectivity, manifested in their failure to narrativize reality adequately, has to do, not at all with the modes of perception that they presuppose, but with their failure to represent the moral under the aspect of the aesthetic? And could we answer that question without giving a narrative account of the history of objectivity itself, an account that would already prejudice the outcome of the story we would tell in favor of the moral in general? Could we ever narrativize without moralizing?

2. The Question of Narrative in Contemporary Historical Theory

In contemporary historical theory the topic of narrative has been the subject of extraordinarily intense debate. Viewed from one perspective, this is surprising; on the face of it, there should be very little to debate about narrative. Narration is a manner of speaking as universal as language itself, and narrative is a mode of verbal representation so seemingly natural to human consciousness that to suggest that it is a problem might well appear pedantic.[1] But it is precisely because the narrative mode of representation is so natural to human consciousness, so much an aspect of everyday speech and ordinary discourse, that its use in any field of study aspiring to the status of a science must be suspect. For whatever else a science may be, it is also a practice that must be as critical about the way it describes its objects of study as it is about the way it explains their structures and processes. Viewing modern sciences from this perspective, we can trace their development in terms of their progressive demotion of the narrative mode of representation in their descriptions of the phenomena that their specific objects of study comprise. And this in part explains why the humble subject of narrative should be so widely debated by historical theorists in our time. To many of those who would transform historical studies into a science, the continued use by historians of a narrative mode of representation is an index of a failure at once methodological and theoretical. A discipline that produces narrative accounts of its subject matter as an end in itself seems theoretically unsound; one that investigates its data in the interest of telling a story about them appears methodologically deficient.[2]

Within the field of historical studies, however, the narrative has been viewed for the most part neither as a product of a theory nor as the basis for a method but rather as a form of discourse that may or may not be used for the representation of historical events, depending upon whether the primary aim is to describe a situation, analyze a historical process, or tell a story.[3] According to this view, the amount of narrative in a given history will vary, and its function will change depending on whether it is conceived as an end in itself or only as a means to some other end. Obviously, the amount of narrative will be greatest in accounts designed to tell a story, least in those intended to provide an analysis of the events of which it treats. Where the aim in view is the telling of a story, the problem of narrativity turns on the issue of whether historical events can be truthfully represented as manifesting the structures and processes of events met with more commonly in certain kinds of "imaginative" discourses, that is, such fictions as the epic, the folk tale, myth, romance, tragedy, comedy, farce, and the like. This means that what distinguishes "historical" from "fictional" stories is first and foremost their content, rather than their form. The content of historical stories is real events, events that really happened, rather than imaginary events, events invented by the narrator. This implies that the form in which historical events present themselves to a prospective narrator is found rather than constructed.

For the narrative historian, the historical method consists in investigating the documents in order to determine what is the true or most plausible story that can be told about the events of which they are evidence. A true narrative account, according to this view, is less a product of the historian's poetic talents, as the narrative account of imaginary events is conceived to be, than it is a necessary result of a proper application of historical "method." The form of the discourse, the narrative, adds nothing to the content of the representation; rather it is a simulacrum of the structure and processes of real events. And insofar as this representation resembles the events that it represents, it can be taken as a true account. The story told in the narrative is a mimesis of the story lived in some region of historical reality, and insofar as it is an accurate imitation, it is to be considered a truthful account thereof.

In traditional historical theory, at least since the mid-nineteenth century, the story told about the past was distinguished from whatever explanation might be offered of why the events related in the story occurred when, where, and how they did. After the historian had discovered the true story of "what happened" and accurately represented it in a narrative, he might abandon the narrational manner of speaking and, addressing the reader directly, speaking in his own voice, and representing his considered opinion as a student of human affairs, dilate on what the story he had told indicated about the nature of the period, place, agents, agencies, and processes (social, political, cultural, and so forth) he had studied. This aspect of the historical discourse was called by some theorists the dissertative mode of address and was considered to comprise a form as well as a content different from those of the narrative.[4] Its form was that of the logical demonstration, and its content the historian's own thought about the events, regarding either their causes or their significance for the understanding of the types of events of which the lived story was an instantiation. This meant, among other things, that the dissertative aspect of a historical discourse was to be assessed on grounds different from those used to assess the narrative aspect. The historian's dissertation was an interpretation of what he took to be the true story, while his narration was a representation of what he took to be the real story. A given historical discourse might be factually accurate and as veracious in its narrative aspect as the evidence permitted and still be assessed as mistaken, invalid, or inadequate in its dissertative aspect. The facts might be truthfully set forth, and the interpretation of them misguided. Or, conversely, a given interpretation of events might be suggestive, brilliant, perspicuous, and so on, and still not be justified by the facts or square with the story related in the narrative aspect of the discourse. But whatever the relative merits of the narrative and the dissertative aspects of a given historical discourse, the former was fundamental, the latter secondary. As Benedetto Croce put it in a famous dictum, "Where there is no narrative, there is no history."[5] Until the real story had been determined and the true story told, there was nothing of a specifically historical nature to interpret.

But this nineteenth-century view of the nature and function of narrative in historical discourse was based on an ambiguity. On the one hand, narrative was regarded as only a form of discourse, a form featuring the story as its content. On the other hand, this form was itself a content insofar as historical events were conceived to manifest themselves in reality as elements and aspects of stories. The form of the story told was supposed to be necessitated by the form of the story enacted by historical agents. But what about those events and processes attested by the documentary record that did not lend themselves to representation in a story but could be represented as objects of reflection only in some other discursive mode, such as the encyclopedia, the epitome, the tableau, the statistical table or series? Did this mean that such objects were "unhistorical," that is, that they did not belong to history; or did the possibility of representing them in a nonnarrative mode of discourse indicate a limitation of the narrative mode and even a prejudice regarding what could be said to have a history?

Hegel had insisted that a specifically historical mode of being was linked to a specifically narrative mode of representation by a shared "internal vital principle."[6] This principle was, for him, nothing other than politics, which was both the precondition of the kind of interest in the past that informed historical consciousness and the pragmatic basis for the production and preservation of the kinds of records that made historical inquiry possible:

> We must suppose historical narrations to have appeared contem-
> poraneously with historical deeds and events. Family memorials,
> patriarchal traditions, have an interest confined to the family and
> the clan. The uniform course of events that such a condition
> implies is no subject of serious remembrance. . . . It is the state
> that first presents a subject matter that not only is *adapted* to the
> prose of history but involves the production of such history in the
> very progress of its own being. (83)

In other words, for Hegel, the content (or referent) of the specifically historical discourse was not the real story of what happened but the peculiar relation between a public present and a past that a state endowed with a constitution made possible.

> Profound sentiments generally, such as love, as well as religious
> intuition and its conceptions, are in themselves complete — con-
> stantly present and satisfying; but that outward existence of a
> political constitution enshrined in its rational laws and customs is
> an *imperfect* present and cannot be thoroughly understood with-
> out a knowledge of the past. (83–84)

Hence the ambiguity of the term *history*. It "unites the objective with the subjective side and denotes the *historia rerum gestarum* quite as much as the *res gestae* themselves" and "comprehends what has *happened* no less than the *narration* of what has happened." This ambiguity, Hegel said, reflects "a higher order than mere outward accident [müseen wir für höhere Art als für eine bloss äusserliche Zufälligkeit anschen]" (83). Narrative per se did not distinguish historiography from other kinds of discourses, nor did the reality of the events recounted distinguish historical from other kinds of narrative.

It was the interest in a specifically political mode of human community that made a specifically historical mode of inquiry possible; and the political nature of this mode of community necessitated a narrative mode for its representation. Thus considered, historical studies had their own proper subject matter, namely, "those momentous collisions between existing, acknowledged duties, laws, and rights and those contingencies that are adverse to this fixed system" (44–45); their own proper aim, namely, to depict these kinds of conflicts; and their own proper mode of representation, the (prose) narrative. When either the subject matter, the aim, or the mode of representation is lacking in a discourse, it may still be a contribution to knowledge, but something less than a full contribution to historical knowledge.

Hegel's views on the nature of historical discourse had the merit of making explicit what was acknowledged in the dominant practice of historical scholarship in the nineteenth century, namely, an interest in the study of political history, which was, however, often hidden behind vague professions of an interest in narration as an end in itself. The *doxa* of the profession, in other words, took the form of the historical discourse—what it called the true story—for the content of the discourse, while the real content, politics, was represented as being primarily only a vehicle for or an occasion of storytelling. This is why most professional historians of the nineteenth century, although they specialized in political history, tended to regard their work as a contribution less to a science of politics than to the political lore of national communities. The narrative form in which their discourses were cast was fully commensurate with this latter aim. But it reflects both an unwillingness to make historical studies into a science and, what is more important, a resistance to the idea that politics should be an object of scientific study to which historiography might contribute.[7] It is in this respect, rather than in any overt espousal of a specific political program or cause, that nineteenth-century professional historiography can be regarded as ideological. For if ideology is the treatment of the form of a thing as a content or essence, nineteenth-century historiography is ideological precisely insofar as it takes the characteristic form of its discourse, the narrative, as a content, namely, narrativity, and treats "narrativity" as an essence shared by both discourses and sets of events alike.

It is within the context of considerations such as these that we may attempt to characterize the discussions of narrative in historical theory that have taken place in the West over the last two or three decades. We can discern four principal strains in these discussions.

First, that represented by certain Anglo-American analytical philosophers (Walsh, Gardiner, Dray, Gallie, Morton White, Danto, Mink), who have sought to establish the epistemic status of narrativity, considered as a kind of explanation especially appropriate to the explication of historical, as against natural, events and processes.[8] Second, that of certain social-scientifically oriented historians, of whom the members of the French *Annales* group may be considered exemplary. This group (Braudel, Furet, Le Goff, Le Roy-Ladurie, and so on) regarded narrative historiography as a nonscientific, even ideological representational strategy, the extirpation of which was necessary for the transformation of historical studies into a genuine science.[9] Third, that of certain semiologically oriented literary theorists and philosophers (Barthes, Foucault, Derrida, Todorov, Julia Kristeva, Benveniste, Genette, Eco), who have studied narrative in all of its manifestations and viewed it as simply one discursive "code" among others, which might or might not be appropriate for the representation of reality.[10] And finally, that of certain hermeneutically oriented philosophers, such as Gadamer and Ricoeur, who have viewed narrative as the manifestation in discourse of a specific kind of time-consciousness or structure of time.[11]

We might have added a fifth category, namely, that of certain historians who can be said to belong to no particular philosophical or methodological persuasion but speak from the standpoint of the *doxa* of the profession, as defenders of a craft notion of historical studies, and who view narrative as a perfectly respectable way of "doing" history (as J. H. Hexter puts it) or "practicing" it (as Geoffrey Elton would have it).[12] But this group does not so much represent a theoretical position as incarnate a traditional attitude of eclecticism in historical studies — an eclecticism that is a manifestation of a certain suspicion of theory itself as an impediment to the proper practice of historical inquiry, conceived as empirical inquiry.[13] For this group, narrative representation poses no significant theoretical problem. We need, therefore, only register this position as the *doxa* against which a genuinely theoretical inquiry must take its rise and pass on to a consideration of those for whom narrative is a problem and an occasion for theoretical reflection.

The *Annales* group have been most critical of narrative history, but in a rather more polemical than a distinctively theoretical way. For them, narrative history was simply the history of past politics and, moreover, political history conceived as short-term, "dramatic" conflicts and crises lending themselves to "novelistic" representations,

of a more "literary" than a properly "scientific" kind. As Braudel put
it in a well-known essay:

> The narrative history so dear to the heart of Ranke offer[s]
> us. . . . [a] gleam but no illumination; facts but no humanity.
> Note that this narrative history always claims to relate "things just
> as they really happened." . . . In fact, though, in its own covert
> way, narrative history consists of an interpretation, an authentic
> philosophy of history. To the narrative historians, the life of men
> is dominated by dramatic accidents, by the actions of those excep-
> tional beings who occasionally emerge, and who often are the
> masters of their own fate and even more of ours. And when they
> speak of "general history," what they are really speaking of is the
> intercrossing of such exceptional destinies, for obviously each hero
> must be matched against another. A delusive fallacy, as we all
> know.[14]

This position was taken up rather uniformly by other members of
the *Annales* group, but more as a justification for their promotion of
a historiography devoted to the analysis of "long-term" trends in
demography, economics, and ethnology, that is, "impersonal" processes, than as an incentive to analyze what "narrative" itself consisted
of and the basis of its millennial popularity as the "proper" mode of
historical representation.[15]

It should be stressed that the rejection of narrative history by the
Annalistes was due as much to their distaste for its conventional subject matter, that is, past politics, as to their conviction that its form was
inherently "novelistic" and "dramatizing" rather than "scientific."[16]
Their professed conviction that political affairs did not lend themselves
to scientific study, because of their evanescent nature and status as epiphenomena of processes demand to be more basic to history, was consistent with the failure of modern politology (I thank Jerzy Topolski
for this useful word) to create a genuine science of politics. But the
rejection of politics as a fit object of study for a scientific historiography is curiously complementary to the prejudice of nineteenth-
century professional historians regarding the undesirability of a
scientific politics. To hold that a science of politics is impossible is, of
course, as much of an ideological position as to hold that such a science is undesirable.

But what has narrative to do with all this? The charge leveled by
the *Annalistes* is that narrativity is inherently "dramatizing" or

"novelizing" of its subject matter, as if dramatic events either did not exist in history or, if they did exist, were by virtue of their dramatic nature not a fit object of historical study.[17] It is difficult to know what to make of this strange congeries of opinions. One can narrativize without dramatizing, as the whole of modernist literature demonstrates, and dramatize without theatricalizing, as the modern theater since Pirandello and Brecht makes eminently clear. So how can one condemn narrative on grounds of its "novelizing" effects? One suspects that it is not the dramatic nature of novels that is at issue but a distaste for a genre of literature that puts human agents rather than impersonal processes at the center of interest and suggests that such agents have some significant control over their own destinies.[18] But novels are not necessarily humanistic any more than they are necessarily dramatic. In any case, the free will–determinism question is quite as much an ideological issue as that of the possibility or impossibility of a science of politics. Therefore, without presuming to judge the positive achievement of the *Annalistes* in their effort to reform historical studies, we must conclude that the reasons they adduce for their dissatisfaction with narrative history are jejune.

It may be, however, that what some of them have to say about this topic is only a stenographic reproduction of a much more extensive analysis and deconstruction of narrativity that was carried out by Structuralists and Post-Structuralists in the 1960s, who claimed to demonstrate that narrative was not only an instrument of ideology but the very paradigm of ideologizing discourse in general.

This is not the place for yet another exposition of Structuralism and Post-Structuralism, of which there are more than enough already.[19] But the significance of these two movements for the discussion of narrative history can be briefly indicated. This significance, as I see it, is threefold: anthropological, psychological, and semiological. From the anthropological perspective, as represented above all by Claude Lévi-Strauss, it was not narrative so much as history itself that was the problem.[20] In a famous polemic directed against Sartre's *Critique de la raison dialectique*, Lévi-Strauss denied the validity of the distinction between "historical" (or "civilized") and "pre-historical" (or "primitive") societies, and therewith the legitimacy of the notion of a specific method of study and mode of representing the structures and processes of the former. The kind of knowledge that the so-called historical method was supposed to provide, that is to say, "historical knowledge," was, in Lévi-Strauss's view, hardly distinguishable from the mythic lore of "savage" communities. Indeed, historiography—by which Lévi-Strauss understood traditional, "narrative" historiography—was nothing but the myth of Western and especially modern, bourgeois, industrial, and imperialistic societies. The substance of this myth consisted in the mistaking of a method of representation, narrative, for a content, namely, the notion of a humanity uniquely identified with those societies capable of believing that they had lived the kinds of stories that Western historians had told about them. Lévi-Strauss granted that the historical, which is to say, the *diachronic,* representation of events *was* a method of analysis, but "it is a method with no distinct object corresponding to it," much less a method peculiarly adequate to the understanding of "humanity" or "civilized societies."[21] The representation of events in terms of their chronological order of occurrence, which Lévi-Strauss identified as the putative method of historical studies, is for him nothing but a heuristic procedure common to every field of scientific study, whether of nature or of culture, prior to the application of whatever analytical techniques are necessary for the identification of those events' common properties as elements of a structure.[22]

The specific chronological scale used for this ordering procedure is always culture-specific and adventitious, a purely heuristic device the validity of which depends upon the specific aims and interests of the scientific discipline in which it is used. The important point is that in Lévi-Strauss's view of the matter there is no such thing as *a* single scale for the ordering of events; rather, there are as many chronologies as there are culture-specific ways of representing the passage of time. Far from being a science or even a basis for a science, the narrative representation of any set of events was at best a proto-scientific exercise and at worst a basis for a kind of cultural self-delusion. "The progress of knowledge and the creation of new sciences," he concluded, "take place through the generation of anti-histories which show that a certain order which is possible only on one [chronological] plane ceases to be so on another."[23]

Not that Lévi-Strauss was opposed to narrative as such. Indeed, his monumental *Mythologiques* was intended to demonstrate the centrality of narrativity to the structuration of cultural life in all its forms.[24] What he objected to was the expropriation of narrativity as the method of a science purporting to have as its object of study a humanity more fully realized in its historical than in its pre-historical manifestations. The thrust of his criticism was directed, therefore, at that humanism in which Western civilization took so much pride but whose ethical principles it seemed to honor more in the breach than in the observance. This was the same humanism that Jacques Lacan sought to undermine in his revision of psychoanalytical theory, that Louis Althusser wished to expunge from modern Marxism, and that Michel Foucault had simply dismissed as the ideology of Western civilization in its most repressive and decadent phase.[25] For all of these—as well as for Jacques Derrida and Julia Kristeva—history in general and narrativity specifically were merely representational practices by which society produced a human subject peculiarly adapted to the conditions of life in the modern *Rechtsstaat*.[26] Their arguments on behalf of this view are too complex to be represented here, but the nature of their kind of hostility to the notion of narrative history can be suggested by a brief consideration of Roland Barthes's 1967 essay "The Discourse of History."

In this essay, Barthes challenged the distinction, basic to historicism in all its forms, between "historical" and "fictional" discourse. The point of attack chosen for this argument was the kind of historiography that favored a narrative representation of past events and processes. Barthes asked:

> Does the narration of past events, which, in our culture from the time of the Greeks onwards, has generally been subject to the sanction of historical "science," bound to the underlying standard of the "real," and justified by the principles of "rational" exposition—does this form of narration really differ, in some specific trait, in some indubitably distinctive feature, from imaginary narration, as we find it in the epic, the novel, and the drama?[27]

It is obvious from the manner in which he posed this question—with the placement of the words *science, real,* and *rational* within quotation marks—that Barthes's principal aim was to attack the vaunted objectivity of traditional historiography. And this is precisely what he did—by exposing the ideological function of the narrative mode of representation with which it had been associated.

As in his theoretical appendix to *Mythologies* (1957), Barthes did not so much oppose science to ideology as distinguish between progressive and reactionary, liberating and oppressive, ideologies.[28] In "The Discourse of History" he indicated that history could be represented in a number of different modes, some of which were less "mythological" than others inasmuch as they overtly called attention to their own process of production and indicated the "constituted," rather than "found," nature of their referents. But in his view, traditional historical discourse was more retrograde than either modern science or modern art, both of which signaled the invented nature of their "contents." Historical studies alone among the disciplines pretending to the status of scientificity remained a victim of what he called "the fallacy of referentiality."

Barthes purported to demonstrate that "as we can see, simply from looking at its structure, and without having to invoke the substance of its content, historical discourse is in its essence a form of ideological elaboration, or to put it more precisely, an imaginary elaboration," by which he meant a "speech-act" that was "performative" in nature, "through which the utterer of the discourse (a purely linguistic entity) 'fills out' the place of the subject of the utterance (a psychological or ideological entity)."[29] It should be observed that although Barthes here refers to historical discourse in general, it is historical discourse endowed with "narrative structure" that is his principal object of interest, for two reasons. First, he finds it paradoxical that "narrative structure, which was originally developed within the cauldron of fiction (in myths and the first epics)," should have become, in traditional historiography, "at once the sign and the proof of reality."[30] Second, and more important, narrative was, for Barthes, following Lacan, the principal instrumentality by which society fashions the narcissistic, infantile consciousness into a "subjectivity" capable of bearing the "responsibilities" of an "object" of the law in all its forms.

In the acquisition of language, Lacan had suggested, the child also acquires the very paradigm of orderly, rule-governed behavior. Barthes adds that in the development of the capacity to assimilate "stories" and to tell them, however, the child also learns what it is to be that creature that, in Nietzsche's phrase, is capable of making promises, of "remembering forward" as well as backwards, and of linking his end to his beginning in such a way as to attest to an "integrity" which every individual must be supposed to possess if he is to become a "subject" of (any) system of law, morality, or propriety. What is "imaginary" about any narrative representation is the illusion of a centered consciousness capable of looking out on the world, apprehending its structure and processes, and representing them to itself as having all of the formal coherency of narrativity itself. But this is to mistake a "meaning" (which is always constituted rather than found) for "reality" (which is always found rather than constituted).[31]

Behind this formulation, needless to say, lay a vast mass of highly problematical theories of language, discourse, consciousness, and ideology with which the names of both Jacques Lacan and Louis Althusser especially were associated. Barthes drew upon these for his own purpose, which was nothing less than the dismantling of the whole heritage of nineteenth-century "realism"—which he viewed as the pseudo-scientific content of that ideology that appeared as "humanism" in its sublimated form.

It was no accident, for Barthes, that "realism" in the nineteenth-century novel and "objectivity" in nineteenth-century historiography had developed *pied-à-pied*. What they had in common was a dependency on a specifically narrative mode of discourse, the principal purpose of which was to substitute surreptitiously a conceptual content (a signified) for a referent that it pretended merely to describe. As he had written in the seminal "Introduction to the Structural Analysis of Narrative" (1966):

> Claims concerning the "realism" of narrative are therefore to be
> discounted. . . . The function of narrative is not to "represent," it
> is to constitute a spectacle. . . . Narrative does not show, does not
> imitate. . . . "What takes place" in a narrative is from the referen-
> tial (reality) point of view literally *nothing;* "what happens" is
> language alone, the adventure of language, the unceasing celebra-
> tion of its coming.[32]

This passage refers to narrative in general, to be sure, but the principles enunciated were extendable to historical narrative as well. Whence his insistence, at the end of "The Discourse of History," that "in 'objective' history, the 'real' is never more than an unformulated signified, sheltering behind the apparently all-powerful referent. This situation characterizes what might be called the *realistic effect (effet du réel).*"[33]

Much could be said about this conception of narrative and its supposed ideological function, not least about the psychology on which it is based and the ontology that it presupposes. It is, obviously, reminiscent of Nietzsche's thought about language, literature, and historiography, and insofar as it bears upon the problem of historical consciousness, it does not say much that goes beyond "The Uses and Abuses of History for Life" and *The Genealogy of Morals*. This Nietzschean affiliation is openly admitted by such Post-Structuralists as Derrida, Kristeva, and Foucault, and it is this Nietzschean turn in French thought over the last twenty years or so that serves to distinguish the Post-Structuralists from their more "scientific" Structuralist predecessors, as represented by Lévi-Strauss, Roman Jakobson, and the early Barthes. Needless to say, Post-Structuralism has little in common with the aspirations of those historians among the *Annales* group who dreamed of transforming historical studies into a kind of science. But the "deconstruction" of narrativity carried out by Barthes and the Post-Structuralists is consistent with the objections raised by the *Annalistes* against the narrative mode of representation in historiography.

Barthes's formulation of the problematics of narrative history points up a significant difference, however, between discussions of this subject that developed in France in the 1960s and those that had taken place in the previous two decades in the Anglophone philosophical community, dominated at that time by analytical philosophy. The most apparent difference lies in the consistency with which narrative was defended by the analytical philosophers, as both a mode of representation and a mode of explanation, in contrast to the attacks upon it emanating from France. Different philosophers gave different accounts of the bases for the conviction that narrative was a perfectly valid mode of representing historical events and even of providing an explanation of them. But in contrast to the French discussion, in the Anglophone world narrative historiography was viewed for the most part not as an ideology but rather as an antidote for the nefarious "philosophy of history" à la Hegel and Marx, the presumed ideological linchpin of "totalitarian" political systems.

Here, too, however, the lines of debate were muddied by the issue of history's status as a science and discussion of the kind of epistemic authority that historical knowledge could claim in comparison with the kind of knowledge provided by the physical sciences. There was even a vigorous debate within Marxist circles—a debate that reached a culmination in the 1970s—over the extent to which a Marxist, "scientific" historiography should be cast in a narrativist, as against a more properly analytical, mode of discourse. Issues similar to those that divided the *Annalistes* from their more conventional co-professionals had to be addressed, but here narrativity was much less a matter of concern than was the issue of "materialism *versus* idealism."[34] On the whole, amongst both historians and philosophers and amongst both Marxist and non-Marxist practitioners of these disciplines, no one seriously questioned the legitimacy of distinctively "historical" studies, as Lévi-Strauss had done in France, or the adequacy, at some level, of the narrative to represent veraciously and objectively the "truths" discovered by whatever methods the individual historian happened to have used in his research, as Barthes and Foucault did in France. Some social scientists raised such questions, but given the tenuousness of their own claims to methodological rigor and the exiguousness of their "science," they bore little theoretical fruit with respect to the question of narrative history.[35]

The differences between these two strains of discussions of historical narrative also reflected fundamentally different conceptions of the nature of discourse in general. In literary and lingusitic theory, the discourse is conventionally thought of as any unit of utterance larger than the (complex) sentence. What are the principles of discourse formation corresponding to those rules of grammar that preside over the formation of the sentence? Obviously, these principles are not grammatical themselves, since one can construct chains of grammatically correct sentences that do not aggregate or coalesce into a recognizable discourse.

Obviously, one candidate for the role of organon of discourse formation is logic, the protocols of which preside over the formation of all "scientific" discourses. But logic yields place to other principles in poetic discourse, principles such as phonetics, rhyme, meter, and so on, the exigencies of which may authorize violations of logical protocols in the interest of producing formal coherencies of another kind. And then there is rhetoric, which may be regarded as a principle of discourse formation in those speech events that aim at persuasion or impulsion to action rather than description, demonstration, or explication. In both poetic and rhetorical speech, the communication of a message about some extrinsic referent may be involved, but the functions of "expression" and of "conation" may be given a higher order of importance. Therefore, the distinctions between "communication," "expression," and "conation" permit the differentiation, in terms of function, among different kinds of rules of discourse formation, of which logic is only one and by no means the most privileged.

Everything depends, as Roman Jakobson put it, on the "set" (*Einstellung*) towards the "message" contained in the discourse in question.[36] If the conveyance of a message about an extrinsic referent is the primary aim of the discourse, we can say that the communication function predominates; and the discourse in question is to be assessed in terms of the clarity of its formulation and its truth value (the validity of the information it provides) with respect to the referent. If, on the other hand, the message is treated as being primarily an occasion for expressing an emotional condition of the speaker of the discourse (as in most lyrics) or for engendering an attitude in the recipient of the message, conducing to an action of a particular kind (as in hortatory speeches), then the discourse in question is to be assessed less in terms of its clarity or its truth value with respect to its referent than in terms of its performative force—a purely pragmatic consideration.

This functional model of discourse relegates logic, poetic, and rhetoric alike to the status of "codes" in which different kinds of "messages" can be cast and transmitted with quite different aims in view: communicative, expressive, or conative, as the case may be.[37] These aims are by no means mutually exclusive; indeed, every discourse can be shown to possess aspects of all three of these functions. And this goes for "factual" as well as "fictional" discourse. But considered as a basis for a general theory of discourse, this model permits us to ask how narrative discourse in particular utilizes these three functions. And what is more relevant to our purpose in this essay, it permits us to see how contemporary discussions of the nature of narrative history have tended to ignore one or another of these functions in order either to save narrative history for "science" or to consign it to the category of "ideology."

Most of those who would defend narrative as a legitimate mode of historical representation and even as a valid mode of explanation (at least for history) stress the communicative function. According to this view of history as communication, a history is conceived to be a "message" about a "referent" (the past, historical events, and so on) the content of which is both "information" (the "facts") and an "explanation" (the "narrative" account). Both the facts in their particularity and the narrative account in its generality must meet a correspondence, as well as a coherence, criterion of truth value. The coherence criterion invoked is, needless to say, logic rather than poetic or rhetoric. Individual propositions must be logically consistent with one another, and the principles conceived to govern the process of syntagmatic combination must be consistently applied. Thus, for example, although an earlier event can be represented as a cause of a later event, the reverse is not the case. By contrast, however, a later event can serve to illuminate the significance of an earlier event, but the reverse is not true (for example, the birth of Diderot does not illuminate the significance of the composition of *Rameau's Nephew,* but the composition of *Rameau's Nephew* illuminates, retrospectively as it were, the significance of the birth of Diderot).[38]

The correspondence criterion is another matter. Not only must the singular existential statements that make up the "chronicle" of the historical account "correspond" to the events of which they are predications, but the narrative as a whole must "correspond" to the general configuration of the sequence of events of which it is an account. Which is to say that the sequence of "facts" as they are emplotted in order to make a "story" out of what would otherwise be only a "chronicle" must correspond to the general configuration of the "events" of which the "facts" are propositional indicators.

For those theorists who stress the communication function of narrative historical discourse, the correspondence of the "story" to the events it relates is established at the level of the conceptual content of the "message." This conceptual content may be thought to consist either of the factors linking events in chains of causes and effects or of the "reasons" (or "intentions") motivating the human agents of the events in question. The causes (necessary if not sufficient) or reasons (conscious or unconscious) for events' taking place as they in fact did are set forth in the narrative in the form of the story it tells.[39] According to this view, the narrative form of the discourse is only a medium for the message, having no more truth value or informational content than any other formal structure, such as a logical syllogism, a metaphorical figure, or a mathematical equation. Considered as a code, the narrative is a vehicle rather in the way that the Morse code serves as the vehicle for the transmission of messages by a telegraphical apparatus. Which means, among other things, that thus envisaged, the narrative code adds nothing in the way of information or knowledge that could not be conveyed by some other system of discursive encodation. This is proven by the fact that the content of any narrative account of real events can be extracted from the account, represented in a dissertative format, and subjected to the same criteria of logical consistency and factual accuracy as a scientific demonstration. The narrative actually composed by a given historian may be more or less "thick" in content and more or less "artistic" in its execution; it may be more or less elegantly elaborated—in the way that the touch of different telegraphers is conceived to be. But this, the proponents of this view would have it, is more a matter of individual style than of content. In the historical narrative, it is the content alone that has truth value. All else is ornament.

This notion of narrative discourse fails, however, to take into account the enormous number of kinds of narratives that every culture disposes for those of its members who might wish to draw upon them for the encodation and transmission of messages. Moreover, every narrative discourse consists, not of one single code monolithically utilized, but of a complex set of codes the interweaving of which by the author—for the production of a story infinitely rich in suggestion and variety of affect, not to mention attitude towards and subliminal evaluation ot its subject matter—attests to his talents as an artist, as master

rather than servant of the codes available for his use. Whence the
"density" of such relatively informal discourses as those of literature
and poetry as against those of science. As the Russian textologist Juri
Lotman has remarked, the artistic text carries much more "information" than does the scientific text, because the former disposes more
codes and more levels of encodation than does the latter.[40] At the same
time, however, the artistic text, as against the scientific, directs attention as much to the virtuosity involved in its production as to the "information" conveyed in the various codes employed in its composition.

It is this complex multilayeredness of discourse and its consequent
capacity to bear a wide variety of interpretations of its meaning that
the performance model of discourse seeks to illuminate. From the perspective provided by this model, a discourse is regarded as an apparatus for the production of meaning rather than as only a vehicle for
the transmission of information about an extrinsic referent. Thus
envisaged, the content of the discourse consists as much of its form as
it does of whatever information might be extracted from a reading of
it.[41] It follows that to change the form of the discourse might not be
to change the information about its explicit referent, but it would certainly change the meaning produced by it. For example, a set of events
simply listed in the chronological order of their original occurrence is
not, pace Lévi-Strauss, devoid of meaning. Its meaning is precisely the
kind that any list is capable of producing—as Rabelais's and Joyce's use
of the list genre amply attests. A list of events may be only a "thin"
chronicle (if the items in the list are presented chronologically) or a
"slim" encyclopedia (if organized topically). In both cases the same
information may be conveyed, but different meanings are produced.

A chronicle, however, is not a narrative, even if it contains the
same set of facts as its informational content, because a narrative
discourse performs differently from a chronicle. Chronology is no
doubt a code shared by both chronicle and narrative, but narrative
utilizes other codes as well and produces a meaning quite different
from that of any chronicle. It is not that the code of narrative is more
"literary" than that of chronicle—as many historians of historical
writing have suggested. And it is not that the narrative "explains" more
or even explains more fully than does the chronicle. The point is that
narrativization produces a meaning quite different from that produced
by chronicalization. And it does this by imposing a discursive form on
the events that its own chronicle comprises by means that are poetic
in nature; that is, the narrative code is drawn from the performative
domain of poiesis rather than that of noesis. This is what Barthes

meant when he said: "Narrative does not *show,* does not *imitate.* . . . [Its] function is not to '*represent,*' it is to *constitute* a spectacle" (my italics).

It is generally recognized that one way of distinguishing poetic from prosaic discourse is by the prominence given in the former to patterning—of sounds, rhythms, meter, and so on—which draws attention to the form of the discourse quite apart from (or in excess of) whatever message it may contain on the level of its literal verbal enunciation. The form of the poetic text produces a meaning quite other than whatever might be represented in any prose paraphrase of its literal verbal content. The same can be said of the various genres of *Kuntsprosa* (oratorical declamation, legal brief, prose romance, novel, and so on), of which the historical narrative is undeniably a species, but here the patterning in question is not that of sound and meter so much as it is that of the rhythms and repetitions of motific structures that aggregate into themes and of themes that aggregate into plot structures. This is not to say, of course, that such genres do not also utilize the various codes of logical argumentation and scientific demonstration, for indeed they do; but these codes have nothing to do with the production of the kind of meaning that is effected by narrativization.

Certain narrative discourses may have arguments embedded within them, in the form of explanations of why things happened as they did, set forth in the mode of direct address to the reader in the author's own voice and perceivable as such. But such arguments are more properly considered as a commentary on, rather than a part of, the narrative. In historical discourse, the narrative serves to transform into a story a list of historical events that would otherwise be only a chronicle. In order to effect this transformation, the events, agents, and agencies represented in the chronicle must be encoded as story elements; that is, they must be characterized as the kinds of events, agents, agencies, and so on, that can be apprehended as elements of specific story types. On this level of encodation, the historical discourse directs the reader's attention to a secondary referent, different in kind from the events that make up the primary referent, namely, the plot structures of the various story types cultivated in a given culture.[42] When the reader recognizes the story being told in a historical narrative as a specific kind of story—for example, as an epic, romance, tragedy, comedy, or farce,—he can be said to have comprehended the meaning produced by the discourse. This comprehension is nothing other than the recognition of the form of the narrative.

The production of meaning in this case can be regarded as a performance, because any given set of real events can be emplotted in a number of ways, can bear the weight of being told as any number of different kinds of stories. Since no given set or sequence of real events is intrinsically tragic, comic, farcical, and so on, but can be constructed as such only by the imposition of the structure of a given story type on the events, it is the choice of the story type and its imposition upon the events that endow them with meaning. The effect of such emplotment may be regarded as an explanation, but it would have to be recognized that the generalizations that serve the function of universals in any version of a nomological-deductive argument are the *topoi* of literary plots, rather than the causal laws of science.

This is why a narrative history can legitimately be regarded as something other than a scientific account of the events of which it speaks—as the *Annalistes* have rightly argued. But it is not sufficient reason to deny to narrative history substantial truth value. Narrative historiography may very well, as Furet indicates, "dramatize" historical events and "novelize" historical processes, but this only indicates that the truths in which narrative history deals are of an order different from those of its social scientific counterpart. In the historical narrative the systems of meaning production peculiar to a culture or society are tested against the capacity of any set of "real" events to yield to such systems. If these systems have their purest, most fully developed, and formally most coherent representations in the literary or poetic endowment of modern, secularized cultures, this is no reason to rule them out as merely imaginary constructions. To do so would entail the denial that literature and poetry have anything valid to teach us about reality.

The relationship between historiography and literature is, of course, as tenuous and difficult to define as that between historiography and science. In part, no doubt, this is because historiography in the West arises against the background of a distinctively literary (or rather "fictional") discourse which itself took shape against the even more archaic discourse of myth. In its origins, historical discourse differentiates itself from literary discourse by virtue of its subject matter ("real" rather than "imaginary" events) rather than its form. But form here is ambiguous, for it refers not only to the manifest appearance of historical discourses (their appearance as stories) but also to the systems of meaning production (the modes of emplotment) that historiography shared with literature and myth. This affiliation of narrative historiography with literature and myth should provide no reason for embarrassment, however, because the systems of meaning production shared by all three are distillates of the historical experience of a people, a group, a culture. And the knowledge provided by narrative history is that which results from the testing of the systems of meaning production originally elaborated in myth and refined in the alembic of the hypothetical mode of fictional articulation. In the historical narrative, experiences distilled into fiction as typifications are subjected to the test of their capacity to endow "real" events with meaning. And it would take a *Kulturphilistinismus* of a very high order to deny to the results of this testing procedure the status of genuine knowledge.

In other words, just as the contents of myth are tested by fiction, so, too, the forms of fiction are tested by (narrative) historiography. If in a similar manner the content of narrative historiography is tested to determine its adequacy to represent and explain another order of reality than that presupposed by traditional historians, this should be seen less as an opposition of science to ideology, as the *Annalistes* often seem to view it, than as a continuation of the process of mapping the limit between the imaginary and the real which begins with the invention of fiction itself.

The historical narrative does not, as narrative, dispel false beliefs about the past, human life, the nature of the community, and so on; what it does is test the capacity of a culture's fictions to endow real events with the kinds of meaning that literature displays to consciousness through its fashioning of patterns of "imaginary" events. Precisely insofar as the historical narrative endows sets of real events with the kinds of meaning found otherwise only in myth and literature, we are justified in regarding it as a product of *allegoresis*. Therefore, rather than regard every historical narrative as mythic or ideological in nature, we should regard it as allegorical, that is, as saying one thing and meaning another.

Thus envisaged, the narrative figurates the body of events that serves as its primary referent and transforms these events into intimations of patterns of meaning that any literal representation of them as facts could never produce. This is not to say that a historical discourse is not properly assessed in terms of the truth value of its factual (singular existential) statements taken individually and the logical conjunction of the whole set of such statements taken distributively. For unless a historical discourse acceded to assessment in these terms, it would lose all justification for its claim to represent and provide explanations of specifically real events. But such assessment touches only that aspect of the historical discourse conventionally called its chronicle. It does not provide us with any way of assessing the content of the narrative

itself. This point has been made most tellingly by the philosopher
Louis O. Mink:

> One can regard any text in direct discourse as a logical conjunc-
> tion of assertions. The truth-value of the text is then simply a
> logical function of the truth or falsity of the individual assertions
> taken separately: the conjunction is true if and only if each of the
> propositions is true. Narrative has in fact been analyzed, espe-
> cially by philosophers intent on comparing the form of the narra-
> tive with the form of theories, as if it were nothing but a logical
> conjunction of past-referring statements; and on such an analysis
> there is no problem of *narrative truth.* The difficulty with the
> model of logical conjunction, however, is that it is not a model of
> narrative at all. It is rather a model of a chronicle. Logical con-
> junction serves well enough as a representation of the only order-
> ing relation of chronicles, which is ". . . and then . . . and then
> . . . and then. . . ." Narratives, however, contain indefinitely many
> ordering relations, and indefinitely many ways of *combining* these
> relations. It is such a combination that we mean when we speak
> of the coherence of a narrative, or lack of it. It is an unsolved
> task of literary theory to classify the ordering relations of narra-
> tive form; but whatever the classification, it should be clear that a
> historical narrative claims truth not merely for each of its indi-
> vidual statements taken distributively, but for the complex form of
> the narrative itself.[43]

But the "truth" of narrative form can display itself only indirectly,
that is to say, by means of *allegoresis.* What else could be involved in
the representation of a set of real events as, for example, a tragedy,
comedy, or farce? Is there any test, logical or empirical, that could be
applied to determine the truth value of the assertion by Marx that the
events of "the 18th Brumaire of Louis Buonaparte" constitute a "farcical" reenactment of the "tragedy" of 1789?[44] Marx's discourse is certainly assessable by the criteria of factual accuracy in his representation
of particular events and the logical consistency of his explanation of
why they occurred as they did. But what is the truth value of his figuration of the whole set of events, achieved by narrative means, as a farce?
Are we intended to take this as only a figure of speech, a metaphorical
expression, and therefore not subject to assessment on grounds of its
truth value? To do so would require that we dismiss the narrative
aspect of Marx's discourse, the story he tells about the events, as mere
ornament and not an essential aspect of the discourse as a whole.

Marx's assertion of the farcical nature of the events he describes is made only indirectly (by means of the aphorism that opens his discourse and by his narrativization of the events, the story he makes of them), which is to say, allegorically. This does not mean that we would be justified in assuming that Marx did not intend us to take this assertion seriously and to regard it as truthful in its content. But what is the relation between the assertion of the farcical nature of the events and the facts registered in the discourse, on the one side, and the dialectical analysis of them given in the passages in which Marx, speaking in his own voice and as a putative scientist of society, purports to "explain" them, on the other? Do the facts confirm the characterization of the events as a farce? Is the logic of Marx's explanation consistent with the logic of the narrative? What logic governs this narrativizing aspect of Marx's discourse?

The logic of Marx's explicit argument about the events, his explanation of the facts, is manifestly dialectical; that is, it is his own version of Hegel's logic. Is there another logic presiding over the structuration of the events as a farce? This is the question that the threefold distinction between the chronicle of events, the explanation of them given in direct discourse as commentary, and the narrativization of the events provided by *allegoresis* helps us to answer. And the answer is given the moment we recognize the allegorical aspect of the characterization of the events of "the 18th Brumaire" as a farce. It is not fact that legitimates the representation of the events as a farce, and it is not logic that permits the projection of the fact *as* a farce. There is no way that one could conclude on logical grounds that any set of "real" events *is* a farce. This is a judgment, not a conclusion; and it is a judgment that can be justified only on the basis of a poetic troping of the "facts" so as to give them, in the very process of their initial description, the aspect of the elements of the story form known as farce in the literary code of our culture.

If there is any logic presiding over the transition from the level of fact or event in the discourse to that of narrative, it is the logic of figuration itself, which is to say, tropology. This transition is effected by a displacement of the facts onto the ground of literary fictions or, what amounts to the same thing, the projection onto the facts of the plot structure of one or another of the genres of literary figuration. To put it yet another way, the transition is effected by a process of transcodation, in which events originally transcribed in the code of chronicle are retranscribed in the literary code of the farce.

To present the question of narrativization in historiography in these terms, of course, is to raise the more general question of the truth of literature itself. On the whole, this question has been ignored by the analytical philosophers concerned to analyze the logic of narrative explanations in historiography. This seems to be because the notion of explanation that they brought to their investigation ruled out the consideration of figurative discourse as productive of genuine knowledge. Since historical narratives refer to "real" rather than "imaginary" events, it was assumed that their truth value resided either in the literal statements of fact contained within them or in a combination of these and a literalist paraphrase of statements made in figurative language. It being generally given that figurative expressions are either false, ambiguous, or logically inconsistent (consisting as they do of what some philosophers call category mistakes), it followed that whatever explanations might be contained in a historical narrative should be expressible only in literal language. Thus, in their summaries of explanations contained in historical narratives, these analysts of the form tended to reduce the narrative in question to sets of discrete propositions, for which the simple declarative sentence served as a model. When an element of figurative language turned up in such sentences, it was treated as only a figure of speech the content of which was either its literal meaning or a literalist paraphrase of what appeared to be its grammatically correct formulation.

But in this process of literalization, what gets left out is precisely those elements of figuration—tropes and figures of thought, as the rhetoricians call them—without which the narrativization of real events, the transformation of a chronicle into a story, could never be effected. If there is any "category mistake" involved in this literalizing procedure, it is that of mistaking a narrative account of real events for a literal account thereof. A narrative account is always a figurative account, an allegory. To leave this figurative element out of consideration in the analysis of a narrative is to miss not only its aspect as allegory but also the performance in language by which a chronicle is transformed into a narrative. And it is only a modern prejudice against allegory or, what amounts to the same thing, a scientistic prejudice in favor of literalism that obscures this fact to many modern analysts of historical narrative. In any event, the dual conviction that truth must be represented in literal statements of fact and explanation must conform to the scientific model or its commonsensical counterpart has led most analysts to ignore the specifically literary aspect of historical narrative and therewith whatever truth it may convey in figurative terms.

Needless to say, the notion of literary, even mythical, truth is not alien to those philosophers who continue to work in a tradition of thought that has its modern origin in Hegelian idealism, its continuator in Dilthey, and its recent, existentialist-phenomenological avatar in Heideggerian hermeneutics. For thinkers in this line, history has always been less an object of study, something to be explained, than a mode of being-in-the-world that both makes possible understanding and invokes it as a condition of its own deconcealment. This means that historical knowledge can be produced only on the basis of a kind of inquiry fundamentally different from those cultivated in the (nomological-deductive) physical sciences and the (structural-functional) social sciences. According to Gadamer and Ricoeur, the "method" of the historicogenetic sciences is hermeneutics, conceived less as decipherment than as "inter-pretation," literally "translation," a "carrying over" of meanings from one discursive community to another. Both Gadamer and Ricoeur stress the "traditionalist" aspect of the hermeneutical enterprise, or what amounts to the same thing, the "translational" aspect of tradition. It is tradition that unites the interpreter with the *interpretandum*, apprehended in all the strangeness that marks it as coming from a past, in an activity productive of the establishment of the individuality and communality of both. When this individuality-in-communality is established across a temporal distance, the kind of knowledge-as-understanding produced is a specifically historical knowledge.[45]

So much is familiar to any reader of this tradition of philosophical discourse and, needless to say, utterly foreign to traditional historians, as well as those who wish to transform historiography into a science. And why not? The terminology is figurative, the tone pious, the epistemology mystical — all of the things that both traditional historians and their more modern, social scientifically oriented counterparts wish to expunge from historical studies. Yet this tradition of thought has a special relevance for the consideration of our topic, for it has been left to one of its representatives, Paul Ricoeur, to attempt nothing less than a metaphysics of narrativity.

Ricoeur has confronted all of the principal conceptions of discourse, textuality, and reading on the current theoretical scene. He has, moreover, surveyed exhaustively contemporary theories of historiography and the notions of narrative advanced in both contemporary philosophy of history and social science. On the whole, he finds much to commend in the analytical philosophers' arguments, especially as represented by Mink, Danto, Gallie, and Dray, who view narrative as providing a kind of explanation different from, though not antithetical

to, nomological-deductive explanations. Ricoeur, however, holds that
narrativity in historiography conduces more to the attainment of an
understanding of the events of which it speaks than to an explanation
that is only a softer version of the kind found in the physical and social
sciences. Not that he opposes understanding to explanation: these two
modes of cognition are related "dialectically," he maintains, as the
"unmethodical" and "methodical" aspects of all knowledge that deals
with (human) actions rather than with (natural) events.[46]

The "reading" of an action, according to Ricoeur, resembles the
reading of a text; the same kind of hermeneutic principles are required
for the comprehension of both. Since "history is about the actions of
men in the past," it follows that the study of the past has as its proper
aim the hermeneutic "understanding" of human actions. In the process
of attaining this understanding, explanations of various sorts are called
for, in much the same way that explanations of "what happened" in
any story are called for on the way to the story's full elaboration. But
these explanations serve as a means to understanding "what happened" rather than as ends in themselves. Thus, in the writing of the
historical text, the aim in view should be to represent (human) events
in such a way that their status as parts of meaningful wholes will be
made manifest.[47]

To grasp the meaning of a complex sequence of human events is
not the same as being able to explain why or even how the particular
events that the sequence comprises occurred. One might be able to explain why and how every event in a sequence occurred and still not
have understood the meaning of the sequence considered as a whole.
Carrying over the analogy of reading to the process of understanding,
one can see how one might understand every sentence in a story and
still not have grasped its point. It is the same, Ricoeur maintains, with
our efforts to grasp the meaning of human actions. Just as texts have
meanings that are not reducible to the specific words and sentences
used in their composition, so, too, do actions. Actions produce meanings by their consequences—whether foreseen and intended or unfore-
seen and unintended—which become embodied in the institutions and
conventions of given social formations. To understand historical actions, then, is to "grasp together," as parts of wholes that are "meaningful," the intentions motivating actions, the actions themselves, and
their consequences as reflected in social and cultural contexts.[48]

In historiography, Ricoeur argues, this "grasping together" of the
elements of situations in which "meaningful action" has occurred is

affected by the "configuration" of them through the instrumentality of plot. For him, unlike many commentators on historical narrative, plot is not a structural component of fictional or mythical stories alone; it is crucial to the historical representations of events as well. "Every narrative combines two dimensions in various proportions, one chronological and the other nonchronological. The first may be called the episodic dimension, which characterizes the story made out of events. The second is the configurational dimension, according to which the plot construes significant wholes out of scattered events."[49] But this plot is not imposed by the historian on the events; nor is it a code drawn from the repertoire of literary models and used "pragmatically" to endow what would otherwise be a mere collection of facts with a certain rhetorical form. It is plot, he says, that figures forth the "historicality" of events: "The plot . . . places us at the crossing point of temporality and narrativity: to be historical, an event must be more than a singular occurrence, a unique happening. It receives its definition from its contribution to the development of a plot" (171).

According to this view, a specifically historical event is not one that can be inserted into a story wherever the writer wishes; it is rather a kind of event that can "contribute" to "the development of a plot." It is as if the plot were an entity in process of development prior to the occurrence of any given event, and any given event could be endowed with historicality only to the extent that it could be shown to contribute to this process. And, indeed, such seems to be the case, because for Ricoeur, historicality is a structural mode or level of temporality itself.

Time, it would appear, is possessed of three "degrees of organization": "within-time-ness," "historicality," and "deep temporality." These are reflected, in turn, in three kinds of experiences or representations of time in consciousness: "ordinary representations of time, . . . as that 'in' which events take place"; those in which "emphasis is placed on the weight of the past and, even more, . . . the power of recovering the 'extension' between birth and death in the work of 'repetition'"; and, finally, those that seek to grasp "the plural unity of future, past, and present" (171). In the historical narrative—indeed, in any narrative, even the most humble—it is narrativity that "brings us back from within-time-ness to historicality, from 'reckoning with' time to 'recollecting' it." In short, "the narrative function provides a transition from within-time-ness to historicality," and it does this by revealing what must be called the "plot-like" nature of temporality itself (178).

Thus envisaged, the narrative level of any historical account has a referent quite different from that of its chronicle level. While the chronicle represents events as existing "within time," the narrative represents the aspects of time in which endings can be seen as linked to beginnings to form a continuity within a difference. The "sense of an ending," which links a terminus of a process with its origin in such a way as to endow whatever happened in between with a significance that can only be gained by "retrospection," is achieved by the peculiarly human capacity of what Heidegger called "repetition." This repetition is the specific modality of the existence of events in "historicality," as against their existence "in time." In historicality conceived as repetition, we grasp the possibility of "the retrieval of our most basic potentialities inherited from our past in the form of personal fate and collective destiny" (183–84). And this is why—among other reasons, to be sure—Ricoeur feels justified in holding "temporality to be that structure of existence that reaches language in narrativity and narrativity to be the language structure that has temporality as its ultimate referent" (169). It is this contention that justifies, I think, speaking of Ricoeur's contribution to historical theory as an attempt to contrive a "metaphysics of narrativity."

The significance of this metaphysics of narrativity for historiographical theory lies in Ricoeur's suggestion that the historical narrative must, by virtue of its narrativity, have as its "ultimate referent" nothing other than "temporality" itself. Placed within the wider context of Ricoeur's *oeuvre,* what this means is that he has assigned historical narrative to the category of symbolic discourse, which is to say, a discourse whose principal force derives neither from its informational content nor from its rhetorical effect but rather from its imagistic function.[50] A narrative, for him, is neither an icon of the events of which it speaks, an explanation of those events, nor a rhetorical refashioning of "facts" for a specifically persuasive effect. It is a symbol mediating between different universes of meaning by "configuring" the dialectic of their relationship in an image. This image is nothing other than the narrative itself, that "configuration" of events reported in the chronicle by the revelation of their "plot-like" nature.

Thus, in telling a story, the historian necessarily reveals a plot. This plot "symbolizes" events by mediating between their status as existants "within time" and their status as indicators of the "historicality" in which these events participate. Since this historicality can only be indicated, never represented directly, the historical narrative, like all symbolic structures, "says something other than what it says and

. . . consequently, grasps me because it has in its meaning created a new meaning."[51]

Ricoeur grants that in characterizing symbolic language in this way, he has all but identified it with allegory. This is not to say that it is only fantasy, because for Ricoeur, allegory is a way of expressing that "excess of meaning" present in those apprehensions of "reality" as a dialectic of "human desire" and "cosmic appearance."[52] A historical narrative, then, can be said to be an allegorization of the experience of "within-time-ness," the figurative meaning of which is the structure of temporality. The narrative expresses a meaning "other" than that expressed in the chronicle, which is an "ordinary representation of time . . . as that 'in' which events take place." This secondary, or figurative, meaning is not so much "constructed" as "found" in the universal human experience of a "recollection" that promises a future because it finds a "sense" in every relationship between a past and a present. In the plot of the historical story, we apprehend a "figure" of the "power of recovering the 'extension' between birth and death in the work of 'repetition.'"[53]

For Ricoeur, then, narrative is more than a mode of explanation, more than a code, and much more than a vehicle for conveying information. It is not a discursive strategy or tactic that the historian may or may not use, according to some pragmatic aim or purpose. It is a means of symbolizing events without which their historicality cannot be indicated. One can make true statements about events without symbolizing them — as in a chronicle. One can even explain these events without symbolizing them as is done all the time in the (structural functional) social sciences. But one cannot represent the meaning of historical events without symbolizing them, because historicality itself is both a reality and a mystery. All narratives display this mystery and at the same time foreclose any inclination to despair over the failure to solve it by revealing what might be called its form in "plot" and its content in the meaning with which the plot endows what would otherwise be only mere event. Insofar as events and their aspects can be "explained" by the methods of the sciences, they are, it would seem, thereby shown to be neither mysterious nor particularly historical. What can be explained about historical events is precisely what constitutes their non- or ahistorical aspect. What remains after events have been explained is both historical and meaningful insofar as it can be understood. And this remainder is understandable insofar as it can be "grasped" in a symbolization, that is, shown to have the kind of meaning with which plots endow stories.

It is the success of narrative in revealing the meaning, coherence, or significance of events that attests to the legitimacy of its practice in historiography. And it is the success of historiography in narrativizing sets of historical events that attests to the "realism" of narrative itself. In the kind of symbolization embodied in the historical narrative, human beings have a discursive instrument by which to assert (meaningfully) that the world of human actions is both real and mysterious, that is, is mysteriously real (which is not the same thing as saying that it is a real mystery); that what cannot be explained is in principle capable of being understood; and that, finally, this understanding is nothing other than its representation in the form of a narrative.

There is, then, a certain necessity in the relationship between the narrative, conceived as a symbolic or symbolizing discursive structure, and the representation of specifically historical events. This necessity arises from the fact that human events are or were products of human actions, and these actions have produced consequences that have the structures of texts—more specifically, the structure of narrative texts. The understanding of these texts, considered as the products of actions, depends upon our being able to reproduce the processes by which they were produced, that is, to narrativize these actions. Since these actions are in effect lived narrativizations, it follows that the only way to represent them is by narrative itself. Here the form of discourse is perfectly adequate to its content, since the one is narrative, the other what has been narrativized. The wedding of form with content produces the symbol, "which says more than what it says" but in historical discourse always says the same thing: historicality.

Ricoeur's is surely the strongest claim for the adequacy of narrative to realize the aims of historical studies made by any recent theorist of historiography. He purports to solve the problem of the relationship between narrative and historiography by identifying the content of the former (narrativity) with the "ultimate referent" of the latter (historicality). In his subsequent identification of the content of historicality with a "structure of time" that cannot be represented except in a narrative mode, however, he confirms the suspicions of those who regard narrative representations of historical phenomena as being inherently mythical in nature. Nonetheless, in his attempt to demonstrate that historicality is a content of which narrativity is the form, he suggests that the real subject of any discussion of the proper form of historical discourse ultimately turns on a theory of the true content of history itself.

My own view is that all theoretical discussions of historiography become enmeshed in the ambiguity contained in the notion of history itself. This ambiguity derives, not from the fact that the term *history* refers both to an object of study and to an account of this object, but from the fact that the object of study itself can be conceived only on the basis of an equivocation. I refer, of course, to the equivocation contained in the notion of a general human past that is split into two parts one of which is supposed to be "historical," the other "unhistorical." This distinction is not of the same order as that between "human events" and "natural events," on the basis of which historical studies constitute an order of facts different from those studied in the natural sciences. The differences between a life lived in nature and one lived in culture are sufficient grounds for honoring the distinction between natural events and human events, on the basis of which historical studies and the human sciences in general can proceed to work out methods adequate to the investigation of human events. And once an order of generally human events is conceptualized, and this order is further divided into human events past and human events present, it is surely legitimate to inquire to what extent different methods of study may be called for in the investigation of those designated as past as against those called for in the investigation of events designated as present (in whatever sense *present* is construed). But it is quite another matter, once this human past is postulated, to further divide it into an order of events that is "historical" and another that is "nonhistorical." For this is to suggest that there are two orders of humanity, one of which is more human—because it is more historical—than the other.

The distinction between a humanity or kind of culture or society that is historical and another that is nonhistorical is not of the same order as the distinction between two periods of time in the development of the human species: prehistorical and historical. For this distinction does not hinge on the belief that human culture was not developing prior to the beginning of "history" or that this development was not historical in nature. It hinges rather on the belief that there is a point in the evolution of human culture after which its development can be represented in a discourse different from that in which this evolution in its earlier phase can be represented. As is well-known and generally conceded, the possibility of representing the development of certain cultures in a specifically historical kind of discourse is based on the circumstance that these cultures produced, preserved, and used a certain kind of record, written records.

The possibility of representing the development of certain cultures in a specifically historical discourse is not, however, sufficient grounds for regarding cultures whose development cannot be similarly represented, because of their failure to produce these kinds of records, as continuing to persist in the condition of prehistory, for at least two reasons. One is that the human species does not enter into history only in part. The very notion of human species implies that if any part of it exists in history, the whole of it does. Another is that the notion of the entrance into history of any part of the human species could not properly be conceived as a purely intramural operation, a transformation that certain cultures or societies undergo that is merely internal to themselves. On the contrary, what the entrance into history of certain cultures implies is that their relationships to those cultures that remained "outside" of history have undergone radical transformations, so that what formerly was a process of relatively autonomous or autochthonous relationships now becomes a process of progressive interaction and integration between the so-called historical cultures and those deemed to be nonhistorical. This is that panorama of the domination of the so-called higher civilizations over their "neolithic" subject cultures and the "expansion" of Western civilization over the globe that is the subject of the standard narrative of the world history written from the point of view of "historical" cultures. But this "history" of "historical" cultures is by its very nature, as a panorama of domination and expansion, at the same time the documentation of the "history" of those supposedly nonhistorical cultures and peoples who are the victims of this process. Thus, we could conclude, the records that make possible the writing of a history of historical cultures are the very records that make possible the writing of a history of the so-called nonhistorical cultures. It follows that the distinction between historical and nonhistorical fractions of the human past, based on the distinction between the kinds of records available for their study, is as tenuous as the notion that there are two kinds of a specifically human past, one that can be investigated by "historical" methods, the other investigatable by some "nonhistorical" method, such as anthropology, ethnology, ethnomethodology, or the like.

Insofar, then, as any notion of history presupposes a distinction within the common human past between a segment or order of events that is specifically historical and one that is nonhistorical, this notion contains an equivocation. Because insofar as the notion of history indicates a generally human past, it cannot gain in specificity by dividing this past into a "historical history" and a "nonhistorical history." In this formulation, the notion of history simply replicates the ambiguity contained in the failure to distinguish adequately between an object of study (the human past) and discourse about this object.

Does the recognition of the tissue of ambiguities and equivocations contained in the notion of history provide a basis for understanding recent discussions of the question of narrative in historical theory? I noted earlier that the notion of narrative itself contains an ambiguity of the same kind as that typically found in the use of the term *history*. Narrative is at once a mode of discourse, a manner of speaking, and the product produced by the adoption of this mode of discourse. When this mode of discourse is used to represent "real" events, as in "historical narrative," the result is a kind of discourse with specific linguistic, grammatical, and rhetorical features, namely, narrative history. Both the felt adequacy of this mode of discourse for the representation of specifically "historical" events and its inadequacy as perceived by those who impute to narrativity the status of an ideology derive from the difficulty of conceptualizing the difference between a manner of speaking and the mode of representation produced by its enactment.

The fact that narrative is the mode of discourse common to both "historical" and "nonhistorical" cultures and that it predominates in both mythic and fictional discourse makes it suspect as a manner of speaking about "real" events. The nonnarrative manner of speaking common to the physical sciences seems more appropriate for the representation of "real" events. But here the notion of what constitutes a real event turns, not on the distinction between true and false (which is a distinction that belongs to the order of discourses, not to the order of events), but rather on the distinction between real and imaginary (which belongs both to the order of events and to the order of discourses). One can produce an imaginary discourse about real events that may not be less "true" for being imaginary. It all depends upon how one construes the function of the faculty of imagination in human nature.

The same is true with respect to narrative representations of reality, especially when, as in historical discourses, these representations are of "the human past." How else can any past, which by definition comprises events, processes, structures, and so forth, considered to be no longer perceivable, be represented in either consciousness or discourse except in an "imaginary" way? Is it not possible that the question of narrative in any discussion of historical theory is always finally about the function of imagination in the production of a specifically human truth?

3. The Politics of Historical Interpretation: Discipline and De-Sublimation

The politics of interpretation should not be confused with interpretative practices that have politics itself as a specific object of interest—political theory, political commentary, or histories of political institutions, parties, conflicts, and so on. For in these interpretative practices, the politics that informs or motivates them—politics in the sense of political values or ideology—is relatively easily perceived, and no particular metainterpretative analysis is required for its identification. The politics of interpretation, on the other hand, arises in those interpretative practices that are ostensibly most remote from overtly political concerns, practices carried out under the aegis of a purely disinterested search for the truth or inquiry into the natures of things that appear to have no political relevance at all. This politics has to do with the kind of authority the interpreter claims vis-à-vis the established political authorities of the society of which he is a member, on the one side, and vis-à-vis other interpreters in his own field of study or investigation, on the other, as the basis of whatever rights he conceives himself to possess and whatever duties he feels himself obligated to discharge in his status as a professional seeker of truth. This politics that presides over interpretative conflicts is difficult to identify, because traditionally, in our culture at least, interpretation is conceived to operate properly only as long as the interpreter does not have recourse to the one instrumentality that the politician *per vocationem* utilizes as a matter of course in his practice, the appeal to force as a means of resolving disputes and conflicts.[1]

Interpretative conflicts reach a limit as specifically interpretative ones when political power or authority is invoked in order to resolve them. This suggests that interpretation is an activity that, in principle, stands over against political activity in much the same way that contemplation is seen to stand over against action, or theory over against practice.[2] But in the same way that contemplation presupposes action and theory presupposes practice, so, too, interpretation presupposes politics as one of the conditions of its possibility as a social activity. "Pure" interpretation, the disinterested inquiry into anything whatsoever, is unthinkable as an ideal without the presupposition of the kind of activity that politics represents. The purity of any interpretation can be measured only by the extent to which it succeeds in repressing any impulse to appeal to political authority in the course of earning its understanding or explanation of its object of interest. This means that the politics of interpretation must find the means either to effect this repression or to so sublimate the impulse to appeal to political authority as to transform it into an instrument of interpretation itself.[3]

This may seem an inordinately circuitous and abstract entry into our subject, but it is necessary for my purpose, which is to consider the question of the politics of interpretation within the context of the disciplinization of fields of study in the human and social sciences. The question is, What is involved in the transformation of a field of studies into a discipline, especially in the context of modern social institutions designed for the regulation of knowledge production, in which the physical sciences function as a paradigm for all cognitive disciplines? The question has special importance for any understanding of the social function of the institutionalized forms of study in the human and social sciences, for all of them have been promoted to the status of disciplines without having attained to the theoretical and methodological regimentation that characterizes the physical sciences.[4]

It is often argued that the human and social sciences are precluded from developing into true sciences by virtue of the nature of their objects of study (man, society, culture), which differ from natural objects in their interiority, an autonomy vis-à-vis their environments, and their capacity to change social processes through the exercise of a certain freedom of will. For some theorists, the human possession of this interiority, autonomy, and freedom of will makes it not only impossible but also undesirable even to aspire to the creation of full-blown sciences of man, culture, and society.[5] In fact, one tradition of theory and philosophy of science has it that such an aspiration is politically undesirable. For this tradition, if man, society, and culture are to be objects of disciplined inquiry, the disciplines in question should aim at understanding these objects, not at explaining them, as in the physical sciences.[6]

The field of historical studies may be taken as exemplary of those disciplines in the human and social sciences that rest content with the understanding of the matters with which they deal in place of aspiring to explain them. This is not to say that historians do not purport to explain certain aspects either of the past or of the historical process. It is rather that in general they do not claim to have discovered the kinds of causal laws that would permit them to explain phenomena by viewing them as instantiations of the operations of such laws, in the way that physical scientists do in their explanations. Historians also often claim to explain the matters of which they treat by providing a proper understanding of them. The means by which this understanding is provided is *interpretation. Narration* is both the way in which a historical interpretation is achieved and the mode of discourse in which a successful understanding of matters historical is represented.[7]

The connection between interpretation, narration, and understanding provides the theoretical rationale for considering historical studies as a special kind of discipline and for resisting the demand (made by positivists and Marxists) for the transformation of historical studies into a science. The ideological nature of both is indicated by the politics that each is seen to be able to serve. In general, the demand that historical studies be transformed into a science is advanced in the interest of promoting a politics thought to be progressive—liberal in the case of positivists, radical in the case of Marxists. The resistance to this demand, per contra, is usually justified by appeal to political or ethical values that are manifestly conservative or reactionary.[8] Since the constitution of historical studies as a discipline was carried out in the modern period in the service of political values and regimes that were in general antirevolutionary and conservative, the burden for establishing the feasibility and desirability of treating history as the object of a possible science falls upon those who would so treat it. This means that the politics of interpretation in modern historical studies turns upon the question of the political uses to which a knowledge thought to be specifically historical can or ought conceivably to be put.

My approach here requires that I attempt to specify what was involved in the transformation of historical studies into a discipline that applied rules for construing and studying their objects of interest that were different from the rules of scientific investigation prevailing in the physical sciences. The social function of a properly disciplined study of history and the political interests it served at its inception in the early nineteenth century, the period of the consolidation of the (bourgeois) nation-state, are well-known and hardly in need of documentation. We do not have to impute dark ideological motives to those who endowed history with the authority of a discipline in order to recognize the ideological benefits to new social classes and political constituencies that professional, academic historiography served and, *mutatis mutandis,* continues to serve down to our own time.

The desirability of transforming historical studies into a discipline could be urged on grounds more purely theoretical and epistemological. In an age characterized by conflicts between representatives of a host of political positions, each of which came attended by a "philosophy of history" or master narrative of the historical process, on the basis of which their claims to "realism" were in part authorized, it made eminently good sense to constitute a specifically historical discipline. The purpose of such a discipline would be simply to determine the "facts" of history, by which to assess the objectivity, veridicality, and realism of the philosophies of history that authorized the different political programs. Under the auspices of the philosophy of history, programs of social and political reconstruction shared an ideology with utopian visions of man, culture, and society. This linkage justified both and made a study of history, considered as a recovery of the facts of the past, a social desideratum at once epistemologically necessary and politically relevant. To analyze the elements of this linkage, the epistemological criticism proceeded by opposing a properly disciplined historical method conceived as empirical to a philosophy of history conceived as inherently metaphysical. The political aspect of this analytical effort consisted in opposing a properly disciplined historical consciousness to utopian thinking in all its forms (religious, social, and above all political). The combination of these two aspects of history's disciplinization had the effect of permitting the kind of historical knowledge produced by professional historians to serve as the standard of realism in political thought and action in general.[9]

What politics of interpretation is involved in this transformation of historical studies into a discipline that purports to serve as custodian of realism in political and social thinking? I take issue with a view of the relation between historical and political thinking that has become a commonplace of modern theories of totalitarian ideologies. This view has been forcefully represented by the late Hannah Arendt, and it is shared by many, especially humanistically oriented theorists of totalitarianism who attribute the degeneration of classical politics and its attendant theory to the rise of modern philosophy of history of the sort associated with Hegel, Marx, Nietzsche, Spengler, and so forth. In "The Concept of History," Arendt put the matter in the following terms: "In any consideration of the modern concept of history one of the crucial problems is to explain its sudden rise during the last third of the eighteenth century *and the concomitant decrease* of interest in purely political thinking" (my emphasis).[10]

Leaving aside the question of whether there has actually been a general "decrease of interest in purely political thinking" (not to mention the difficulty of distinguishing between a thinking that is purely political and one that is not), we may accept as generally valid Arendt's linkage of history and politics in those ideologies that took shape in the wake of the French Revolution and continue, in one form or another, to contaminate even the most chaste efforts to contrive a theory of politics free of the charge of being ideological in either motivation or effect. But Arendt leads us astray, I think, in identifying "the modern concept of history" with those philosophies of history that take their rise in Hegel's effort to use historical knowledge as a basis for a metaphysics adequate to the aims and interests of the modern secular state. For while it is true that, as Arendt says, Marx went even further than Hegel and sought to give direction to "the aims of political action," it was not his "influence" alone (or even primarily) that "politicalized" both "the historian and the philosopher of history," thereby causing the "decrease in purely political thinking" that she laments.[11] The politicalization of historical thinking was a virtual precondition of its own professionalization, the basis of its promotion to the status of a discipline worthy of being taught in the universities, and a prerequisite of whatever "constructive" social function historical knowledge was thought to serve. This was true especially of professional, academic, institutionalized (or to use Nietzsche's term, "incorporated") historical studies, that approach to the study of history that defined its aims in opposition to those of philosophy of history, that limited itself to the unearthing of the facts relevant to finite domains of the past, contented itself with the narration of "true stories," and eschewed any temptation to construct grandiose "metahistorical" theories, to find the key to the secret of the whole historical process, to prophesy the future, and to dictate what was both best and necessary for the present.

The "politics" of this disciplinization, conceived, as all disciplinization must be, as a set of negations, consists of what it marks out for repression for those who wish to claim the authority of discipline itself for their learning. What it marks out for repression in general is utopian thinking—the kind of thinking without which revolutionary politics, whether of the Left or the Right, becomes unthinkable (insofar, of course, as such thinking is based on a claim to authority by virtue of the knowledge of history that informs it). To be sure, positivists and Marxists claimed to transcend the opposition of historical thinking and utopian thinking by virtue of their claims to have provided the basis of a genuinely scientific study of history capable of revealing the laws of historical process. From the standpoint of a properly disciplined historical consciousness, however, such claims simply evidenced the presence in positivism and Marxism of the philosophy of history which a properly disciplined historical consciousness was supposed to guard against. The fact that Marxism especially claimed to be a science of history that both justified the hope for and would help to bring about the revolution of bourgeois society only attested to the utopian nature of Marxism and its putative science of history.

Now I am against revolutions, whether launched from "above" or "below" in the social hierarchy and whether directed by leaders who profess to possess a science of society and history or be celebrators of political "spontaneity."[12] Like Arendt, I would wish that in political and social matters both politicians and political thinkers were guided by the kind of realism to which a disciplined historical knowledge conduces. But on the level of interpretative theory, where the matter under contention is the politics inherent in alternative conceptions of what historical discipline itself consists of, one cannot seek to resolve differences of opinion by an appeal either to political values or to some criterion of what a properly disciplined historical knowledge consists of. For it is political values and what constitutes historical discipline that are at issue. The problem lies, however, not with philosophy of history, which is at least openly political, but with a conception of historical studies that purports to be above politics and at the same time rules out as unrealistic any political program or thought in the least tinged with utopianism. And it does so, moreover, by so disciplining historical consciousness as to make realism effectively identical with antiutopianism. One is at least obliged to try to clarify the nature of the politics implicit in the disciplinization of a field of studies undertaken with the express purpose of recuperating its objects of study from the "distortions" of political ideology in general.

It may seem perverse, however, to characterize as a politics of interpretation the disengagement of historical thought from utopian thinking, the de-ideologization of its discipline which modern historical studies values most highly. Those who value the kinds of works that professional historians typically produce must regard the philosophy of history (à la Hegel, Marx, and so on) as a pernicious, when not deluded, activity—even if, unlike many modern humanists, they do not regard it as a mainstay of totalitarian ideologies. But the fight between historians and philosophers of history is really more in the nature of a family feud than a conflict between practitioners of different disciplines or between a discipline properly practiced and one improperly practiced. For historians and philosophers of history do have the same objects of study in common, and the fight between them is over what a properly disciplined study of those objects should consist of. Since this dispute cannot be arbitrated on the grounds of any appeal to "what history teaches" (since this is what is at issue), it becomes incumbent upon us to attempt to characterize what constitutes the notion of disciplined historical reflection itself, the general belief in the possibility of which both parties share. The problem can be narrowed to that of characterizing the positive content of the historical object for which philosophy of history is conceived to be the "undisciplined" (or what amounts to the same thing, the "overdisciplined") counterpart. And this problem can be approached by asking, What is ruled out by conceiving the historical object in such a way that *not* to conceive it in that way would constitute prima facie evidence of want of "discipline"?

In order to get a handle on this question, we must recall what was considered "undisciplined" about historical studies prior to the nineteenth century. Throughout the eighteenth century, historical studies had no discipline proper to itself alone. It was for the most part an activity of amateurs. Scholars *per vocationem* were trained in ancient and modern languages, in how to study different kinds of documents (a discipline known as diplomatic), and in mastering the techniques of rhetorical composition. Historical writing, in fact, was regarded as a branch of the art of rhetoric. These constituted the methods of the historian.[13]

The eighteenth-century historian's field of phenomena was simply "the past," conceived as the source and repository of tradition, moral examplars, and admonitory lessons to be investigated by one of the modes of interpretation into which Aristotle divided the kinds of rhetorical discourse: ceremonial, forensic, and political.[14] The preliminary ordering of this field of phenomena was consigned to the "disciplines" of chronology and the techniques of ordering documents for study in the form of "annals." As for the uses to which historical reflection was to be put, these were as wide as rhetorical practice, political partisanship, and confessional variation admitted. And as for what history, considered as a record of human development, told about human society, this either fell under the charge of Christian myth or its secular, Enlightenment counterpart, the myth of Progress, or displayed a panorama of failure, duplicity, fraud, deceit, and stupidity.

When Kant turned to the consideration of what could be known from the study of history, so as to be able to determine what mankind could legitimately hope on the basis of that knowledge, he identified three kinds of equally pertinent conclusions. These were that (1) the human race was progressing continually; (2) the human race was degenerating continually; and (3) the human race remained at the same general level of development continually. He called these three notions of historical development "eudaemonism," "terrorism," and "farce," respectively; they might just as well be called comedy, tragedy, and irony (if considered from the standpoint of the plot structures they impose upon the historical panorama) or idealism, cynicism, and skepticism (if considered from the standpoint of the world-views they authorize).[15]

Whatever names we attach to them, Kant's three conceptualizations of the process of historical development indicate that all of the types of philosophy of history subsequently developed in the nineteenth century were not distinctively "modern" (as Arendt argues) but were already conceptually present in historical thinking of the premodern period. Moreover, far from being a modern innovation, the "politicalization" of the historian and philosopher of history was the rule rather than the exception. The important point is that the variety of uses to which written history's subordination to rhetoric permitted it to be put exposed historical thinking to the threat of being conceived solely in terms of Kant's third type, the farce: as long as history was subordinated to rhetoric, the historical field itself (that is, the past or the historical process) had to be viewed as a chaos that made no sense at all or one that could be made to bear as many senses as wit and rhetorical talent could impose upon it. Accordingly, the disciplining of historical thinking that had to be undertaken if history considered as a kind of knowledge was to be established as arbitrator of the realism of contending political programs, each attended by its own philosophy of history, had first of all to consist of a rigorous de-rhetoricization.

The de-rhetoricization of historical thinking was an effort to distinguish history from fiction, especially from the kind of prose fiction represented by the romance and the novel. This effort was, of course, a rhetorical move in its own right, the kind of rhetorical move that Paolo Valesio calls "the rhetoric of anti-rhetoric."[16] It consisted of little more than a reaffirmation of the Aristotelian distinction between history and poetry—between the study of events that had actually occurred and the imagining of events that might have occurred, or could possibly occur—and the affirmation of the fiction that the "stories" historians tell are found in the evidence rather than invented. Thus the whole question of the composition of the historian's discourse was moot: it appeared to be solely a function of the rigorous application of "rules of evidence" to the examination of the "historical record." In point of fact, the narratives produced by historians lend themselves to analysis in terms of their rhetorical *topoi,* which in general have been canonized in the classical notion of the so-called middle style of declamation.

The subordination of historical narrative to the deliberative mode of the middle style entails stylistic exclusions, and this has implications for the kinds of events that can be represented in a narrative. Excluded are the kinds of events traditionally conceived to be the stuff of religious belief and ritual (miracles, magical events, godly events), on the one side, and the kinds of "grotesque" events that are the stuff of farce, satire, and calumny, on the other. Above all, these two orders of exclusion consign to historical thinking the kinds of events that lend themselves to the understanding of whatever currently passes for educated common sense. They effect a disciplining of the imagination, in this case the historical imagination, and they set limits on what constitutes a specifically historical event. Moreover, since these exclusions effectively set limits on rules of description (or descriptive protocols), and since a "fact" must be regarded as "an event under a description," it follows that they constitute what can count as a specifically historical fact.[17]

The imagination was discussed in the late eighteenth century in terms of the notions of taste and sensibility and the question, addressed by the newly constituted field of aesthetics, of the difference between the ideas of "the beautiful and the sublime." If, as Arendt suggested, the disciplinization of historical studies must be considered in terms of its relation to political thinking, then it must also be considered in terms of its relation to aesthetic theory and especially to the notions of "the beautiful and the sublime." For insofar as the disciplinization of history entailed regulation, not only of what could count as a proper object of historical study but also of what could count as a proper representation of that object in a discourse, discipline consisted in subordinating written history to the categories of the "beautiful" and suppressing those of the "sublime."

Because history, unlike fiction, is supposed to represent real events and therefore contribute to knowledge of the real world, imagination (or "fancy") is a faculty particularly in need of disciplinization in historical studies. Political partisanship and moral prejudice may lead the historian to misread or misrepresent documents and thus to construct events that never took place. On the conscious level, the historian can, in his investigative operations, guard against such errors by the judicious employment of "the rules of evidence." The imagination, however, operates on a different level of the historian's consciousness. It is present above all in the effort, peculiar to the modern conceptualization of the historian's task, to enter sympathetically into the minds or consciousnesses of human agents long dead, to empathize with the intentions and motivations of actors impelled by beliefs and values that may differ totally from anything the historian might himself honor in his own life, and to understand, even when he cannot condone, the most bizarre social and cultural practices. This is often described as putting oneself in the place of past agents, seeing things from their point of view, and so forth, all of which leads to a notion of objectivity that is quite different from anything that might be meant by that term in the physical sciences.[10]

This notion is quite specific to modern historical theory, and it is typically thought to be imaginative rather than rational. For it is one thing to try to be rational, in the sense of being on guard against unwarranted inferences or one's own prejudices, and quite another to think one's way into the minds and consciousnesses of past actors whose "historicity" consists in part in the fact that they acted under the impulsion of beliefs and values peculiar to their own time, place, and cultural presuppositions. But imagination is dangerous for the historian, because he cannot know that what he has "imagined" was actually the case, that it is not a product of his "imagination" in the sense in which that term is used to characterize the activity of the poet or writer of fiction. Here, of course, the imagination is disciplined by its subordination to the rules of evidence which require that whatever is imagined be consistent with what the evidence permits one to assert as a "matter of fact." Yet "imagination," precisely in the sense in which it is used to characterize the activity of the poet or novelist, is operative in the work of the historian at the last stage of his labors, when it becomes necessary to compose a discourse or narrative in which to represent his findings, that is, his notion of "what really happened" in the past. It is at this point that what some theorists call the style of the historian, considered now as a writer of prose, takes over and an operation considered to be exactly like that of the novelist, an operation that is openly admitted to be literary, supervenes.[19] And since it is literary, the disciplinization of this aspect of the historian's work entails an aesthetic regulation. What is the nature of a disciplined historical style?

Here again we must recall that discipline consists less of prescriptions of what must be done than of exclusions or proscriptions of certain ways of imaging historical reality. And this is where the late-nineteenth-century debate over what Edmund Burke called "our ideas of the sublime and the beautiful" becomes relevant to our understanding of what was involved in the disciplinization of historical sensibility.[20] This debate, as it extends into the nineteenth century, is complex and was rendered more so by the particular obsessions the Romantics brought to their considerations of issues considered relevant to it. For our purposes, however, the crucial turn in this discussion has to do with the progressive demotion of the sublime in favor of the beautiful as a solution to the problems of taste and imagination. For the most part, these problems were construed in terms of the imagination's response to different kinds of natural phenomena: those that possessed the capacity to "charm,"and those that "terrified" (by their grandeur, extent, awesomeness, and so forth).[21] While he likened the feeling of the sublime to what the subject must feel in the presence of political majesty, Burke did not explicitly address the question of the sublime and the beautiful with respect to historical or social phenomena.[22] Indeed, he condemned the French Revolution as a "strange chaos of levity and ferocity" and a "monstrous tragi-comic scene" that could only fill its observers with "disgust and horror" rather than with that feeling of "astonishment" that the sublime in nature inspired or that feeling of respect for sheer "power" that he took to be the essence of religious awe.[23] Viewed as a contribution to the aesthetics (or what amounts to the same thing, the psychology) of historical consciousness, Burke's *Reflections on the Revolution in France* can be seen as one of many efforts to exorcise the notion of the sublime from any apprehension of the historical process, so that the "beauty" of its "proper" development, which for him was given in the example of the "English constitution," could be adequately comprehended.[24]

It was quite otherwise with Schiller, who, in his theory of the imagination, equated the "attraction" of the "bizarre savagery in physical nature" to the "delight" one might feel in contemplating "the uncertain anarchy of the moral world."[25] Meditation on the "confusion" that the "spectacle" of history displayed could produce a sense of a specifically human "freedom," and insofar as it did, "world history" appeared to him "a sublime object" (204–5). The feeling of the sublime, Schiller believed, could transform the "pure daemon" in humankind into grounds for belief in a "dignity" unique to man. The sublime, then, was a necessary "complement" to the beautiful if "aesthetic education" were to be made into a "complete whole" (210). Because the beautiful ruled over the "ceaseless quarrel between our natural and rational vocations, it took precedence over the sublime in this education, constantly returning us to "our *spiritual* mission" which has its sphere in "the world of sense" and "action to which we are after all committed" (210–11).

Schiller's linkage of the beautiful with the sphere of "sense" and "action" anticipated what was to become a commonplace of nineteenth-century aesthetics and had important consequences for both historical thought and political theory, radical as well as conservative. The gradual displacement of the sublime by the beautiful in a generally accredited aesthetic theory, as uncritically accepted by Marxists as by their conservative and liberal opponents, had the effect of restricting speculation on any ideal social order to some variant in which freedom was apprehended less as an exercise of individual will than as a release of beautiful "feelings." Yet Schiller himself joined the notion of the historical sublime to the kind of response to it that would authorize a totally different politics:

> Away then with falsely construed forebearance [*sic*] and vapidly effeminate taste which cast a veil over the solemn face of necessity and, in order to curry favor with the senses, *counterfeit* a harmony between good fortune and good behavior of which not a trace is to be found in the actual world. . . . We are aided [in the attainment of this point of view] by the terrifying spectacle of change which destroys everything and creates it anew, and destroys again. . . . We are aided by the pathetic spectacle of mankind wrestling with fate, the irresistible elusiveness of happiness, confidence betrayed, unrighteousness triumphant and innocence laid low; of these history supplies ample instances, and tragic art imitates them before our eyes. (209–10)

This could have been written by Nietzsche.

Hegel saw the dangers in such a conception of history, and in the introduction to his *Philosophy of History* he subjects it to scathing criticism on both cognitive and moral grounds.[26] Cognitively, such a conception remains on the level of appearances and fails to subject the phenomena to the critical analysis that would reveal the laws governing their articulation. Morally, such a conception could lead, not to the apprehension of human freedom and dignity, but to pessimism, lassitude, and submission to fate. The sublimity of the spectacle of history had to be transcended if it was to serve as an object of knowledge and deprived of the terror it induced as a "panorama of sin and suffering."[27]

Kant's "analytic of the sublime," in the *Critique of Judgment,* relates the apprehension of anything merely "powerful" (which belonged to what he called "the dynamical sublime") to our feeling of possessing a freedom and dignity uniquely human, but he grounds this feeling in the faculty of the reason alone.[28] Thus envisaged, the sublime is effectively cut free from the aesthetic faculty, which remains under the sway of judgments appropriate to the "beautiful," in order to be relegated to the rule of the cognitive and moral faculties.[29] And this for obvious reasons: Kant had no faith in the capacity of reflection on history to teach anything that could not be learned—and learned better—from reflection on present human existence or, indeed, on the experience of a single socialized individual.

Although Hegel took up the question of the sublime, both explicitly in his *Aesthetics* and implicitly in the *Philosophy of History,* he subordinated it to the notion of the beautiful in the former and to the notion of the rational in the latter. It was this demotion of the sublime in favor of the beautiful that constituted the heritage from German idealism to both radical and conservative thought about the kind of utopian existence mankind could justifiably envisage as the ideal aim or goal of any putatively progressive historical process. Here is a prime example of a certain kind of "politics of interpretation" which produces an "interpretation of politics" with distinct ideological implications. It is the aesthetics of the beautiful that, as Thomas Weiskel suggests, undercuts the radical impulse of this tradition.[30] This undercutting may account in part for the weak psychological appeal of the "beautiful life" as a project to be realized in political struggles and, what is more important, for the apparent incapacity of political regimes founded on Marxist principles to sustain their professed programs for the radical transformation of society in anything but the most banal ways.

What must be recognized, however, is that for both the Left and the Right, this same aesthetics of the beautiful presides over the process in which historical studies are constituted as an autonomous scholarly discipline. It takes little reflection to perceive that aestheticism is endemic to what is regarded as a proper attitude towards objects of historical study in a certain tradition, deriving from Leopold von Ranke and his epigones, which represents the nearest thing to an orthodoxy that the profession possesses. For this tradition, whatever "confusion" is displayed by the historical record is only a surface phenomenon: a product of lacunae in the documentary sources, of mistakes in ordering the archives, or of previous inattention or scholarly errors. If this confusion is not reducible to the kind of order that a science of laws might impose upon it, it can still be dispelled by historians endowed with the proper kind of understanding. And when this understanding is subjected to analysis, it is always revealed to be of an essentially aesthetic nature.

This aestheticism underwrites the conviction (periodically reaffirmed when history fails to provide a knowledge that can legitimately claim the title "scientific") that historical studies are, after all, a branch of belles-lettres, a calling suitable for a kind of gentleman-scholar for whom "taste" serves as a guide to comprehension, and "style" as an index of achievement. When the notions of taste and style are given a specifically moral connotation, as they inevitably are when they serve as the basis of a professional ethics, they authorize the attitudes that the socially responsible historian properly assumes before his designated objects of study. These attitudes include respect for the "individuality," "uniqueness," and "ineffability" of historical entities, sensitivity to the "richness" and "variety" of the historical field, and a faith in the "unity" that makes of finite sets of historical particulars comprehensible wholes. All this permits the historian to see some beauty, if not good, in everything human and to assume an Olympian calm in the face of any current social situation, however terrifying it may appear to anyone who lacks historical perspective. It renders him receptive to a genial pluralism in matters epistemological, suspicious of anything smacking of reductionism, irritated with theory, disdainful of technical terminology or jargon, and contemptuous of any effort to discern the direction that the future development of his own society might take.

Viewed as the positive content of a program for transforming history into a discipline, these attitudes and the values they imply are undeniably attractive; they possess all the "charm" that an esthetics of the beautiful might prescribe for a scholarly discipline. And they were undeniably effective in blocking any impulse to use history as the basis for a science or as a basis for justifying a visionary politics. At the same time, the establishment of these attitudes and values as an orthodoxy for professional historical studies made of history (conceived as a body of established learning) a repository of the kinds of facts that could serve as the subject matter of those human and social sciences called into existence to de-ideologize thought about man, society, and culture in the late nineteenth century. Historical facts are politically domesticated precisely insofar as they are effectively removed from displaying any aspect of the sublime that Schiller attributed to them in his essay of 1801. By this I mean nothing more than the following: insofar as historical events and processes become understandable, as conservatives maintain, or explainable, as radicals believe them to be, they can never serve as a basis for a visionary politics more concerned to endow social life with meaning than with beauty. In my view, the theorists of the sublime had correctly divined that whatever dignity and freedom human beings could lay claim to could come only by way of what Freud called a "reaction-formation" to an apperception of history's meaninglessness.

Let me try to put this somewhat more clearly. It seems to me that the kind of politics that is based on a vision of a perfected society can compel devotion to it only by virtue of the contrast it offers to a past that is understood in the way that Schiller conceived it, that is, as a "spectacle" of "confusion," "uncertainty," and "moral anarchy." Surely this is the appeal of those eschatological religions that envision a "rule of the saints" that is the very antithesis of the spectacle of sin and corruption that the history of a fallen humanity displays to the eye of the faithful. But the appeal of these religions must be quite different from that of secular ideologies, radical and reactionary alike, which seek to justify the obligations they lay upon their devotees by virtue of their claim to have divined the pattern, plan, or meaning of the historical process for which a humanity that is neither inherently corrupt nor fallen from an originally Edenic condition, but simply "unenlightened," is responsible. But modern ideologies seem to me to differ crucially from eschatological religious myths in that they impute a meaning to history that renders its manifest confusion comprehensible to either reason, understanding, or aesthetic sensibility. To the extent that they succeed in doing so, these ideologies deprive history of the kind of meaninglessness that alone can goad living human beings to make their lives different for themselves and their children, which is to say, to endow their lives with a meaning for which they alone are fully responsible. One can never move with any politically effective confidence from an apprehension of "the way things actually are or have been" to the kind of moral insistence that they "should be otherwise" without passing through a feeling of repugnance for and negative judgment of the condition that is to be superseded. And precisely insofar as historical reflection is disciplined to understand history in such a way that it can forgive everything or at best to practice a kind of "disinterested interest" of the sort that Kant imagined to inform every properly aesthetic perception, it is removed from any connection with a visionary politics and consigned to a service that will always be antiutopian in nature. Indeed, this is as true of a Marxist view of the way things are or have been in the past as it is of the bourgeois historians' concern with the study of the past "for itself alone."

It is bound to seem paradoxical to suggest that Marxism is inherently antiutopian as a philosophy of history, especially inasmuch as professional academic historiography in the West derives much of its political prestige from its proven capacity to counter the kind of utopian thinking that Marxism is supposed to exemplify. But Marxism is antiutopian insofar as it shares with its bourgeois counterpart the conviction that history is not a sublime spectacle but a comprehensible process the various parts, stages, epochs, and even individual events of which are transparent to a consciousness endowed with the means to make sense of it in one way or another.

I am not suggesting that Marxists have got history wrong and their bourgeois opponents have it right, or vice versa. Nor am I suggesting that the claim merely to understand history rather than to explain it, which non-Marxist humanist historians make, is a more appropriate way to approach the study of history than that recommended by Marxists and that therefore Marxism can be dismissed as either tactless or arrogant. Everyone recognizes that the way one makes sense of history is important in determining what politics one will credit as realistic, practicable, and socially responsible. But it is often overlooked that the conviction that one can make sense of history stands on the same level of epistemic plausibility as the conviction that it makes no sense whatsoever. My point is that the kind of politics that one can justify by an appeal to history will differ according to whether one proceeds on the basis of the former or the latter conviction. I am inclined to think that a visionary politics can proceed only on the latter conviction. And I conclude that however radical Marxism may be as a social philosophy and especially as a critique of capitalism, in its aspect as a philosophy of history it is no more visionary than its bourgeois counterpart.

Prior to the nineteenth century, history had been conceived as a spectacle of crimes, superstitions, errors, duplicities, and terrorisms that justified visionary recommendations for a politics that would place social processes on a new ground. Philosophies of history such as Voltaire's and Condorcet's constituted the basis of the Enlightenment's contribution to a progressive political theory. Schiller caught the spirit of this conception when he wrote:

> For where is the man whose moral disposition is not wholly degenerate who can read about the determined yet vain struggle of Mithradates, of the collapse of Syracuse and Carthage, or in the presence of like events can refrain from paying homage with a shudder to the grim law of necessity, or from instantly curbing his desires and, shaken by the perpetual infidelity of all sensuous objects, can avoid fastening upon the eternal in his breast?[31]

But this "shudder," occasioned by reflection on this historical spectacle, and the "fastening upon the eternal" that it was supposed instinctively to call up were progressively consigned to the class of errors to which the Romantics in general and Romanticist historians in particular—Michelet and Carlyle above all—were singularly prone.[32] In fact, the extent to which historical studies were disciplinized can be measured by the extent to which professional practitioners on both sides of the political barricades succeeded in identifying as errors the attitudes with which the Romantics approached history. The domestication of historical thinking required that Romanticism be consigned to the category of well-meaning but ultimately irresponsible cultural movements which used history for only literary or poetic purposes. Michelet and Carlyle looked to history for neither understanding nor explanation but rather for inspiration—the kind of inspiration, moreover, that an older aesthetics called sublime. Their demotion by professional historians to the status of thinkers who should be read for their literary style rather than for any insight that they might have had into history and its processes is the measure of the price paid in utopian aspiration for the transformation of history into a discipline.[33]

In the politics of contemporary discussions of historical interpretation, the kind of perspective on history that I have been implicitly praising is conventionally associated with the ideologies of fascist regimes. Something like Schiller's notion of the historical sublime or Nietzsche's version of it is certainly present in the thought of such philosophers as Heidegger and Gentile and in the intuitions of Hitler and Mussolini. But having granted as much, we must guard against a sentimentalism that would lead us to write off such a conception of history simply because it has been associated with fascist ideologies. One must face the fact that when it comes to apprehending the historical record, there are no grounds to be found in the historical record itself for preferring one way of construing its meaning over another. Nor can such grounds be found in any putative science of man, society, or culture, because such sciences are compelled simply to presuppose some conception of historical reality in order to get on with their program of constituting themselves as sciences. Far from providing us with grounds for choosing among different conceptions of history, the human and social sciences merely beg the question of history's meaning, which, in one sense, they were created to resolve. Therefore, to appeal to sociology, anthropology, or psychology for some basis for determining an appropriate perspective on history is rather like basing one's notion of the soundness of a building's foundations on the structural properties of its second or third story. The human and social sciences, insofar as they are based on or presuppose a specific conception of historical reality, are as blind to the sublimity of the historical process and to the visionary politics it authorizes as is the disciplinized historical consciousness that informs their investigative procedures.

The domestication of history effected by the suppression of the historical sublime may well be the sole basis for the proud claim to social responsibility in modern capitalist as well as in communist societies. While this pride derives in part from the claim to see through the distortions and duplicities of fascist ideologies, it is possible that fascist politics is in part the price paid for the very domestication of historical consciousness that is supposed to stand against it. Fascist social and political policies are undeniably horrible, and they may well be a function of a vision of history that sees no meaning in it and therefore imposes a meaning where none is to be found. But the appeal of fascism not only to the masses but to any number of intellectuals who had certainly been exposed to a culture of history that explained and understood the past to the very depths of all possibility leaves us with the necessity of trying to understand why this culture provided so weak an impediment to fascism's appeal.

The problem of fascism's appeal to modern political constituencies is certainly not to be solved by intellectual historical inquiry, by the history of ideas, or, if what I have suggested thus far regarding the politics of interpretation in the human and social sciences is correct, by historical inquiry in general. The events that make up fascism's history occupy a domain of human experience far removed from the kinds

of theoretical questions addressed here. But fascism in its Nazi incarnation and especially in its aspect as a politics of genocide constitutes
a crucial test case for determining the ways in which any human or
social science may construe its "social responsibilities" as a discipline
productive of a certain kind of knowledge.

It is often alleged that "formalists" such as myself, who hold that
any historical object can sustain a number of equally plausible descriptions or narratives of its processes, effectively deny the reality of the
referent, promote a debilitating relativism that permits any manipulation of the evidence as long as the account produced is structurally
coherent, and thereby allow the kind of perspectivism that permits
even a Nazi version of Nazism's history to claim a certain minimal
credibility. Such formalists are typically confronted with questions
such as the following: Do you mean to say that the occurrence and
nature of the Holocaust is only a matter of opinion and that one can
write its history in whatever way one pleases? Do you imply that any
account of that event is as valid as any other account so long as it meets
certain formal requirements of discursive practices and that one has no
responsibility to the victims to tell the truth about the indignities and
cruelties they suffered? Are there not certain historical events that tol-
erate none of that mere cleverness that allows criminals or their ad-
mirers to feign accounts of their crimes that effectively relieve them of
their guilt or responsibility or even, in the worst instances, allows them
to maintain that the crimes they committed never happened? In such
questions we come to the bottom line of the politics of interpretation
which informs not only historical studies but the human and social
sciences in general.

These questions have been given a new urgency by the appearance
in recent years of a group of "revisionist" historians of the Holocaust
who indeed argue that this event never occurred.[34] The claim is as
morally offensive as it is intellectually bewildering. It is not, of course,
bewildering to most Jews, who have no difficulty recognizing in it
another instance of the kind of thinking that led to the implementation
of the "final solution" in Germany in the first place. But it has proven
bewildering to some Jewish scholars who had thought that fidelity to
a rigorous "historical method" could not possibly result in a conclusion so monstrous. For, indeed, as Pierre Vidal-Naquet has recently
written, the revisionist case features as an important element of its
brief that massive research in the archives and pursuit of documentary
and oral testimony that are the mainstays of this "method."[35]

Vidal-Naquet takes it as a matter requiring nothing more than its assertion that the "research" that has gone into the putative search for anyone or anything that could "prove" that the Holocaust actually "happened" is not genuinely "historical" but rather "ideological." The aim of this research "is to deprive a community of what is represented by its historic memory." But he is confident that "on the terrain of positive history . . . true opposes false quite simply, independent of any kind of interpretation," and that when it is a matter of the occurrence of events (he cites the taking of the Bastille on 14 July 1789 as an example), there is no question of alternative interpretations or "revisionist" hypotheses. Such an occurrence is simply a matter of fact, and therefore a positive historiography can always set a limit on its interpretation that permits of no transgression and distinguishes well enough between a genuinely historical account and a fictive or mythic deformation of "reality." Vidal-Naquet extends his criticism of such deformations to include a Zionism that "exploits this terrible massacre in a way that is at times quite scandalous." "Finally," he writes, "it is the duty of historians to take historical facts out of the hands of ideologists who exploit them" and set limits on "this permanent rewriting of history that characterizes ideological speech." For him, these limits are approached when one encounters the kind of manifest "total lie" produced by the revisionists (75, 90–91).

This is clear enough, although the distinction between a lie and an error or a mistake in interpretation may be more difficult to draw with respect to historical events less amply documented than the Holocaust. What is less clear is the relative validity of an interpretation of the Holocaust that, according to Vidal-Naquet, has been produced by "the Israelis, or rather their ideologists," for whom "Auschwitz was the ineluctable, logical outcome of life lived in the Diaspora, and all the victims of the death camps were destined to become Israeli citizens," which he labels less a lie than an "untruth" (90). Here the distinction seems to turn, for Vidal-Naquet at least, on the difference between an interpretation that would "have profoundly transformed the *reality* of the massacre" and one that would not. The Israeli interpretation leaves the "reality" of the event intact, whereas the revisionist interpretation de-realizes it by redescribing it in such a way as to make it something other than what the victims know the Holocaust to have been. The phenomenon in question is rather like that met with in A. J. P. Taylor's controversial interpretation of Hitler as a run-of-the-mill European statesman whose methods were a bit excessive but whose ends were respectable enough, given the conventions of European politics in his time.[36] The theoretical point to be taken, however, is that an interpretation falls into the category of a lie when it denies the reality of the events of which it treats, and into the category of an untruth when it draws false conclusions from reflection on events whose reality remains attestable on the level of "positive" historical inquiry.

There is a question of interpretative tact that should be raised at this point. It must seem unconscionably pedantic, arguably eristic, and conceivably tasteless to be fiddling with what appear to be points of method in the context of a question having to do with an event so horrendous that those who experienced it, as well as their relatives and descendants, can hardly bear to hear it spoken of, much less turned into an occasion for a purely scholarly discussion of the politics of interpretation. But if this question is not a crucial example of how the politics of interpretation arises from an interpretation of politics, especially in matters historical, how could we imagine a better one? The cause of taste and sensitivity to the feelings of those who have a living investment in the memory of this event could be served by taking an example more remote in time—the French Revolution, the American Civil War, the Wars of Religion, the Crusades, the Inquisition— events remote enough in time to permit us to disengage whatever emotional weight they might have had for the people who experienced them from our purely intellectual "interest" in what they were or how they happened. But this very temptation to discuss the problem of the politics of interpretation in historical studies in the context of a consideration of events remote in time should itself enliven us to the morally domesticating effects of consigning an event definitively to "history."

Vidal-Naquet eloquently dilates on the poignant moment at which a people or group is forced, by the death of its members, to transfer an experience, existentially determinative of its own image of the nature of its existence as a historical entity, from the domain of memory to that of history. The resolution of the Holocaust question, he says, does not lie in the direction of simply exposing the "fraudulence" of the revisionists' "version" of history.

> For whatever the circumstances, today we are witnessing the transformation of memory into history. . . . My generation, people of about fifty, is probably the last one for whom Hitler's crimes are still a memory. That both disappearance and, worse still, depreciation of this memory must be combated seems to me obvious. Neither prescription nor pardon seems conceivable. . . . But what

are we going to do with this memory that, while it is our memory, is not that of everybody? (93–94)

What indeed? In the answer that a historian gives to that question is contained an entire politics of interpretation — and not only for historical studies. Vidal-Naquet's own efforts to answer it are instructive and illuminate some of the points I have been trying to make here. His remarks warrant full quotation, for they return us to the relevance of the historical sublime to the larger questions of historical interpretation:

> It is hard for me to explain myself on this point. I was brought up with an elevated — some might say megalomaniacal — conception of the task of the historian, and it was during the war that my father made me read Chateaubriand's famous article in the *Mercure* of July 4, 1807:
>
> In the silence of abjection, when the only sounds to be heard are the chains of the slave and the voice of the informer; when everything trembles before the tyrant and it is as dangerous to incur his favor as to deserve his disfavor, this is when the historian appears, charged with avenging the people.
>
> I still believe in the need to remember and, in my way, I try to be a man of memory; but I no longer believe that historians are "charged with avenging the people." We must accept the fact that "the war is over," that the tragedy has become, in a way secularized, even if this carries with it for us, I mean for we who are Jewish, the loss of a certain privilege of speech that has largely been ours since Europe discovered the great massacre. And this, in itself, is not a bad thing; for what can be more intolerable than the pose of certain personages draped in the sash of the Order of Extermination, who believe that in this way they can avoid the everyday pettiness and baseness that are our human lot? (94)

I find these words moving, not least because over and above the humaneness to which they attest, they attest to the politically domesticating effects of a historical attitude that is always much too prone to equate the consignment of an event to history with the end of a war. In point of fact, for French anti-Semites the war was far from over, as the attack on the synagogue in the rue Copernic in October 1980 (which postdated the composition of Vidal-Naquet's article) amply indicated. It is less easy than Vidal-Naquet suggests to neutralize human memory by the consignment of an event or experience of it to history. What he condemns as ideology may be nothing other than the treatment of a historical event as if it were still a memory of living men; but a memory, whether real or only felt to be so, cannot be deprived of the emotional charge and the action it seems to justify by presenting a historical-real that has remembrance as its only purpose.

Vidal-Naquet is inclined—too hastily, I think—to consign the Zionist interpretation of the Holocaust (or his version of that interpretation) to the category of untruth. In fact, its truth, as a historical interpretation, consists precisely of its effectiveness in justifying a wide range of current Israeli political policies that, from the standpoint of those who articulate them, are crucial to the security and indeed the very existence of the Jewish people. Whether one supports these policies or condemns them, they are undeniably a product, at least in part, of a conception of Jewish history that is conceived to be meaningless to Jews insofar as this history was dominated by agencies, processes, and groups who encouraged or permitted policies that led to the "final solution" of "the Jewish Question." The totalitarian, not to say fascist, aspects of Israeli treatment of the Palestinians on the West Bank may be attributable primarily to a Zionist ideology that is detestable to anti-Zionists, Jews and non-Jews alike. But who is to say that this ideology is a product of a distorted conception of history in general and of the history of Jews in the Diaspora specifically? It is, in fact, fully comprehensible as a morally responsible response to the meaninglessness of a certain history, that spectacle of "moral anarchy" that Schiller perceived in "world history" and specified as a "sublime object." The Israeli political response to this spectacle is fully consonant with the aspiration to human freedom and dignity that Schiller took to be the necessary consequence of sustained reflection on it. So far as I can see, the effort of the Palestinian people to mount a politically effective response to Israeli policies entails the production of a similarly effective ideology, complete with an interpretation of their history capable of endowing it with a meaning that it has hitherto lacked (a project to which Edward Said wishes to contribute).

Does this imply that historical knowledge, or, rather, the kind of discourses produced by historians, finds the measure of its validity in its status as an instrument of a political program or of an ideology that rationalizes, when it does not inspire, such a program? And if so, what does this tell us about the kind of historical knowledge that comes attended by a claim to have forgone service to any specific political cause and simply purports to tell the truth about the past as an end in itself and *sine ira et studio,* to provide "understanding" of what

cannot be perfectly "explained," and to lead to tolerance and forbear-
ance rather than reverence or a spirit of vengefulness?

In answer to the first question, one must grant that while it is
possible to produce a kind of knowledge that is not explicitly linked
to any specific political program, all knowledge produced in the human and social sciences lends itself to use by a given ideology better
than it does to others. This is especially true of historical knowledge
of the conceptually underdetermined sort that appears in the form of
a conventional narrative. Which brings us back to the question of the
political or ideological implications of narrativity itself as a modality
of historical representation of the sort that Barthes associates with
nineteenth-century bourgeois notions of realism.[37] Is narrativity itself
an ideological instrument? It is sufficient here to indicate the extent to
which a number of contemporary analysts of narratology, among
whom must be numbered Julia Kristeva, think it to be so.[38] If, by contrast, it is possible to imagine a conception of history that would signal
its resistance to the bourgeois ideology of realism by its refusal to
attempt a narrativist mode for the representation of its truth, is it possible that this refusal itself signals a recovery of the historical sublime
that bourgeois historiography repressed in the process of its disciplinization? And if this is or might be the case, is this recovery of the
historical sublime a necessary precondition for the production of a
historiography of the sort that Chateaubriand conceived to be desirable in times of "abjection"? a historiography "charged with avenging
the people"? This seems plausible to me.

As for the second question, namely, what all of this might imply
for any effort to comprehend that politics of interpretation in historical
studies that instructs us to recognize that "the war is over" and to forgo
the attractions of a desire for revenge, it seems obvious to me that such
instruction is the kind that always emanates from centers of established
political power and social authority and that this kind of tolerance is
a luxury only devotees of dominant groups can afford. For subordi-
nant, emergent, or resisting social groups, this recommendation—that
they view history with the kind of "objectivity," "modesty," "realism,"
and "social responsibility" that has characterized historical studies
since their establishment as a professional discipline—can only appear
as another aspect of the ideology they are indentured to oppose. They
cannot effectively oppose such an ideology while only offering their
own versions, Marxist or otherwise, of this "objectivity" and so forth
that the established discipline claims. This opposition can be carried

forward only on the basis of a conception of the historical record as being not a window through which the past "as it really was" can be apprehended but rather a wall that must broken through if the "terror of history" is to be directly confronted and the fear it induces dispelled.

Santayana said that "those who neglect the study of the past are condemned to repeat it." It is not so much the study of the past itself that assures against its repetition as it is how one studies it, to what aim, interest, or purpose. Nothing is better suited to lead to a repetition of the past than a study of it that is either reverential or convincingly objective in the way that conventional historical studies tend to be. Hegel opined that "the only thing anyone ever learned from the study of the study of history is that no one ever learned anything from the study of history." But he was convinced, and demonstrated to the satisfaction of a number of students of history more sapient than I, that one could learn a great deal, of both practical and theoretical worth, from the study of the study of history. And one of the things one learns from the study of history is that such study is never innocent, ideologically or otherwise, whether launched from the political perspective of the Left, the Right, or the Center. This is because our very notion of the possibility of discriminating between the Left, the Right, and the Center is in part a function of the disciplinization of historical studies which ruled out the possibility—a possibility that should never be ruled out of any area of inquiry—that history may be as meaningless "in itself" as the theorists of the historical sublime thought it to be.

4. Droysen's *Historik:* Historical Writing as a Bourgeois Science

Historical theory in West Germany since World War II, Georg Iggers tells us, was divided among three principal interpretative strategies: neopositivist, hermeneuticist, and Marxist.[1] These strategies represented alternative choices for those younger German scholars who still believed that history had something to teach a people that had once prided itself on its historical sense but had plunged blindly, nonetheless, into the *Walpurgisnacht* of Nazism. Among social theorists, however, history was in bad odor. In a nation that, although politically divided, had managed to effect a virtually unprecedented economic recovery, the study of the past did not seem to matter very much. The general orientation of the social theory that took shape in the 1960s, even among many Marxists, was pragmatist: practical and presentist rather than historicist.[2] It is instructive, therefore, to reflect on the recent revival of interest in the work of Johann Gustav Droysen (1808–84), who today is ranked along with Marx and Dilthey as one of the nineteenth-century thinkers from whom modern Germany may learn how to return to history and possibly even to come to terms with its own problematic past.

Droysen is usually presented as one of the founders, along with Treitschke and Sybel, of the Prussian Historical School.[3] He usually appears in histories of historiography as a critic of Rankean objectivism, celebrator of Prussian power, and defender of political relativism as a principle of historical writing. In the late 1920s, Meinecke sought to soften the conventional characterization by stressing the moral orientation of Droysen's thought. He interpreted the three concepts that Droysen had virtually invented—*Hellenismus, Prussentum,*

83

and *historik* — as aspects of a single effort to fuse cultural, political, and *wissenschaftliche* ideas into a program for German revival, after Olmütz and the failure of the Frankfort Assembly, that would be both moral and modern at the same time.[4] After World War II, the philosopher Hans-Georg Gadamer hailed Droysen as the founder of a distinctively modern hermeneutics, different from those of Schleiermacher, Hegel, and Dilthey, and as anticipating the thought of Martin Heidegger.[5] The success of this effort at redemption was reflected in Georg Iggers's authoritative study *The German Conception of History* and in the works of a number of younger German scholars.[6] Since the appearance of Jörn Rüsen's *Begriffene Geschichte* and Karl-Heinz Spieler's *Untersuchungen zur Johan Gustav Droysens "Historik,"* Droysen's thought has figured prominently in both historiographical and social scientific discussions in West Germany.[7] He is now generally regarded as the founder of a discourse that, while both theoretical and systematic, is consistent with the ideals of the humanistic tradition incarnated for many Germans in the figure of Goethe.

The current prestige of Droysen is reflected in the publication of a new edition of his most famous theoretical work, *Historik,* edited with the greatest care, precision, and comprehensiveness by Peter Leyh and projected to comprise three massive volumes.[8] When completed, this edition will certainly supplant that of Rudolf Hübner, first issued in 1937 and now in its eighth edition,[9] and further contribute to the fame of its author as a historical theorist of classic stature. The first volume of Leyh's edition contains a full reconstruction of Droysen's lectures for his courses on *Historik* delivered at the universities of Jena and Berlin between 1857 and 1883, two versions of the *Grundriss der Historik* (the earliest manuscript version of 1857/58 and the last published version of 1882), and three essays on theoretical and methodological issues which Droysen appended to the published versions of the *Grundriss.*

This first volume is dedicated to Jörn Rüsen, who made his mark in a study of Droysen's historical works, showing how the theories presented systematically in *Historik* were implicit in his historiographical practice from the beginning. Meinecke had argued that Droysen had been driven to theory out of disillusionment caused by the Prussian defeat at Olmütz and a fear of the French threat to Germany represented by Louis Bonaparte's restoration of the Empire in 1852. Rüsen showed that no such "epistemological break" occurred, that the problem of the relation between theory and practice, culture and politics, had informed Droysen's studies of Alexander the Great, Hellenistic culture, and Prussian politics from early on. This orientation would have been consistent with the interests of Droysen's intellectual models (Hegel, August Boeckh, and Wilhelm von Humboldt); and in fact while still a student Droysen had conceived the project of writing a work that would provide a theoretical basis for history's claim to autonomy as a distinct discipline. He was no doubt drawn to the study of Hellenistic culture by his perception of the "Hellenistic" nature of his own cultural epoch (that Hellenistic flavor that Burckhardt lamented and Nietzsche took as a presupposition of his own "nihilism") and to the figure of Alexander the Great by his recognition that in his own time nation building had to be the work of a strong state rather than a spontaneous process. All of this, Rüsen showed, made him as critical of the newer, Rankean, "objectivist" historiography as he was inclined to be by temperament of any merely "antiquarian" study of the past.[10]

Droysen always insisted that the best historiography would arise out of the historian's concerns with the problems of his own epoch. A historiography fully sensitized to the ineluctable link between theory and praxis could contribute, he maintained, to the articulation of the principles of a (Kantian) "practical reason" in terms relevant to an age that was more different from its past than it was similar to it. Historiography, Droysen believed from the first, had to be an ethical enterprise, not in the spirit of Plato but in that of the Sophists.[11] Like the latter, he desired a realistic ethics, which meant a "historicist" ethics; and he saw in the thought of Wilhelm von Humboldt a model that had been betrayed by the Rankean ideal of "objectivity," which favored "criticism" at the expense of "interpretation" as a hermeneutic principle (51–53).

Given this brand of realism, which combines Sophistic skepticism with morality, it is not surprising that Droysen's *Historik* was unappreciated in its own time. Leyh notes that Droysen's courses on *Historik,* given over a quarter of a century, were always sparsely attended by students; and Droysen himself remarked that his whole enterprise was regarded by his professional colleagues with utter bemusement ("Vorwart," ix and n. 4). The *Grundriss* of the *Historik,* which Droysen first distributed to his friends and students and then published in three editions, was too condensed to appeal to theorists and much too aphoristic, even gnomic, to yield methodological principles that could be used as guides to research. In his review of Hübner's first edition of the *Vorlesungen,* Erich Rothacker (who had himself published a fourth edition of the *Grundriss* in 1925) claimed a magisteriality for Droysen's theories which linked them to most of the currents of German philoso-phy in the late nineteenth and early twentieth centuries.[12] But until recently, interest in Droysen's work tended to concentrate on his politi-cal ideas and theories of state-building rather than on his *Historik*. Outside of Germany, Croce in Italy and Collingwood in Britain dis-missed the *Grundriss* peremptorily.[13] Not until Gadamer hailed *Historik* as a precursor of Heideggerian philosophy did the work come into its own. In current historiographical-philosophical debate in Ger-many, "its own" appears to be to function as a basis for a "bourgeois" alternative to Marx and to Nietzsche. Against Marx, Droysen appears as an eminently respectable, if bourgeois, philosopher of social praxis; against Nietzsche, he appears as an equally respectable, but gratify-ingly sophisticated, bourgeois "genealogist of morals."

In fact, Droysen's *Historik* provides nothing less than an explica-tion of the theoretical principles of bourgeois ideology in its national-industrial phase. Thus envisaged, it can be viewed as a textbook for producing bourgeois ideology in the post-Revolutionary era. This may be why it received such scant public notice in the nineteenth century. It is "in house" discourse, product of a discussion within the dominant class on how to give its own historically determinate existence the odor of ideality. Unlike those historians who simply manifest their ideo-logical allegiances in their historical writings, as Ranke, Treitschke, and Mommsen did, Droysen—from a perspective within ideology—turns his critical powers upon its operations and examines ways by which ideology can achieve a desirable, socially domesticating effect through the production of a certain kind of historical discourse. To put it in contemporary critical-theoretical terms, Droysen shows how a cer-tain kind of "writing activity," in this case the writing of history, can engender a certain kind of reading subject who will identify with the moral universe incarnated in "the Law" of a society organized politi-cally as a nation-state and economically as a part of an international system of production and exchange.

I wish to stress that in characterizing Droysen's work as ideologi-cal, I do not intend to derogate it. Since Althusser,[14] we have learned to think of ideology less as a distortion or false account of "reality" than as a certain practice of representation whose function is to create a specific kind of reading or viewing subject capable of inserting him-self into the social system that is his historically given potential field of public activity. It is obvious that any society, in order to sustain the practices that permit it to function in the interests of its dominant groups, must devise cultural strategies to promote the identification of its subjects with the moral and legal system that "authorizes" the society's practices. Seen from this perspective, a given kind of art, literature, or historiography need not be construed as a consciously constructed instrument for convincing the members of a society of the truth of certain doctrines, for indoctrinating them into certain beliefs of an economic or political kind. On the contrary, the ideological element in art, literature, or historiography consists of the projection of the kind of subjectivity that its viewers or readers must take on in order to experience it as art, as literature, or as historiography.[15] Art and literature have a domesticating effect when they project as possible subjectivities for their consumers the figure of the "law-abiding" citizen; this is their moral aspect, whatever subject matter they may deal with and whatever stylistic genius they may manifest.[16] Pornography gains its effects—both as titillation and scandal—precisely by the projection of the "law-abiding" citizen as its potential consumer. Similarly, art and literature become "revolutionary" or at least socially threatening, not when they set forth specific doctrines of revolt or depict sympathetically revolutionary subjects, but precisely when they project—as Flaubert did in *Madame Bovary*—a reading subject alienated from the social system of which the prospective reader is a member. Dominant social groups will therefore favor public representational practices that produce the mentality of the "law-abiding" citizen, whatever their own private preferences in art, literature, or morality. And this is why the important theoretical issues in fields like historiography, literary criticism, and philosophy—the mainstays of the humanities in the modern era—have always had to do with formal matters, problems of representation, rather than material (subject matter) or methodological (research procedures) problems.

This can be seen most clearly in the history of historiography, which has played a dominant role in the political economy of the humanities since the French Revolution. Historiography is, by its very nature, the representational practice best suited to the production of the "law-abiding" citizen. This is not because it may deal in patriotism, nationalism, or explicit moralizing but because in its featuring of narrativity as a favored representational practice, it is especially well suited to the production of notions of continuity, wholeness, closure, and individuality that every "civilized" society wishes to see itself as incarnating, against the chaos of a merely "natural" way of life. In order to read appreciatively the kinds of works produced by the majority of modern historians, amateur or professional, one must assume the mental stance of a subjectivity that believes in these notions not only as values but also as the categories best suited to the conceptualization of the "reality" one lives. Such a subjectivity is prepared to adopt a specific morality as the criterion for endowing the events of history with whatever meaning they can be construed "objectively" to possess. When this morality is identified with the actual practices of the society to which the reader belongs, these notions and the representational practices that project them as the basis for understanding "reality" correctly can be labeled "ideological" in the broader, analytical sense in which Althusser has presented this concept.

Now, Droysen's *Historik* is unique among nineteenth-century tracts on historical thinking inasmuch as it openly embraces this ideological function as an aim or purpose. This is what drives Droysen to push beyond the "critical" methods refined by Ranke and the Historical School to the consideration of the alternative ways that one might legitimately write different accounts of the same set of historical events. This emphasis on historiographical composition makes the work original in its own right, since modern historical theory offers very little instruction in this regard — and this can be said as much of Marxist as of bourgeois historical theory. But Droysen is even more original, for it can be seen on reflection that what he offers is less a theory of historiographical composition than a kind of phenomenology of historical reading. He instructs historians in how to produce different readings of history so as to engender different kinds of moral perspectives in their readers, but reconciling them with respect to the current social system and its *doxa* in every case.

The act of reading requires that the subject assume a particular position vis-à-vis the discourse, on the one side, and the system of beliefs, values, ideals, and so on, that comprise his cultural horizons, on the other. To acquiesce in the adequacy of a given way of representing "reality" is already to acquiesce implicitly to a certain standard for determining the value, meaning, or worth of the "reality" thus represented. This standard, in turn, is incarnated in the system of symbolic relationships under the aegis of which all forms of "legitimate" authority are offered for the subject. The purpose of the canonical representational practices of a given society, then, is to produce a subjectivity that will take this symbolic structure as the sole criterion for assessing the "realism" of any recommendation to act or think one way and not another.

Historical representation is especially well suited to the production of such a subjectivity, since it purports to deal with "the real" rather than the merely "imaginary" (as "literature" is supposed to do) but distances this "reality" by construing it under the modality of a "pastness" both distinct from and continuous with "the present." As distinct from the present, the past is alien, exotic, or strange; as continuous with it, this past is familiar, recognizable, and potentially fully knowable. The historical past is, in a word, "uncanny," both known and unknown, present and absent, familiar and alien, at one and the same time. Thus construed, the historical past has all the attributes that we might ascribe to the psychological sphere of "the imaginary," the level of infantile fantasies and narcissistic projections that feeds off dreams of uninhibited mastery and control of objects of desire. On this level, cognitive problems, problems connected with the question of "how we know" and "if we know," do not arise or are suppressed. On the contrary, as past, everything arising within this sphere is "fixed" forever, located eternally in a tableau of finished actions whose natures are indistinguishable from the places they occupy in the tableau. These places, in turn, are not merely spatial locations but moral ones especially, *topoi* or *loci* defined by the "symbolic system" by reference to which they are identified. In contemplating the historical past, the reading subject is treated to a spectacle that allows him to exercise his fantasies of freedom under the aspect of a fixed order, or conflict under the aspect of resolution, of violence under the aspect of an achieved peace, and so on. In other words, historical representation permits the reader to give free reign to "the imaginary" while remaining bound to the constraints of a "symbolic system," but in such a way as to engender in him a sense of "reality" that is "more comprehensible" than his present social existence. Indeed, historical representation can produce in the subject a sense of "the real" that can be used as a criterion for determining what shall count as "realistic" in his own present. It is thus a necessary element in every modern ideology that, whether radical or reactionary, revolutionary or conservative, must have some such criterion for "fixing" the subject within a given system of social praxis. All this is recognized more or less explicitly by Droysen in his reflections on "Historik," his proposed "organon" for historical thought and the theory by which he proposed to raise history to the status of a "disziplin" (43, 53).

The notion of a "historics" that would be to historiography what poetics was for fiction, and rhetorics for oratory, had been raised by the liberal German historian and publicist G. C. Gervinus in 1837 in a work entitled *Grundzüge der Historik*.[17] A historian of literature and culture, Gervinus discriminated among the possible kinds of historiographical representation on the analogy of the traditional distinctions among the poetic modes of Epic, Lyric, and Dramatic. Droysen regarded this move as leading to the assimilation of history to belles-lettres and argued that if history was different from science and philosophy, it was also different from literature (217). "Historics," in his view, had to address the (Kantian) question, How is history possible? with the word *history* carrying the full ambiguity of designating both a mode of specifically human existence and a specific way of representing that mode in discourse. In effect, Droysen turns the ambiguity of the word *history* into a principle for organizing his analysis of all the problems connected with historical representation. Accordingly, he divides his work into two principal parts: (1) *Methodik,* having to do with the forms and contents of a distinctively historical mode of thinking ("heuristic," "criticism," "interpretation," and "representation"); and (2) *Systematik,* having to do with the forms and contents of a distinctively historical mode of existence (the "Ethical Powers" that inform historical being and the concepts of "Man and Humanity" that history's basis and goal, respectively, comprise).

It will be readily observed that in this schema Droysen does not simply divide history into form and content, in the manner of many theorists who identify the latter with facts and the former with narrative or manner of composition. On the contrary, in his discussion of the problem of representation, Droysen makes clear that he regards the content of the historian's discourse, not as the facts or events that comprise his manifest referent, but as his understanding of these facts and the moral implications he draws from their contemplation. As a matter of fact (if one may be permitted that expression in this context), Droysen's analysis of historical representation allows us to speak of the "content of the form" of a historical discourse, analogously to the way we might speak of the content of a given form of historical existence. For considered as an entity, object, or monument, the historian's discourse is something quite other than the referent about which it speaks; it is, to use modern critical terminology, a discursive event that differs in both form and content from other kinds of events, such as wars, revolutions, economic undertakings, and the like, by virtue of its status as a verbal performance. And thus envisaged, the historical discourse has a content which we might call the aim or purpose of the discourse, not to be confused with its subject matter, or referent.

Historical discourses with the same referent, say, the French Revolution, may have many different possible contents. This is why, in his discussion of the forms of historical discourse, Droysen distinguishes among four kinds—*investigative, narrative, didactic,* and *discussive*—on the basis of the different degrees to which they relate to current debates over public policy, social struggles, and the like (217–22 ff.). The same set of events could be the subject, in the sense of the referent, for each and all of these modes of representation; and any given historical discourse may contain elements of all of them. Indeed, the historical classic would be defined as a discourse that integrated all of these modes into its elaboration. But the modes of representation can be ranked, and Droysen ranks them with respect to the discussive form, which he regards as the highest of all (271–83). And it is highest because it explicitly addresses itself to the relevance that our knowledge of the past might have with respect to the social praxis of the society to which the writer or reader of history belongs.

This is a manifestation of Droysen's presentism, his insistence that the subject matter of historical investigation, the interpretative framework used to disclose some meaning for it, and the representational mode chosen to insert it into current theoretical and practical activities are not given by the data themselves but are chosen by the historian—in response to imperatives more or less conscious in a given historian but immanent always in the current praxis that defines the historian's social horizon. This presentism is reflected as well in Droysen's notion of the nature of historical data. The past, he says, can be known only insofar as it has continued to exist in the present. The events that make up the past are gone and can never be the object of a present perception. But the past can be conceived to have continued to exist in the present in two forms: as *Überreste,* "remains," in the form of documents and monuments, and as elements of social praxis inherited from the past in the form of conventions, ideas, institutions, beliefs, and so on (71–87). Thus envisaged, every putative investigation of the past is and can only be a meditation on that part of the present that is really either a trace or a sublimation of some part of the past.

It would be too much to say that Droysen has anticipated the Freudian notion of history as the study of materials given in the "return of the repressed" of society, but the idea is similar. The "content" of present existence is the praxis of the society to which the individual belongs. This content appears as the product of a mediation between a past only vaguely known and a future only vaguely anticipated. This gives the "form" of a specifically historical existence, which is nothing other than the sense of the historicity of the present engendered by the intuition that we are at once continuous with our past and distinctively different from it. Historians contribute to this sense of the historicity of the present by representing the past in discourses that more or less consciously "situate" the reader in a position of activity or passivity with respect to the social forces that represent his current horizon of expectations (159–63).

This is where interpretation comes in. Interpretation is called for after the work of heuristic and criticism has been done. By heuristic we "determine an object for our activity," and by criticism, of the sort that Ranke had brought to perfection, "we make it ready for understanding (*Verständnis*)." Then, by interpretation, "bemächtigen wir uns seines Inhalts" (65). We do so, not by providing an "explanation" (*Erklärung*) of the events, discovering their causes or presenting them as manifestations of some ontologically prior ground or power, but by submitting them to conceptualization under the categories of the "Understanding (*das Verständnis*)." Droysen is quite explicit on this matter: "Das Wesen der geschichtlichen Methode ist forschend zu Verstehen, ist die Interpretation." And to understand historical events is to conceptualize them under "the same ethical and intellectual categories which . . . have their expression in the thing that is to be understood" (22).

This sounds like the historicist instruction to view events and actors of the past "in their own terms"— as if determining what these "terms" might be were a process different from the investigation of the past that had provided the objects to be so understood. But for Droysen, "the . . . ethical and intellectual categories" that are to be used for understanding historical events have already been located in the historian's own present, as "remains" or "sublimations" of past practices. So what is involved is not the explication of principles that are endemic to the past only and alien to the present but the application of the categories operative in our own present situation (as egos trying, with a combination of material and spiritual means, to live a distinctively human life) to materials that are equally present to perception. These means consist of (1) the individual's immediate practical aims and needs, (2) the material conditions of his time and place, (3) the character type and elements of personal will of the individual, and (4) the moral principles (*der sittlichen Ideen*) of the culture to which the individual belongs (206–15). Whether the historian stresses one or another of the categories that each of these means presupposes will determine the kind of "interpretation" he will be inclined to use for "understanding" his object of study. There are thus four fundamental types of historical interpretation:

1. *Pragmatic,* concentrating on the immediate aims of the actors in the historical drama;
2. *Conditional,* stressing the material conditions within which the drama unfolds;
3. *Psychological,* dealing in character types and stressing the element of personality and will in the individual and the masses; and
4. *Ethical,* contemplating the events under the categories that determine the three spheres of the moral life: material (familial, national, human), ideal (the good, the true, and the beautiful), and practical (law, politics, and economics). (163–66)

In his consideration of the modes of interpretation, Droysen insists that they are not mutually exclusive and that all are more or less present in any historical account of classical stature, such as Thucydides' history of the Peloponnesian Wars. But the ethical type stands at the pinnacle and constitutes a standard by which the other types, singly or combined, can be judged: "Mit dieser Interpretation der [sittlichen] Ideen ist das historischen Verständnis vollendet" (166). It is ethical interpretation that closes the hermeneutic circle by which the part of the historical process is used to illuminate the whole, and the whole to illuminate the part; and it is this type of interpretation that underlies that mode of representation, the discussive, that alone can wed the form with the content of a discourse in order to make reflection on its referent seem relevant to both knowledge and current social praxis (215).

In his discussion of historical interpretation and representation, Droysen reveals that he had anticipated two insights on which post-Marxist critiques of nineteenth-century bourgeois "realist" ideology had been based. First, what appears in a given historical representation as a direct portrayal of events is actually a mediated portrayal, the determinateness of which derives from the incompleteness of historical materials, the dramatistic instincts of the narrator, his didactic purpose, and his deepest interests in the problems of his own times. Second, what appears to be a "realistic" representation of the facts is always actually based on a criterion, not of truth, but of plausibility, which has reference to the social practices of the historian's own time, place, and circumstances. If Droysen's system is a science, it is a science of the plausible, the verisimilar, the *Wahrscheinlich,* rather than the *Wahre.* But the "plausible," which is a socially given category, is quite different from the "possible" revealed to us by science and the "imaginary" revealed to us by literature and art. It is in this sense that Droysen departs from Aristotle, who viewed history, which dealt in the "actual," as inferior to philosophy, which dealt in the "true," and poetry, which dealt in the "possible."[18] What is plausible, we know since Freud, is that which conscience, the distillation of social authority, tells us we should desire against that which need or instinct tells us we do desire. The plausible is the distillate of the conflict between social restraints, introjected as the "symbolic system" of the culture to which we belong, on the one side, and the "imaginary," acting under the impulsions of the libido and instincts, on the other. The distilled "plausibility" is our lived "reality," more real to us than any absolute intelligence might discern in any objective perception of "the way things are." More real even than what the ego, operating in accordance with the "reality principle," tells us is "possible."

It was because Droysen realized that historical reflection deals in the plausible rather than in the true that he gave such prominence to the problem of historical representation, to the historian's production of an image of the past and of a discourse capable of assimilating that image to the reader's understanding. Droysen does not regard representation as being primarily a "literary" problem, a matter of "style" or rhetoric (see esp. the essay, "Kunst und Methode," 480. ff., and *Vorlesungen,* 217) because, among other things, the historian's materials do not lie before him in the manner of a landscape or spectacle that he could depict in the way a painter would do. The past is both present and absent to the historian: present as remains and inherited practices, absent as a prior human existence indicated by these. It follows that the historian's principal task cannot be simply to resurrect the past; rather, it is to explicate (*erschliessen*) the past through an unveiling (*Enthüllung*) and exaltation (*Erhebung*) of the present that was latent within it, or, conversely, to enrich (*bereichen*) the present through explication (*Erschliessung*) and illumination (*Aufklärung*) of the past that inheres within it (219). From the "Doppelnatur des Erforschten" (*Vorlesungen,* 219; *Grundriss,* 445) derives the "verschiedenen Formen der Darstellung" (219). And these forms are the following:

1. *Investigative (die Untersuchende),* which provides a mimesis of the research process by which a given object was located and identified (222–29);
2. *Narrative (die Erzählende),* which provides a mimesis of the course of development that that object followed, and as discovered by the research (229–49);

3. *Didactic* (*die Didaktische*), which draws the "moral" of the story set forth in the narrative account, especially for pedagogical purposes (249–65); and
4. *Discussive* (*die Diskussive* or *Erörtende*), which relates the moral teachings drawn from the didactic exercise to the contemporary social problems and practical concerns of the reader (265–80).

As with the kinds of interpretation, each kind of representation has its own proper object of study, aim or purpose, appropriate materials, and rhetorical stance. They must be judged, therefore, "nach der Aufgabe wird sich die eine oder andere als geeigneter, ja als die gebotene zeigen." (221). But the forms can be, and are, ranked by Droysen with respect to their comprehensiveness and service to the ultimate historical value, which is the cultivation of a "proper" historical consciousness in the reader (280).

It should be stressed that the four forms of representation do not correspond in any obvious way to the four forms of interpretation earlier set forth. The four interpretative modes (pragmatic, conditional, psychological, and ethical) can appear in any and all of the representational forms. It is less a matter of matching any given form of interpretation to a given form of rerpesentation than it is a matter of making clear to the historian what can and what cannot be achieved as an effect upon the reader of a given form of either. These effects are conceived to be more or less "appropriate" as they move the reader out of a position as mere spectator of the human drama into that of a self-conscious representative of "the ethical powers" (*die sittlichen Mächte*) which have their incarnation in a given system of social practice. The aim is not to produce an "objective," in the sense of "unparteilich," perception of reality. Indeed, historical objectivity is and can only be "parteilich." And Droysen raises the whole question of objectivity within the context of his discussion of the aims of historical narrative only in order to dismiss it with the following aphorism: "Die objektive Unparteilichkeit . . . ist unmenschlich. Menschlich ist die vielmehr, parteilich zu sein" (236). Since man has his historical existence in his membership in a number of fragmentary circles of "commonality" (*Gemeinsamkeit*)—natural, ideal, and practical—his perspective on reality is necessarily "parteilich." In explicating the past of his own society, the historian should assume a position vis-à-vis its ongoing structures that is similarly "parteilich," even while pointing his reader's attention to the "higher thought" (*ein höhere Gedanke*) in which all merely historical conflict is "versöhnt" (249). This higher thought is an image of unity in which the parts are assimilated to the whole, be-speaking a "totality" in which all spheres of human life are appre-hended "in ihrem Zusammenhang, ihrer Gegenseitigkeit, ihrem allseits rastlosen Fortschreiten" (264–65).

There are no changeless truths, then, except that everything changes; and no absolute progress in human culture save the progress of the idea of progress itself. But Droysen does not stop here. In discerning the possibility of conceiving history under the "higher thought" of change in general, he has only indicated the form the didactic representation should take. It remains to specify the content of this form, and this content is given in his discussion of the discussive form of historical representation (*Vorlesungen,* 265; *Grundriss* I, 406; *Grundriss,* 448). Here historical reflection is set over against every merely practical goal of every finite institution, including the state; every speculatively given ideal end; and above all "public opinion"– as a control and brake (273–77). Here historical consciousness is identi-fied with those principles that in the *Systematik* are set forth as the "content" of historical being: "die sittlichen Mächte." The "practical" significance of "our science (*Wissenschaft*)" is revealed, "nicht als wenn sie sich erst so empfehlen und rechtfertigen müsste, sondern weil unsere methodische Betrachtung erst damit ihren Kreish vollendet, dass, sie, aus der Gegenwart rückwarts arbeitend, das Erarbeitete in die Gegenwart und in deren Mittleben und Mitschaffen zuruckführt" (280). The aim of historical understanding is ultimately only the deep-ening of the faculty of the understanding itself—which has its origins in the praxis of society in general and its manifestation in the current praxis of the historian's own society (283). Historical theory thus envisaged is nothing but a sublimation, a raising to consciousness, of the practice of society itself. In designating these practices as "die sittlichen Mächte," the ethical powers, Droysen closes the gap between morality and society, between *ethos* and *kratos,* which in classical humanism had always been conceived to stand in opposition to one another, as effectively as Nietzsche in *The Genealogy of Morals* or Freud in *Totem and Taboo.*

Droysen's ideological orientation is clearly manifested in his defense of a secular version of Christian providentialism, the idea of a historical "dialectic" that turns private vice into public advantage; in his open defense of modern historical thought over all of its proto-types; and in his celebration of the praxis of bourgeois society as a standard for measuring the achievements of earlier social formations. But he rises above other bourgeois ideologues in his attempt to correlate possible ways of representing historical structures and processes with the exigencies of a social system that simultaneously honors competition, egotism, and force while celebrating the ideals of cooperation, self-sacrifice, and peace. In order to effect this *Gleichschaltung,* two theoretical moves of the utmost originality are made, one on a formal, the other on a material plane. In the section on *Methodik,* the theoretical move on the formal plane consisted of the elevation of "Interpretation" over "Criticism" in the interest of establishing the "Understanding" (versus "Reason" and "taste") as the human faculty best suited to historical reflection. Then, in the section on *Systematik,* the theoretical move on the material plane consists of the elevation of "the practical commonalities" (*die praktischen Gemeinsamkeiten*) over both their "natural" and their "ideal" counterparts. The "practical commonalities" comprise the domains of economics, law, and politics, and these are defined as having the function of mediating between the "natural commonalities" of the family, tribe, and folk and the "ideal commonalities" of language, art, science, and religion. History is thereby given a specific content that can be identified with the social praxis of the historian's own lived present.

My own condensed schematization of the relationships conceived to exist between these three "circles of commonalities" conveys nothing of the subtlety and depth of the explication given in the *Historik.* But the last version of the *Grundriss* clearly displays the intent of the explication, which achieves a comprehensive reformulation, in the direction of their *embourgoisement,* of Aristotle's *Ethics* and *Politics* (f. *Grundriss,* 436). Here the historical process is presented as a product of labor (*die Arbeit*) in which every individual (however unconscious), every institution (however narrow), and every class (however base) has a necessary place and function in a universal dialectic of the "individual Ego" and the "general Ego." The categories of Aristotle are used to define the elements of this dialectic in the following way. The "material" (*Stoff*) of history is "the natural commonalities"; its forms (*Formen*) are provided by the "ideal" and "practical" commonalities; its immediate cause, the "workers" (*Arbeitern*), which is "everyman" (*jeder Mensch*); and its final cause, aim, or purpose, nothing but "history" itself and the consciousness thereof (*Grundriss I,* 407–11). Thus, history is the "species notion" (*Gattungsbegriff*) of humanity, "its knowledge of itself" (*das Wissen der Menschheit von sich*), and its "self-certainty" (*ihre Selbstgewissheit*) (*Grundriss,* 444).

In the celebration of historical consciousness as being at once the product of the human evolutionary process and the species concept of humankind, Droysen provides a secular equivalent of that theology of history that in its Augustinian form had, in his view, made possible the idea of freedom as a universal human value (364–66). This is not the same kind of process that Löwith analyzed, in which the principles of Christian *Heilsgeschichte* are simply translated into secular terms, à la Hegel.[19] History is not conceived to serve some "higher power"; it is conceived to be a process in which "secularity" itself becomes its own means and ends simultaneously: "Historie ist das γνῶθι σαυτόν der sittlichen Welt und ihr Gewissen" (41). This self-identity of means and ends is what effectively undercuts any impulse to "prophesy" the future or to "idealize" the past for reactionary purposes (163). It promotes a feeling of satisfaction for "things as they are" in any given "present" by showing that whatever they are, they have their necessary reasons for being this way and not another. This is the basis of Droysen's "realism" and of the point of view that allows him to claim for historical knowledge the status, not of art, science, or philosophy, but of a *Disziplin* of the plausible, a discipline that is empirical and speculative at one and the same time.

By vesting the criterion of adequacy for any vision of the real in the social praxis of the time and the specific institutions that incarnate that praxis, Droysen articulates a standard of plausibility by which any radical or reactionary version of historical "reality" can be judged and found wanting. Droysen clearly perceived the weakness of any conception of realism founded upon an empirical epistemology. By vesting the concept of the historically real, not in a referent, but in "the ethical powers," he shows that he saw through the claims of the so-called human sciences which were beginning to take shape in his own time. The historically real is never given by naked "experience"; it is always already worked up and fashioned by a specific organization of experience, the praxis of the society from within which the picture of reality is conceptualized. This is why, no doubt, he placed such emphasis on the possibility of conceiving alternative but equally valid images of historical reality and sought to classify them and to rank them by type. Such images would be as various as the kinds of socially organized experience permitted by the praxis of any given age. And this, in turn, is why the problem of representing the historically real concerned him in a way that only Nietzsche among his contemporaries reflected on systematically. But Droysen faced this problem much more directly than Nietzsche, for he wrote from a standpoint of one who valued the very bourgeois ideals that Nietzsche, among others, was concerned to unmask and criticize as mere "fictions."

It remains to ask in what context one should locate the question of Droysen's achievement as a historical theorist. Simply to set his thought over against that of Marx or Nietzsche—as a distinctively "bourgeois" defense of a certain kind of liberal providentialism—does not so much resolve the question as merely raise the further one of the criterion to be used for assessing alternative ways of conceptualizing history and its theoretical problems. It will not do to take one's stance within a specific conception of historical objectivity, such as Marxism or neopositivism, and point out that Droysen is not objective, since Droysen not only raises the question of what a specifically historical objectivity might consist in but also explicitly defends a notion of historical objectivity different from any scientistic kind. Nor would it do to assume a Nietzschean perspective, which locates every form of human inquiry on a spectrum of "fictionality" according to whether it serves the needs of "life" or the "will to power" or not, because Droysen explicitly raises the question of how the line between fiction and fact, possibility and truth, is to be drawn. The main theoretical question that Droysen poses, however, is not that of objectivity and truth in historical thinking but rather that of the autonomy of historical thought with respect to other forms of thinking and of historical studies to other disciplines.

Droysen's is surely the most sustained and systematic defense of the autonomy of historical thought ever set forth—including the attempts of Croce and Collingwood in this century. And claims for the autonomy of a way of thinking or a discipline are not really theoretically arbitrable, since in order for such claims to be assessed, one must assume a point of view outside the way of thinking of the discipline being so defended, which already begs the question of autonomy itself. In this respect, claims for the autonomy of a discipline are like claims for the autonomy of a community, folk, or state, establishable finally only in the practical realization thereof.

The question of the nature of Droysen's achievement, then, must turn on the problem of the ideological function or value attached to the claims for history's autonomy vis-à-vis other ways of thinking and disciplines. Why, in short, should modern historians wish to claim for their "discipline" an autonomy that had never seemed to be an issue at any earlier time? History ("the past") had always been studied under the press of imperatives of either a generally cultural or specifically extra-historical kind down to the nineteenth century: philosophical, pedagogical, rhetorical, religious, political, and so on. Why now should "history" in the sense of past human acts and historical questions (What happened? when? where? why? with what significance?) be marked out as a special field of inquiry, with its own proper objects of study and its own proper methodology—especially when it was obvious that such "methods" differed not at all from those that had been used in humanistic studies in general since the Renaissance?

Of course, the obvious answer to this question lies in part in the crystallization in the nineteenth century of a new social order, the experience of millenarian hope and frustration that attended the French Revolution, Romanticism, and the emergence of new secular ideologies all of which based their claims to authority on particular versions of the historical process. But all of this, which is conventionally invoked to account for the "new" interest in history that characterized the early nineteenth century, could just as easily have led to a rejection of history's claims to a unique place among the human sciences rather than to its elevation as *magistra vitae* and putative arbitrator among other, merely ideological accounts of the historical process. As Droysen clearly saw, there was nothing in Ranke's "critical method" that had not been practiced in historical jurisprudence, philology, and *Altertumswissenschaft* by the *érudits* of the late eighteenth century. And although the Historical school founded by Ranke took a relatively new object for its basic unit of study, namely, the nation-state, rather than the region or a given institution (as Möser and the Göttingen Circle did), this was a matter more of pragmatic, than of theoretical and methodological, moment (50–51).

To be sure, not many historians systematically set forth and defended claims to the autonomy of history as a *Wissenschaft*. They simply assumed that autonomy and criticized anyone who imported interpretative methods into history from other fields and used them to guide the formation of either their narratives or their explanations of what really had happened in the past. This was an effective tactic, since it permitted the practice of historians to substitute for the theory that their enterprise lacked. But it does not account for the "authority" the study of history came to enjoy during the nineteenth century, an authority that was much more effective than any theory could have been in establishing history's claims to autonomy. And this consideration permits us to shift our attention from the theory and practice of historical studies to a consideration of historical writing as a particular kind of discourse within the spiritual economy of the social formations of that age.

If, as most would agree, history is not a science, then it must be seen as part and parcel of the cultural superstructure of an age, as an activity that is more determined by than determinative of social praxis. This does not mean that it functions merely to rationalize the social status quo or provide retroactive justifications for actions intended to sustain or undermine that status quo, although as the history of historical writing amply demonstrates, it can have this function often enough. But the historiographical classics of the nineteenth century, the kind of historical reflection that is recognized as a "timeless" contribution to Western culture, the kind produced by Ranke, Michelet, Tocqueville, Burckhardt, and so on, has a different function which is less to rationalize a given social system than to serve as the very paradigm of realistic discourse by which any putative "realism" threatening to the social status quo can be dismissed as utopian, idealist, mythical, illusory, reductionist, or otherwise distorted.

Nineteenth-century historical discourse, precisely by the celebration of the uniqueness of its objects of study, the richness and variety of its "contents," that "unity in disunity" that can be suggested to exist by its narrative line, the multiplicity of points of view from which the genealogy of anything can be perceived, its claims to "Einfühlung" and "objectivity" at one and the same time, to being both an art and a science, to being cosmopolitan in scope and morally instructive in its effects, and so on—all this generates neither a method nor a theory so much as a model of discourse against which any generalization about society, as well as any intuitive insight claimed by art, can be judged for its "realism." The authority of this model of discourse is surely what underlies the assertions made by a host of nineteenth-century realistic novelists, of which Balzac and Flaubert were foremost, that they were writing "history" in their novels. It was the historical discourse that they emulated that made them "realistic" in their own eyes.

When Lukács suggests that bourgeois literary consciousness in its modern form can only describe the world and never narrate it effectively, and then proceeds to treat this as grounds for dismissing this consciousness as "unrealistic,"[20] he can do so only by privileging the discursive model which has its prototypes in the best bourgeois historians of the nineteenth century—a model to which Marx himself in his specifically historical works (such as *The 18th Brumaire*) remained faithful. In point of fact, both narration *and* description function as essential elements of historical discourse—in Tocqueville no less than in Ranke, in Burckhardt as much as in Macaulay. For "realism" does not consist exclusively in narration *or* description any more than it does in either analysis *or* synthesis. The essence of nineteenth-century realism is to be found, whether in historical or novelistic discourse, in the representational practice which has the effect of constituting an image of a current social praxis as the criterion of plausibility by reference to which any given institution, activity, thought, or even a life can be endowed with the aspect of "reality."

Of course, to say this is to say no more than that "history" functioned in the nineteenth century in the way that "God" had done in the Middle Ages or "Nature" had done in the eighteenth century. We have little difficulty today discerning the symbolic function—by which I mean the power to confer a kind of transcendental authority upon a given system of social praxis—of the notions of God and Nature in the periods referred to. But how the notion of history could function in this way in the nineteenth century, between desire and its potential objects, so as to specify what can be "legitimately" desired and what can be "realistically" hoped for, is difficult to perceive because in order to see it in its nineteenth-century form, we have to use "history" itself to retrieve it. In fact, however, during the nineteenth century, "history" became the very incarnation of the law, which, unless it is internalized in the citizen, turning him in his innermost being into a "subject," a "conscience" rather than a mere "consciousness," must inspire resistance, rebellion, and anarchy as a consequence.

The law is always arbitrary, being grounded as it is in the power of finite and limited groups rather than in some transcendental sphere of Being or some absolute Origin, as it always claims to be.[21] What better substitute for this absolute ground than reality itself, but now identified with history rather than with God or Nature? Essential to this sleight of hand, however, is the necessity of hiding the fact that all history is the study, not of past events that are gone forever from perception, but rather of the "traces" of those events distilled into documents and monuments, on the one side, and the praxis of present social formations, on the other. These "traces" are the raw materials of the historian's discourse, rather than the events themselves. It is equally necessary for the historians to hide—especially from themselves—the fact that their own discourses are not reflections or mimetic reproductions of events but processings of these "traces" so as to endow them with "symbolic" significance—which means to gather them under the categories of the very same law of which both the historian and his readers are "subjects."

Droysen's originality, as compared with that of his teacher Hegel, on the matter of historical writing was to have perceived the constructivist and essentially practical function of historical reflection in an age that was as suspicious of philosophy as it was of theology as possible queen of the sciences. A further claim to originality can be advanced for his recognition that history was a discourse, rather than an absolute ground of being, an objective process, or an empirically observable structure of relationships — a discourse capable of inserting its readers within the circle of moral conceptions that defined their practical social horizons; of leading them to identify this circle as their own conscience and guarantor of the integrities of their selfhood; and of impelling them to affirm this circle of moral conceptions as the reality that they could offend only at the risk of their "humanity."

5. Foucault's Discourse: The Historiography of Anti-Humanism

The work of Michel Foucault, conventionally labeled as Structuralist but consistently denied by him to be such, is extraordinarily difficult to deal with in any short account. This is not only because his oeuvre is so extensive but also because his thought comes clothed in a rhetoric apparently designed to frustrate summary, paraphrase, economical quotation for illustrative purposes, or translation into traditional critical terminology.

In part, the idiosyncrasy of Foucault's rhetoric reflects a general rebellion of his generation against the *clarté* of their Cartesian heritage. Against the Atticism of the older tradition, the new generation is adamantly "Asiatic." But the thorniness of Foucault's style is also ideologically motivated. His interminable sentences, parentheses, repetitions, neologisms, paradoxes, oxymorons, alternation of analytical with lyrical passages, and combination of scientist with mythic terminology—all appear to be consciously designed to render his discourse impenetrable to any critical technique based on ideological principles different from his own.

It is difficult, however, to specify Foucault's own ideological position. If he detests liberalism because of its equivocation and service to the social status quo, he also despises conservatism's dependence on tradition. And although he often joins forces with Marxist radicals in

This essay was written six years before Foucault's death in 1984. I have added a section on the two volumes of his *History of Sexuality* that appeared in that year. I refer throughout to the English translations of Foucault's works where they were available to me. These and the French originals are listed at the end of the essay.

specific causes, he shares nothing of their faith in science. The anarchist Left he dismisses as infantile in its hopes for the future and naive in its faith in a benign human nature. His philosophical position is close to the nihilism of Nietzsche. His discourse begins where Nietzsche's, in *Ecce Homo,* left off: in the perception of the "madness" of all "wisdom" and the "folly" of all "knowledge." But there is nothing of Nietzsche's optimism in Foucault. His is a chillingly clear perception of the transiency of all learning, but he draws the implications of this perception in a manner that has nothing in common with Nietzsche's adamantine rigor.

And this because there is no center to Foucault's discourse. It is all surface—and intended to be so. For even more consistently than Nietzsche, Foucault resists the impulse to seek an origin or transcendental subject that would confer any specific meaning on existence. Foucault's discourse is willfully superficial. And this is consistent with the larger purpose of a thinker who wishes to dissolve the distinction between surfaces and depths, to show that wherever this distinction arises it is evidence of the play of organized power and that this distinction is itself the most effective weapon power possesses for hiding its operations.

The multifold operations of power are, in Foucault's view, at once most manifest and most difficult to identify in what he takes to be the basis of cultural praxis in general, namely, discourse. *Discourse* is the term under which he gathers all of the forms and categories of cultural life, including, apparently, his own efforts to submit this life to criticism. Thus envisaged, and as he himself says in *The Archeology of Knowledge* (1969), his own work is to be regarded as "a discourse about discourse" (205). It follows, then, that if we are to comprehend his work on its own terms, we must analyze it *as* discourse—and with all the connotations of circularity, of movement back and forth, that the Indo-European root of this term (*kers*) and its Latinate form (*dis-,* "in different directions," + *currere,* "to run") suggest. Accordingly, I have sought entry into the thicket of Foucault's work and, I hope, a way out of it by concentrating on its nature as discourse.

My approach will be generally rhetorical, and my aim will be to characterize the style of Foucault's discourse. I think we will find a clue to the meaning of his discursive style in the rhetorical theory of tropes. This theory has served as the organizing principle of Foucault's theory of culture, and it will serve as the analytical principle of this essay. Briefly, I argue that the authority of Foucault's discourse derives primarily from its style (rather than from its factual evidence or rigor of argument); that this style privileges the trope of catachresis in its own elaboration; and that, finally, this trope serves as the model of the world-view from which Foucault launches his criticisms of humanism, science, reason, and most of the institutions of Western culture as they have evolved since the Renaissance.

At the end of *The Archeology of Knowledge,* Foucault's systematic exposition of the analytical principles informing his earlier studies of madness, clinical medicine, and the human sciences, he states that his intention is "to free the history of thought from its subjection to transcendence . . . to cleanse it of all transcendental narcissism; [and free it] from [the] circle of the lost origin" (203). This statement, with its combination of extravagance and obscurity, is typical of Foucault's style and suggests the difficulty of translating his discourse into any other terms. The statement occurs in the course of an imagined exchange between Foucault and his critics (or between two sides of Foucault's own intellectual persona), in which the methods of the Structuralists and those of Foucault are juxtaposed and the differences between them clearly marked.

One issue in the exchange hinges upon what Foucault takes to be the crisis of Western culture. This is a crisis

> that concerns that transcendental reflection with which philosophy since Kant has identified itself; which concerns the theme of the origin, that promise of the return, by which we avoid the difference of our present; which concerns an anthropological thought that orders all these questions around the question of man's being, and allows us to avoid an analysis of practice; which concerns all humanistic ideologies; which, above all, concerns the status of the subject. (204)

Structuralism seeks to avoid discussion of this crisis, Foucault says, by "pursuing the pleasant games of genesis and system, synchrony and development, relation and cause, structure and history." The imagined Structuralist (or Foucault's counter-persona) then asks the questions that still remain unanswered in most discussions of Foucault's work: "What then is the title of your discourse? Where does it come from and from where does it derive its right to speak? How could it be legitimated?" (ibid.).

These are fair questions, even when addressed to a thinker to whom fairness is simply another rule imported from the domain of ethics to set restrictions on the free play of desire; and Foucault's answers to them seem curiously weak. It is to his credit as a serious thinker that he even raises them in his own text, but he takes away in his answers as much as he gives in permitting the questions to be raised. His own discourse, he says, "far from determining the locus in which it speaks, is avoiding the ground on which it could find support." It "is trying to operate a decentering that leaves no privilege to any center . . . it does not set out to be a recollection of the original or a memory of the truth. On the contrary, its task is to *make* differences . . . it is continually making *differentiations,* it is a *diagnosis*" (205–6). And he adds, in that constant repetition of "the same in the different" which is the distinguishing mark of his discourse: "It is an attempt . . . to show that to speak is to do something—something other than to express what one thinks; to translate what one knows, and something other than to play with the structures of a language [*langue*]" (209).

What this "something other" may be, however, is more easily defined by what it is not, in Foucault's view. And he ends *The Archeology of Knowledge* with a negative definition of his central object of study in the form of a "message" to his readers:

> Discourse is not life: its time is not your time; in it, you will not be reconciled to death; you may have killed God beneath the weight of all that you have said; but don't imagine that, with all that you are saying, you will make a man that will live longer than he. (211)

This "message," consisting of nothing but a series of negations, is also typical of Foucault's discourse, which always tends toward the oracular and intimations of apocalypse. His imagination is "always at the end of an era." But the vision is of what cannot be expected at the end of time. This supreme antiteleologist resists the lure of any definitive ending, just as he delights in beginnings that open in "free play," discoveries of paradoxes, and intimations of the folly underlying any "will to know."

If, however, Foucault's discourses begin in paradox and end in negative apocalypse, their middles are heavy with what Foucault calls "positivity," wide (if seemingly capricious) erudition, solemn disclosures of the "way things really were," aggressive redrawings of the map of cultural history, confident restructurings of the chronicle of "knowledge." And even the most sympathetic reader can legitimately ask, How do these middles relate to the beginnings and endings of Foucault's discourse? Their status is difficult to specify in conventional critical terms, for although these middles do mediate between the

paradoxes that open and the oracular utterances that typically close
Foucault's discourses, they have neither the weight of the middle term
of a syllogistic argument nor the plausibility of the peripeteia in a
narrative.

In fact, Foucault rejects the authority of both logic and conventional narrative. His discourses often suggest a story, but they are never
about the same "characters," and the events that comprise them are
not linked by laws that would permit us to understand some as causes
and others as effects. Foucault's "histories" are as fraught with discontinuities, ruptures, gaps, and lacunae as his "arguments." If he continues to fascinate (some of) us, then, it is not because he offers a
coherent explanation or even interpretation of our current cultural in-
coherence but because he denies the authority that the distinction
coherence/incoherence has enjoyed in Western thought since Plato. He
seeks, not the "ground," but rather the "space" within which this distinction arose.

Because he seeks a space rather than a ground, Foucault's discourse unfolds seemingly without restraint, apparently without end.
There are now nine books, many essays and interviews, prefaces to
reprints of older works, manifestoes, and so forth—a flood of what he
calls "utterances" (*énoncés*) which threaten to swamp even the most
admiring reader. He has recently published the first of a projected six-
volume *History of Sexuality*. What are we to make of this interminable
"series" of texts? How are we to receive it? What are we to do with it?

If we were to follow what Foucault claims to be his own critical
principles, we should not be able to refer the whole body of texts, the
oeuvre, to any presiding authorial intention, to any originating event
in the life of the author, or to the historical context in which the discourse arises. We should not even be able to speak about its impact or
influence on a specific group of readers or to situate Foucault himself
within a tradition of discourse. We could not ask, as his most hostile
critics have done, whether his statements of fact are true or false,
whether his interpretations are valid, or whether his reconstructions of
the historical record are plausible. And this because Foucault denies
the concreteness of the referent and rejects the notion that there is a
reality that precedes discourse and reveals its face to a prediscursive
"perception." We cannot, as he reminds us in the passages quoted
above, ask, On what authority do you speak? because Foucault sets the
free play of his own discourse over against all authority. He aspires to
a discourse that is free in a radical sense, a discourse that is self-
dissolving of its own authority, a discourse that opens upon a "silence"

in which only "things" exist in their irreducible difference, resisting every impulse to find a sameness uniting them all in any order whatsoever.

One conventional critical concept appears to escape Foucault's meta-critical ire: the concept of style. He does not explicitly make much of this concept, but he invokes it often enough without qualification to permit its use in the effort to characterize, at least in a preliminary way, the nature of his own discourse. Also, when we have eliminated all of the possible "authorities" to whom we might ordinarily appeal in order to delineate the ground of his discourse, we are still left with the constancies that give to his various texts a unitary tone, mode of address, manner of speaking, attack upon the process of *énonciation,* what, in his essay on Robbe-Grillet, he calls its "aspect" and what in other places he calls simply "style."

In an aside in *The Archeology of Knowledge,* Foucault defines style as "a certain constant manner of utterance."[1] This definition is revealing of what we should look for in our attempts to characterize Foucault's own, obviously highly self-conscious style. We should not fall victim, however, to any banal distinction in his own terms between style and content, or distinguish between "what is said" and "how it is said," because the saying, the "utterance" (*énonciation*), is what constitutes a "content," a "referent," or an "object" of discourse. Until discourse arises against the silence of mere existence or within the "murmur" of a prelinguistic agitation of things, there is no distinction between signifier and signified, subject and object, sign and meaning. Or rather, these distinctions are products of the discursive "event." But this event remains oblivious to its real purpose, which is merely to be and to mask the arbitrariness of its existence as simple utterance. And the manner of this simultaneous disclosure and concealment in discourse is its style.

Discourse need not have come into existence at all, Foucault tells us. That it did come into existence at a certain time in the order of things suggests its contingency—and points to a time when, like that "humanity" which is a hypostatization of the fictive subject of discourse, it will come to an end. Meanwhile, discourse eludes all determination, logical, grammatical, or rhetorical, precisely insofar as such determinations are themselves products of discourse's capacity to hide its origin in a play of signifiers that are their own signifieds. It is the mode of this play that constitutes the essence of style. When it displays a "certain constant manner" of elaboration, we are in the presence of a discourse with style. And the highest style, it would seem, is that which self-consciously makes of this play its own object of representation.

So much is shown by Foucault himself in the only one of his works that can legitimately be classified as a stylistic analysis in the conventional sense of the term, his study of the proto-Surrealist writer Raymond Roussel. Here, after a discussion of the traditional rhetorical theory of tropes as set forth by Dumarsais, he remarks: "Le style, c'est, sous le nécessité souveraine des mots employés, la possibilité, masquée et désigné à la fois, de dire la même chose, mais autrement" (*Raymond Roussel*, 25). Foucault goes on to characterize Roussel's language, in terms that we can apply to his own discourse, as "style renversé," which seeks "a dire subrepticement deux choses avec les même mots." Roussel makes of the "twist [*torsion*], that easy turn of words which ordinarily permits them to 'lie' [*bouger*] by virtue of a tropological movement and allows them to enjoy their profound freedom, . . . a pitiless circle which leads words back to their point of departure by the force of a compelling law." The "bending [*flexion*] of the style becomes its circular negation" (25).

This notion of a reversed style would seem to be apt for characterizing the presuppositions of Foucault's own discourse, because like Roussel, Foucault does not wish "doubler le réel d'un autre monde, mais dans les redoublements spontanés du langage, *découvrir* un espace insoupçonné et le *recouvrir* de choses encore jamais dites" (25). Foucault's own discourse takes its source in that "tropological space" which he, like Roussel, considers "comme un blanc ménage dans le langage, et qui ouvre a l'intérieur même du mot son vide insidieux, désertique et piégé." Finally, also like Roussel, Foucault considers this void as "une lacune à étendre le plus largement possible et a mesurer meticuleusement." This "absence" at the heart of language Foucault takes to be evidence of "an absolute vacancy of being, which it is necessary to invest, master, and fill up [*combler*] by pure invention" (24–25).

The idea of style used to characterize Roussel's discourse appears increasingly in Foucault's own works as a way of characterizing discourse in general. A "certain constant manner of utterance," arising in the "tropological space" which at once reflects and refuses the "vacancy of being," finding its own rule of dispersion in the capacity of words to say the same thing in different ways or to say different things with the same words, circling back upon itself to take its own modality of articulation as its signified, coming to an end as arbitrarily as it began, but leaving a verbal something in the place of the nothing that occasioned it—all this can stand for discourse as well as style in Foucault's thought. To conceive discourse in this way, Foucault tells us in his inaugural lecture in the Collège de France in 1971, *L'Ordre du discours,* would be to free it from subjection to the myth of "signification."

Eight years earlier, in *The Birth of the Clinic* (1963), he had asked: "But must the things said, elsewhere and by others, be treated exclusively in accordance with the play of signifier and signified, as a series of themes present more or less implicitly to one another?" And he had concluded that if the "facts of discourse" were "treated not as autonomous nuclei of multiple significations, but as events and functional segments gradually coming together to form a system," then "the meaning of an utterance [*énoncé*] would be defined not by the treasure of intentions that it might contain, revealing and concealing it at the same time, but by the difference that articulates it upon the real or possible statements, which are contemporary with it or to which it is opposed in the linear series of time" (xvii).

The crucial terms in this passage, which points to the possibility of "a systematic history of discourses," are *events, functional segments, system,* and the notion of the play of *difference* within the system thus constituted. The "regulatory principles of analysis" of discourse, Foucault then makes clear in *L'Ordre du discourse,* are the notions of "event, series, regularity, and the possible conditions of existence" (230). *Style* is the name we will give to the mode of existence of word-events arranged in a series displaying regularity and having specifiable conditions of existence. These conditions of existence are not to be sought in some correlation of "what is said" with an "order of things" that preexists and sanctions one "order of words" as against another. They are to be found in two kinds of restraint placed on discourse since the time of its domestication by the Greeks: external, consisting of the repressions or displacements corresponding to those governing the expression of desire or the exercise of power, and internal, consisting of certain rules of classification, ordering, and distribution and certain "rarefactions" which have the effect of masking discourse's true nature as "free play."

What is always at work in discourse—as in everything else—is "desire and power," but in order for the aims of desire and power to be realized, discourse must ignore its basis in them. This is why discourse, at least since the rout of the Sophists by Plato, always unfolds in the service of the "will to truth." Discourse wishes to "speak the truth," but in order to do this, it must mask from itself its service to desire and power, must indeed mask from itself the fact that it is itself a manifestation of the operations of these two forces (218–20).

Like desire and power, discourse unfolds "in every society" within the context of "external restraints" that appear as "rules of exclusion," rules that determine what can be said and not said, who has the right to speak on a given subject, what will constitute reasonable and what "foolish" actions, what will count as "true" and what as "false" (216–17). These rules limit the conditions of discourse's existence in different ways in different times and places. Whence the distinction, arbitrary but taken for granted in all societies, between "proper," reasonable, responsible, sane, and truthful discourse, on the one side, and "improper," unreasonable, irresponsible, insane, and erroneous discourse, on the other. Foucault himself vacillates between the impulse to justify the discourse of madness, criminality, and sickness (whence his celebration of Sade, Hölderlin, Nietzsche, Artaud, Lautréamont, Roussel, Bataille, Blanchot, and so on), on the one hand, and his constantly reaffirmed aim to probe beneath the distinction between proper and improper discourse in order to explicate the ground on which the distinction itself arises, on the other. Despite this vacillation, his probings take the form of "diagnoses" intended to reveal the "pathology" of a mechanism of control that governs discursive and nondiscursive activity alike.

As for the internal restraints placed on discourse, the "rarefactions" noted above, all these are functions of the distinction, as false as it is insidious, between an order of words and an order of things, which makes discourse itself possible. What is at work here is some principle of subordination, the vertical equivalent, we might say, of the horizontal principle of exclusion operative in the external restraints. At the base of every principle of subordination operative in discourse is the distinction between the signifier and the signified, or rather the fiction of the adequacy of the former to the latter in every "proper" discourse. Whence the conventionalist theories of discourse that seek to obscure its status as mere event in order to ground it in a subject (the author), an originating experience (such as writing or reading), or an activity (discourse conceived as mediation between perception and consciousness, or between consciousness and the world, as in philosophical or scientific theories of language).

These conventionalist theories, Foucault argues, must be dismissed as mere manifestations of the power of discourse to nullify itself by "placing itself at the disposal of the signifier" (228). All of this, reflective of a profound "logophobia" (229) in Western culture, has the effect of averting the very real "powers and dangers" of discourse (216). These derive from the capacity of discourse to reveal, in the free play of words, the arbitrariness of every rule and norm, even those on which society itself, with its rules of exclusion and hierarchical order, is founded. In order to free discourse from these restraints and to open it up once more to the Sadean project of saying everything that can be said in as many ways as it can be said—in order to preside over the dissolution of discourse by closing the gap opened up by the distinction between "words and things"—Foucault undertakes to expose the dark underside of every discursive formation purporting to serve "the will of truth."

This was the more or less clearly stated purpose of Foucault's earlier books, *Madness and Civilization* (1961), *The Birth of the Clinic* (1963), and *The Order of Things* (1966). These dealt with the discourses of psychiatry, medicine, and the human sciences, respectively, and the ways that official discourse perceived, classified, and distributed such insubstantial "things" as "sanity," "health," "knowledge" at different times in the history of Western culture. These books sought to demonstrate that the distinctions between madness and sanity, sickness and health, and truth and error were always a function of the modality of discourse prevailing in centers of social power at different periods. In Foucault's view, this modality was, in turn, less a product of an autonomous exchange between hypothesis and observation, or theory and practice, than the basis of whatever theory and practice prevailed in a given period. And it followed for him that, finally, the modern history of Western man's "will to knowledge" had been less a progressive development towards "enlightenment" than a product of an endless interaction between desire and power within the system of exclusions which made different kinds of society possible.

This structure of deception and duplicity underlying all discourse was more systematically explicated in *The Archeology of Knowledge* and *The Discourse on Language;* and it has been further illuminated and specified in the two books that have appeared since these two essays: *Surveiller et punir: Naissance de la prison* (1975); and *La Volonté de savoir,* the first volume of the projected *History of Sexuality* (1976). The two most recent works are manifestly studies of the relation between the desire for power and the power of desire as revealed in the controls exercised by society over two social types that have threatened its authority throughout time: the criminal and the sexual deviant. In the practices of incarceration and exclusion, respectively, the power of discourse is confirmed by its creation of the human types with which these practices are intended to deal. Thus envisaged, both works are studies of the "discourse of power" in conflict with the "discourse of desire."

Wherever Foucault looks, he finds nothing but discourse; and wherever discourse arises, he finds a struggle between those groups that claim the "right" to discourse and those groups that are denied the right to their own discourse. In *Surveiller et punir* and *La Volonté de savoir,* Foucault comes out more fully on the side of the victims of this discourse of power and against the "authority" of those who exercise the power of "exclusion" under the guise of a simple service to "truth." But the authority of his own discourse still remains unspecified. What, we may still ask, are its modality, its "right," and its relation to the order of discourse of the time and place in which it arises?

Thus far, I have touched only the surface of Foucault's own discourse and suggested that its claim to authority must, according to his own theory, derive from the "certain constant manner of utterance," that is to say, the style, that characterizes it. This style, again on his own terms, cannot be identified as that of a discipline, because Foucault refuses the conventional titles philosopher, historian, sociologist of knowledge, and so forth. It cannot be identified with those looser groupings that he calls "fellowships of discourse," since in his major works he resolutely ignores the work of most of his contemporaries (*Discourse on Language,* 225–26). And most certainly it cannot be linked to any doctrinal orthodoxy of a religious or sectarian sort.

If Foucault were writing this, he might situate his discourse, and classify its style, by reference to what he himself calls the *épistème* of our age, that is to say, "the total set of relations that unite, at a given period, the discursive practices that give rise to epistemological figures, sciences, and possibly formalized systems" of knowledge (*Archeology of Knowledge,* 191). But once more, according to Foucault's theory, the *épistème* of an age cannot be known by those who work under its aegis. In any event, according to him, we are at the end of one epistemic configuration and at the beginning of another. We exist in the gap between two *épistèmes,* one dying, the other not yet born — of which, however, the "mad" poets and artists of the last century and a half were the heralds.

The virtually unquestioned authority that Foucault grants to these heralds suggests the tradition of discourse to which he would wish to belong — if *tradition* were an honorific term to him, and if it could be used to classify a group of artists as different as Hölderlin, Goya, Nietzsche, Van Gogh, Rilke, Artaud, Bataille, Blanchot, and above all Sade. Foucault values the brilliant opacity, the dark superficiality, the casual profundity of those writers who inhabit the silent places left by the discourse of "normal" men. His debt to them would permit us to place him among the anarchists—if he shared their utopian optimism—or among the nihilists—if he possessed any standard by which to justify his preference for "nothing" over "something." But Foucault has none of the directness of his heroes. He cannot say anything directly, because he has no confidence in the power of words to represent either "things" or "thoughts."

It is not surprising, then, that Foucault's own discourse tends to assume the form of what Northrop Frye calls the "existential projection" of a rhetorical trope into a metaphysics. This rhetorical trope is catachresis, and Foucault's style not only displays a profusion of the various figures sanctioned by this trope, such as paradox, oxymoron, chiasmus, hysteron proteron, metalepsis, prolepsis, antonomasia, paronomasia, antiphrasis, hyperbole, litotes, irony, and so on; his own discourse stands as an abuse of everything for which "normal" or "proper" discourse stands. It looks like history, like philosophy, like criticism, but it stands over against these discourses as ironic antithesis. It even assumes a position superior to that of Foucault's own heroes, for Foucault's "discourse about discourses" seeks to effect the dissolution of Discourse itself. This is why I call it catachretic.

In traditional rhetorical theory, the notion of catachresis (in Latin, *abusio;* in English, *misuse*) presupposes the distinction between the literal and the figurative meanings of words, or more generally, the validity of the distinction between "proper" and "improper" usage. Since for Foucault all words have their origin in a "tropological space" in which the "sign" enjoys a "freedom . . . to alight" upon any aspect of the entity it is meant to signify, then the distinction between literal and figurative meanings goes by the board—except as an indication of the power of discourse to constitute "literality" through the application of a consistent rule of signification. This means that all verbal constructions are basically catachretic, inasmuch as no union of any signifier with any signified is "natural" or given by "necessity." Literal meaning, like "proper" usage, is the product of the application of a norm, social in nature, hence arbitrary, rather than a result of the operation of a law (see *The Order of Things*, 110–15).

But Foucault seems to agree with the eighteenth-century rhetoricians and with Pierre Fontanier, the nineteenth-century systematizer of their theories, that the kinds of relationships the sign may have with the entity it is intended to represent are limited to four, depending on whether the sign "alights" on (1) "some internal element" of the entity to be represented by it, (2) some point "adjacent" to the entity, (3)some figure "similar" to the entity, or (4) some figure manifestly "dissimilar" to it. This classification yields what Foucault himself calls the "fundamental figures so well known to rhetoric: synecdoche, metonymy, and catachresis (or metaphor, if the analogy is less immediately perceptible)" (113–14). Each represents a different modality of construing the relation between signs and the things they are meant to signify.

Catachresis enjoys a privileged place in Foucault's own conception of tropes, because for him, no two things are similar to one another in their particularity. All language therefore constitutes an abuse insofar as it gives a single name to things different in their "internal natures," their location in space, or their external attributes. It is all catachretic in origin, although the myth of literal or "proper" meaning obscures this origin and thereby permits the reduction of catachresis to the status of a figure of rhetoric that arises out of a simple misuse of "proper" speech. It follows that if discourse takes its origin in a "tropological space," it must unfold within one or another of the fundamental modalities of figuration in which a relationship between "words and things" can be construed. Consequently, the style of a discourse, its "certain constant manner of utterance," can be characterized in terms of the dominant trope that establishes the originary relation between "words and things" and determines "what can be said" about things in "proper" discourse.

Foucault goes even further: the dominant trope of a given community of discourse determines both "what can be seen" in the world and "what can be known" about it. Tropology thus constitutes the basis of what Foucault calls the *épistème* of an age in the history of thought and expression. It also provides him with a way of characterizing the sequence of *épistèmes* that makes up the "history" of thought about the topics he has analyzed in his major books: madness, clinical medicine, the human sciences, incarceration, and sexuality. This theory of tropes is what underlies and therefore clarifies his own characterization of his "archeological" method: "What archeology wishes to uncover is primarily the play of analogies and difference" (*Archeology of Knowledge*, 160).

"Analogies and differences. . . ." In the beginning, Foucault's enabling myth tells us, everything was simply what it was. "Sameness," or analogy, arose with speech, the gathering of different things under a single name. This gave birth to the concepts of the type, the proposition, and knowledge conceived as the classification of the Different in terms of Sameness, Similitude, or Resemblance. "All error," says Kant in his *Logic,* echoing Bacon and anticipating Darwin, "has its origin in resemblance." Foucault expands this dictum. For him, resemblance is also the source of everything that passes for truth or knowledge. The perception of the Same in the Different, or of Sameness in the interplay of Similarities and Differences as it appears in any aggregate of entities, lies at the base of myth, religion, science, and philosophy alike. But not only this: the perception of Sameness is the basis of social praxis too, of that manipulation of Sameness and Difference which permits the social group, first, to identify itself as a unity and, then, to disperse itself into a hierarchy of more or less different groupings, some "more alike" than others, some more sane, more healthy, more rational, more normal, more human, than others.

The perception of "the Same in the Different" and of "the Different in the Same" is the origin of all hierarchy in social practice, as it is the origin of syntax in grammar and logic in thought. Hierarchy itself derives from that Fall of man into language, and the capacity of speech to "say two things with the same words" or "the same thing with different words." Discourse arises when this capacity of speech becomes highly developed, formalized, submitted to rules, and unfolds under the aegis of a normative concept such as "the permitted versus the prohibited," "the rational versus the irrational," or "the true versus the false." But the limit on what can be said, and *a fortiori* what can be seen and thought, is set by the "error" that resides at the heart of any verbal representation of the "real."

This limit is reached when Difference asserts its rights against Sameness, or as Nietzsche says, when Dionysiac individuation rebels against Apollonian unities. Then discourse, motivated by the "will to truth" which informs it, shifts to another mode of construing the relation between "words and things." Typically, in Foucault's schema, every "discursive" formation undergoes a finite number of such shifts before reaching the limits of the *episteme* that sanctions its operations. This number corresponds to the fundamental modes of figuration identified by the theory of tropology: metaphor, metonymy, synecdoche, and irony (which is here understood as self-conscious catachresis).

Thus, for example, in *Madness and Civilization,* the "discourse on madness" that unfolds in the West between the late Middle Ages and our own time is shown to go through four phases. First, in the sixteenth century, madness is removed from its status as a sign of sanctity, repository of a divine truth, and simultaneously differentiated from and identified with a specifically human wisdom, as in the character of the Wise Fool and the *topos* of the "praise of folly." Then, in the seventeenth and eighteenth centuries, what Foucault calls the Classical age, madness is set over against reason in the mode of contiguity or adjacency, in the way that, in the formal thought of the age, humanity was set over against bestiality, or reason against unreason. This mode of conceiving the relation between madness and sanity is reflected in (and finds its confirmation in) the treatment of those designated as insane, who are not only expelled from society by virtue of their "differentness" but also "confined" in special places at the limits of society, "hospitals," where they are imprisoned and "treated" along with those other "dangerous" deviants from the social norm, criminals and paupers.

Then, in the nineteenth century, the relationship between madness and sanity changes again, reflected in the reforms of Pinel and Tuke, who "liberated" the insane from association with criminals and paupers, defined them as simply "sick" rather than esentially different from their "healthier" counterparts, and identified their "illness' with a phase in the development of the human organism, as either an arrested form of, or regression to, childhood. The insane were thus at once re-identified with "normal" humanity, by being identified with one of the latter's phases of development, hence defined as being essentially the same as the latter and at the same time differentiated from it as requiring a special kind of treatment, usually punitive but always physical, cultivated in the special "asylums" set up for the insane.

Finally, in the twentieth century, a new way of construing the relation between madness and sanity crystallizes, represented above all by Freud and psychoanalysis, in the theory of which the distinction between sanity and insanity is once more weakened, and the similarities between the two stressed; and the notion of neurosis is elaborated as intermediary between the two extremes. Foucault honors Freud as the first modern man to "listen" to what the insane were saying, to try to find the reason in their unreason, the method in their madness. On the other hand, while Freud delivered the patient from "the existence of the asylum," he did not liberate him from the authority of the doctor himself, that combination of scientist and thaumaturge. In the "psychoanalytical situation," Foucault maintains, "alienation becomes disalienating because, in the doctor, it becomes a subject" (278).

The failure to abolish this authoritarian structure, he concludes, both sets the limit on what psychoanalysis can achieve and reveals the "irony" of its claims to liberate, because although psychoanalysis can "unravel some of the forms of madness, it remains a stranger to the sovereign enterprise of unreason" (278). The extent of its alienation from this "enterprise" is to be measured by its failure to comprehend the heralds of radical freedom, those seers whom sane society nullifies under the name of the "mad artist."

> Since the end of the 18th century, the life of unreason no longer manifests itself except in the lightning-flash of works such as those of Hölderlin, of Nerval, of Nietzsche, or of Artaud—forever irreducible to those alienations that can be cured, resisting by their own strength that gigantic moral imprisonment which we are in the habit of calling, doubtless by antiphrasis, the liberation of the insane by Pinel and Tuke. (278)

Foucault's own catachretic reflection on the condition of sanity in the modern world takes its authority from those "lightning-flashes" which, in the works of art where they appear, "open a void, a moment of silence, a question without an answer, [and] provoke a breach without reconciliation where the world is forced to question itself" (288). His celebration of madness is "beyond irony," since it credits the existence of a "silence" before the "differentiation" of madness and sanity occurred.

> Ruse and new triumph of madness: the world that thought to measure and justify madness through psychology must justify itself before madness, since in its struggles and agonies it measures itself by the excess of works like those of Nietzsche, of Van Gogh, of Artaud. And nothing in itself, especially not what it can know of madness, assures the world that it is justified by such works of madness. (289)

Arising in that "tropological space" in which words can "alight" freely on whatever aspect of the thing they are intended to signify, the history of the "discourse on madness" displays the possible modalities of this "alightment." The modes and the tropes that underlie them are, successively, resemblance (metaphor), adjacency (metonymy), essentiality (synecdoche), and what might be called doubling (irony). In its modern phase the discourse on madness takes the form of a duplicity, of a doubling effect, in which madness is identified with both normality and genius, is at once brought back into the world in the form of the patient and further alienated from it in the form of the mad poet;

at once defined as sickness and deviation from the norm and tacitly recognized as a standard against which the norm can be measured. Foucault takes his stand in the breach, the gap, the void that opens up between these two faces of madness and asks, By what authority do we presume to "speak" of either?

The question of authority, the assumption of the power to force conformity to social norms, has increasingly moved to the center of Foucault's own discourse in the books that followed *Madness and Civilization,* from his study of the "discourse on sickness" (*The Birth of the Clinic*) to his studies of the "discourse on criminality" (*Surveiller et punir*) and the "discourse on sexuality" (*Histoire de la sexualité*). And it is this question that is at the heart of his most influential work, his study of the "discourse on humanity" (*The Order of Things*).

The Order of Things is about the use and abuse of the "authority" of the "human sciences." In it Foucault wishes to show that the disciplines that deal with man as a social and cultural being are as little scientific as those conceptions of the body that have successively informed medical practice from the sixteenth century to our own day. *The Order of Things* is denser than Foucault's other "historical" books, because in it he deals with discourses that are more theoretical than practical, or at least discourses that do not have the immediate applicability that such discourses as "psychiatry, medicine, and penology" do. Consequently, he is compelled to consider the epistemological authority of the theoretical disciplines that the "human sciences" comprise. This authority he invests in the *épistème* of an age or a community of discourses, the deep but unacknowledged mode of relating "words and things" that gives to these discourses their coherence, within and between themselves.

As in the book on madness, so, too, in *The Order of Things* Foucault identifies four distinct periods of epistemic coherency: the sixteenth century, the *âge classique,* the nineteenth century, and our own age. Each period is studied "vertically," that is, archeologically, rather than "horizontally" or historically. The strategy is to work from texts or fragments of texts produced during a given period, without any concern for the biographies of the authors who wrote them, with the sole aim of identifying a distinctive "discursive mode" shared by all the important texts of an age or epoch.

An "important" text, of course, is one that displays evidence of the appearance of a discursive mode different from that which prevailed in the preceding age. Foucault is less concerned with the "classic" text, the text that is fully systematized and realized in accordance with the *épistème* that sanctions its discourse, than with the text that marks out a new domain of inquiry, or rather constitutes new "positivities" and "empiricities" on the basis of a new conceptualization of consciousness's relation to the world. Thus, for example, in his analyses of the sciences of biology, economics, and philology in the nineteenth century, he is less interested in—indeed, all but ignores—Darwin, Marx, and Wilamowitz than in Cuvier, Ricardo, and Bopp. The latter trio are regarded as the true "inventors" of the new domains of inquiry—biology, economics, and philology, respectively.

Before the appearance of these three thinkers, Foucault argues, the "sciences" of biology, economics, and philology did not exist. No more than "man" existed as an object of study prior to the late eighteenth century. Before this time, "natural history," "wealth," and "general grammar" were the principal domains of the field of "human sciences," just as before the late eighteenth century, the concept of "man" was obscured by the more general concept of "creation" or the "order of things" of which the "human thing" was but one, and by no means a privileged, instance.

It is folly, then, Foucault argues, to imagine, as conventional historians of ideas are inclined to do, that there are discrete disciplines developing over long periods of time that have the same objects of inquiry, with only the names by which these objects are called changing and the laws governing them progressively becoming clearer as "error" is eliminated and "fact" replaces "superstition" or mere "speculation." For what shall count as error and what as truth, what as fact and what as fancy—these change as arbitrarily as the modes of discourse and the originating *épistèmes* undergo "mutation."

One can, of course, speak of the "influence" of one thinker or another, of precursors and incarnators of intellectual traditions, and even of "genealogies" of ideas, if one wishes; but one should do so with the full realization that such concepts are legitimate only within the epistemic presuppositions of nineteenth-century discourse, a discourse that is not even that of our intellectual fathers but, at best, that of our grandfathers. For new "master disciplines" in the human sciences were constituted on the eve of our own era, in ethnology, psychoanalysis, and linguistics, all of which orient their "true" practitioners, not along the horizontal axis of "befores and afters," as nineteenth-century historicist disciplines did, but along the vertical axis of "surfaces and depths"—and continually point to the insoluble mystery that the notion of a depth without a bottom calls forth.

Knowledge in the human sciences thus no longer takes the form of the search for Similarities and Resemblances (as it did in the sixteenth century), Contiguities and Tables of Relationships (as it did in the Classical age), or Analogies and Successions (as it did in the nineteenth century), but rather Surfaces and Depths—generated by the return to consciousness of the nameless "silence" which underlies and makes possible the forms of all discourse, even that of "science" itself. This is why, in our age, knowledge tends to take the form either of Formalizations or Interpretations and unfolds within an awareness of consciousness's incapacity ever to locate its own origin and of language's inability to reveal a subject; and this because of the inevitable interposition of discourse between the Subject and its putative subject matter. This is why "the whole curiosity of our thought now resides in the question: What is language, and how can we find a way round it in order to make it appear in itself, in all its plenitude?" (*Order of Things,* 306).

But this curiosity can never be satisfied, Foucault maintains, because "the object of the human sciences is not language (though it is spoken by men alone); it is that being [man] which, from the interior of language by which he is surrounded, represents to himself, by speaking, the sense of the words or propositions he utters, and finally provides himself with a representation of language itself" (353). Not even the modern science of linguistics can specify "what language must be in order to structure . . . what is . . . not in itself either word or discourse, and in order to articulate itself on the pure forms of knowledge" (382). Indeed, it is not in science at all but in literature, and a literature "dedicated to language," that "we are led back to the place that Nietzsche and Mallarmé signposted when the first asked: Who speaks?, and the second saw his glittering answer in the Word itself" (382).

A literature so dedicated "gives prominence, in all their empirical vivacity, to the fundamental forms of finitude," the most fundamental form of which is death (383–84). This literature, which presses beyond madness to "that formless, mute, unsignifying region where language can find its freedom" (383), signals the "disappearance of Discourse" (385), and with it, the "disappearance of man." For "man had been a figure occurring between two modes of language; or, rather, he was constituted only when language, having been situated within representation and, as it were, dissolved in it, freed itself from that situation only at the cost of its own fragmentation: man composed his own figure in the interstices of that fragmented language" (386).

That "man" of which humanists speak so eloquently and confidently is thus considered to have no specific being in the world, no essence, no objectivity. The history of the human sciences shows us efforts to locate the nature of "man" in his being as "living, producing, and speaking" animal; but these "living, producing, speaking" themselves dissolve and escape identification, behind the discourses intended to reveal their substance—only to reappear in a new guise, as the subject of new "sciences," when a given notion of "life, labor, or language" finds its limit in language itself.

The crucial change, or rather "mutation," in the history of Western thought, Foucault contends in *The Order of Things,* is that which "situated language within representation," charged words with the task of serving as transparent and unambiguous signs of the "things" that made up "reality." This elevation of words to a special status among "things" created a gap within which "Classical" discourse, the discourse of the Enlightenment, could unfold. Hidden behind its status as simple "representation" of the real, this discourse was able to offer its own form as the obscure content of reality. And because discourse was thus privileged, reality inevitably took on the aspects of the linguistic mode in which it was presented to consciousness. Since in the eighteenth century language was regarded as timeless, as having no history, and universal, as being governed everywhere by the same grammatical and syntactical rules, then not only knowledge but also its object, "man," was considered to be characterized by this same timelessness and universality of determination. Accordingly, knowledge aspired to the construction of "Tables," in which the vocabulary, grammar, and syntax of "reality" would be revealed, its simple elements named, its species and genera unambiguously determined, and its combinatory rules made manifest.

This dream of a *mathesis universalis* has remained the legacy of the sciences, both physical and social, ever since. Its inadequacy to reality became evident, however, at the furthest limit of its development in the nineteenth century, when names were seen to be variable in what they could designate, when the taxonomies revealed their incapacity to accommodate certain "borderline" cases or "monsters," and when the combinatory rules failed of all precise prediction. In the early nineteenth century, it dawned on Western man that not only he but language also had a "history." But Foucault does not view this intensification of "historical consciousness" as an advance in learning, a progressive movement in the history of thought caused by the realization of the "error" contained in the earlier conception of knowledge

(329). On the contrary, the new historical sense was a function of a profound "time-anxiety," a realization that the Classical age had no place for time in its *épistème,* or rather, that it had purchased its certitude at the expense of any awareness of the reality of time, of the finitude of existence.

Whence the radical reconstitution of the whole domain of knowledge in the nineteenth century, its reconceptualization in terms, not of Contiguity and the (spatialized) Table, but of Analogy and (temporal) Succession (218–19)—evidence of a hope that "things" were at least affiliated in time if not related in space. Whence, too, therefore, the proliferation of those great philosophies of history (of Hegel, Marx, and so many others) and of even more of those concrete "historical narratives" (of Ranke, Mommsen, Michelet, and so on), in which the age abounded (334). "Life, labor, and language" were also historicized in the nineteenth century, in the hope that by the study of their evolution in time, their deeper unities would be discovered. But this enterprise, carried out most completely in biology, economics, and philology, was as doomed to failure as that of the Classical age. For the "origin" that it relentlessly pursued just as relentlessly receded from any positive identification (333). The historical approach to the study of "life, labor, and language" revealed neither the Origin nor the Subject of these activities; all it revealed, wherever "knowledge" looked, was infinite Difference and endless Change.

This apprehension of the play of Difference and Change, Foucault maintains, motivates the leading "human sciences" of our century: ethnology, psychoanalysis, and linguistics. All of these disciplines privilege language and hence approach closer to the void in which discourse arises than did their earlier counterparts (382). However, in their propensity to divide their objects (culture, consciousness, and language) into a "surface" and a "depth," and in their faith in their capacity to discover a Subject lurking in those depths, they too reveal their bondage to the myth of Sameness (340). This is why Foucault, in the preface to *The Order of Things,* characterizes his book as "a history of resemblance, . . . a history of the Same" (xxiv); and why, at the end of this book, he writes: "It is apparent how modern reflection . . . moves towards a certain thought of the Same—in which Difference is the same thing as identity" (315). Over against the Same-Different distinction (or rather, meta-distinction, for this dyad is what justifies 'distinction" itself) he sets the notion of the Other, whose history provides the ironic antithesis to that of the Same. This Other's history is inscribed within the "discourses" on madness, sickness, criminality, and sexuality, on the basis of which it has always been "shut away" (xxiv).

Foucault's work since *The Order of Things* can thus be understood as a specification and amplification of the insight with which that book ended:

> Man has not been able to describe himself as a configuration in the *épistème* without thought at the same time discovering, both in itself and outside itself, at its borders yet also in its very warp and woof, an element of darkness, an apparently inert density in which it is embedded, an unthought which it contains entirely, yet in which it is also caught. The unthought (whatever name we give it) is not lodged in man like a shrivelled-up nature or a stratified history; it is, in relation to man, the Other: the Other that is not only a brother but a twin, not of man, nor in man, but beside him and at the same time, in an identical newness, in an unavoidable duality. (326)

The Order of Things is a "history of the Same—of that which, for a given culture, is both dispersed and related, therefore to be distinguished by kinds and to be collected together into identities." *Surveiller et punir* and *La Volonté de savoir,* like *Madness and Civilization* and *The Birth of the Clinic,* are histories of "the Other," that which is "shut away" and hidden "in order to reduce its otherness," that which is regarded, always pre-judicially, as the abnormal (xxiv).

In 1973, Foucault published the results of a collective investigation, made by his students in a seminar, of a famous early nineteenth-century murder, *Moi, Pierre Rivière, ayant égorgé ma mère, ma soeur et mon frère.* . . . This was a case study of the ways in which different kinds of discourse—medicopsychiatric, legal, journalistic, and political—revealed the workings of "power" in their "analyses" and recommended "treatment" of the murderer. Foucault's own interest in this case stemmed, obviously, from the insight it provided into the function of "murder" in marking the limits between legality and illegality. After all, he reminds us, society distinguishes between different kinds of killing: criminal, martial, political (the assassination), and accidental. In the bourgeois society taking shape in the early nineteenth century, however, "murder" had an especial fascination; and accounts of murders, such as Pierre Rivière's famous *memoire* of his crime, an especial popularity.

The "universal success" of these *récits* manifests "the desire to know and to tell how men have been able to rebel against [*se lever contre*] power, break the law, to expose themselves to death by means of death" (271). What these *récits* and their universal popularity reveal, Foucault concludes, is a "battle which was taking shape, on the eve of revolutionary struggles and imperialist wars, over two rights, less different than they appear at first sight: the right to kill and have killed; [and] the right to speak and to recount" (271–72). Apparently, popular and official opinion alike were more outraged by Rivière's presumption in writing about his crime than they were by his committing it (266). His discourse seemed to have "doubled" the crime, making him the "author" of it twice over—first "in fact," second in "history" (274). Rivière did not try to excuse himself from the crime; rather he tried to situate it in the "discourse of murder" which in its official form both sanctioned and prohibited "killing." In daring to give his own account of the crime, Rivière set his own discourse over against every official one—legal, medical, political, and folkloric.

The fact that his act included a parricide brought it close to the fundamental concerns of society: the similarity of parricide to regicide or, indeed, any kind of political assassination had long been recognized in folklore and law alike. The nature of the crime, therefore, had both social and political implications, since it raised the question of the authority of the parent over the child in the family, in the first instance, and that of the state over the citizen, in the second. In setting his own "discourse" over against all official discourses, Rivière effectively claimed a freedom to act however he wished, in conformity to his own desires; and by implication he challenged the authority of society, whether vested in the family, the state, the law, science, or popular opinion, to judge him on its terms.

By remanding the sentence of death and consigning Rivière to life imprisonment, the state in the person of the king reasserted its authority while simultaneously masking it behind an act of grace. In deciding that Rivière had been insane and not, therefore, the *auteur* of his crime, it also nullified his claims to be the *auteur* of his own discourse about it. Instead of being *auteur,* he was defined simply as *autre* and put away in the prison, which, in the modern, totalitarian state, is the potential destiny of any deviant from the norms of society. Foucault had sought to show in his studies of the discourses of penology, psychiatry, and medicine that all deviancy is implicitly considered to be criminal, insane, or sick. That the notion of deviancy as crime, madness, and sickness arises within the economy of discourse itself, in the distinction between proper and improper discourse, is also the explicit message of *Moi, Pierre Rivière, ayant égorgé ma mère, ma soeur et mon frère.* . . .

This contention is further documented in *Surveiller et punir* and *La Volonté de savoir.* The historical framework of the two arguments presented in these books is the same as that found in earlier works: the transition from the *épistème* of the Classical age to that of the nineteenth century (or rather the mutation of the latter out of the former) is the center of interest. The celebration of the relative openness of sixteenth-century society vis-à-vis criminality, on the one side, and sexuality, on the other, is found in these works also, as is the suggestion that our own time is undergoing another change of momentous impact. And as in *The Birth of the Clinic* especially, here too changes in medical and psychiatric discourse are linked to the impulse towards totalitarian control which Foucault conceives to be intrinsic to modern society. But in *La Volonté de savoir* especially, this totalitarian impulse is represented as being more powerful, more fraught with consequences, more apocalyptic than it appears in his earlier works. This is because the "discourse on sexuality" in our time unfolds in the effort to gain total control over the whole individual—over the body, to be sure, but over the psyche also.

Surveiller et punir prepares us for this analysis of totalitarianism by explicating the function of the prison in modern society. Product of the modern "discourse on criminality," the prison serves as a model of the *société disciplinaire,* of which it is the first institutional manifestation. Invented in the nineteenth century, different from the dungeons and châteaux of incarceration that littered the landscape of the Classical age, the prison is committed less to the hiding and confinement of criminals than to their "reformation" into ideal types of what the citizen outside them should be. The prison reforms of the nineteenth century, however, far from being the evidence of growing enlightenment and humanitarianism that they are conventionally presented as being, reflect a new conception of the ideal society, a new conception of deviancy, and new ways of dealing with it.

In the totally ordered, hierocratized space of the nineteenth-century prison, the prisoner is put under constant surveillance, discipline, and education in order to transform him into what power as now organized in society demands that everyone become: docile, productive, hard-working, self-regulating, conscience-ridden—"normal" in every way. Similar reforms, seemingly inspired by the new, enlightened conception of the citizen as a "responsible" human being, were carried out during the same period in schools, military systems, and places of work. Justified by the new social sciences which supposedly promoted a new and more enlightened idea of human nature, culture, and society, these new disciplinary apparatuses (Foucault's word is the virtually untranslatable *dispositifs*) secretly conceal within their several "discourses" the ideal of the prisons organized on their bases. In the sixteenth century, Foucault argues, criminals and heretics were publicly tortured, mutilated, and put to death in a "spectacle" intended to remind the "subject" of the sovereign's right to punish, his right to "kill." But at least this treatment was open and direct, exacted on the body of the prisoner rather than on his whole being, and possessed at its worst the not unenviable virtue of "candor." By its nature, torture taught that authority was based on force and showed by implication that the subject had a "right" to take the law into his own hands and to answer force with force, if he had the power to do so.

Modern legal systems and the penal systems they serve (rather than the reverse) represent a social authority that masks itself behind professions of humanistic concern for the citizen, humanitarian principles of social organization, and altruistic ideals of service and enlightenment. But this authority, as sovereign in practice as any absolute monarch claimed to be in theory, seeks to make society into an extended prison, in which discipline becomes an end in itself; and conformity to a norm that governs every aspect of life, and especially desire, becomes the only principle of both law and morality.

Thus summarized, this sounds very much like the kind of ranting we normally associate with conservative opponents of the power of the centralized state, or a liberal defense of the individual against a "society" intent on violating his rights. It sounds a little like Camus in *The Rebel,* opposing "totalitarianism" and holding up the prospect of an amiable anarchy as a desirable alternative. But if in *Surveiller et punir* Foucault seems to be defending the individual against society, it is not because he credits any idea of natural rights or the sanctity of a contract between the members of society, or between them and their government. Far from honoring the notions of rights and contract, Foucault abandons the notion of the natural itself.

In fact, he argues that wherever it appears in the discourses of the human sciences, the natural always conceals within it the aspect of a "norm," so that any "law" supposedly derived from study of the natural can always be shown to be nothing more than a "rule" by which to define the "normal" and to justify the "disciplining" of those who deviate from the norm, by punishment, incarceration, education, or some other form of "moral engineering." The play of the concepts "normality" and "deviancy" and their functioning in the social discourse of our own time are never more clearly seen than in the modern human sciences' concern with "perversion" and the "pervert." And this concern is never more apparent than in the modern "discourse on sexuality." To show that these concepts and this concern are simply elements in a never-ending conflict between power and desire is the aim of his *History of Sexuality*. To show how this conflict, in turn, is masked behind a simple "desire for knowledge" is the aim of the first volume.

The title of this volume, *La Volonté de savoir* (published in English as *The History of Sexuality*), indicates the matrix of the larger work: the complex relationships that have taken shape in Western society, since the sixteenth century but especially in the nineteenth and twentieth centuries, between power, desire, and knowledge. The stated aim of the extended work is to analyze the *mise en discours* of sex and to relate this to the "polymorphous techniques of power" (20). We are to be enlightened, we are promised, about the "productive processes" that engender "sex, power, and knowledge" (21) to the end of constructing a veritable "political economy" of Western man's "will to know" (98). The principal subject of analysis will be, not sex itself, sexual practices, or the folklore of sex, but rather a "discourse" that substitutes the abstraction "sexuality" for the "body and pleasure" as a "drive" that supposedly underlies every aspect of life and as the "mystery" that clothes the "secret" of life itself (49, 91–94).

If, however, in succeeding volumes Foucault follows the outline given in the first, the work will represent a significant departure from the notions of cultural history that he has promoted up till now. First of all, he seems no longer interested in defending the notion of historical discontinuity, rupture, or mutation on which he has insisted in previous works. He presents the nineteenth-century discourse on sexuality as importantly new in what it aspires to and achieves, but he finds its institutional origins in medieval monastic discipline, the "confessional" culture of post-Tridentine religion, and the "technology of sex" developed in the eighteenth century. Second, more overtly than in previous works, Foucault grounds the "discourse on sexuality" in the larger "discourse of power," so much so that he seems finally to have reached a bottom in his efforts to plumb the *abîme* out of which discourse in general arises. He will, he promises us in his methodological remarks, analyze "a certain knowledge of sex, in terms not of repression or of law, but of power" (121); and he then proceeds to define power in such a way as to endow it with all the mystery, all the meta-physicality with which he claims that power endows sex.

"Power," Foucault says, "is everywhere" (123). Moreover, it is not a thing that can be acquired; its relations are immanent in all other kinds of relations (economic, political, and so on); it "comes from below"; and its relations are both "intentional and nonsubjective" (123–24). This suggests that we should not expect from him in future an analysis of the general "discourse of power." The more so inasmuch as he insists that the principal characteristic of power is always to manifest itself in a discourse about something other; power can only be effective—and tolerated—when some part of it is hidden (113). Power, it seems, has a capacity of infinite displacement; accordingly, it can only be caught "on the wing," analyzed in the places it both in-habits and vacates simultaneously, and hence viewed only indirectly. But sexuality is the place to grasp it most effectively, for the discourse on sexuality, actively promoted by the "apparatus of power" (*dispositif du pouvoir*) in modern Western society, gives access to the human body and, through the body, to the control of the group, the species, and finally "life" itself (184–88).

The third way in which this book differs from others by Foucault is in the radicalism of its attack on "knowledge" in all its forms. The studies of madness, clinical medicine, the human sciences, and even that of "the archeology of knowledge" had continued to suggest that there was some ground, consisting perhaps of a theory of discourse itself, that might be used as a staging area for some positive conception of "knowledge." Hope for the discovery of this ground is now realized. Everything is seen to consist in "power," but power itself is viewed as indeterminable. Even the "discourse about discourse" offers only an indirect insight into its nature. No sooner is power fixed in a "meta-discourse" than it "slips" to another domain, perhaps even to that of "meta-discourse" itself. When knowledge is conceived to be so satu-rated with power that it is no longer distinguishable from it, the only recourse left is to a kind of power that eschews "knowledge" of every sort. The nature of such a power is only hinted at here, in Foucault's designation of the "base" (*point d'appui*) for a counterattack against the apparatus of sexuality: "the body and pleasures" (208). How this base is to be constituted, however, is not made clear.

Finally, this work differs from others in Foucault's corpus by vir-tue of its overtly political tone and open orientation towards contem-porary political questions. The same apocalyptical mood colors the end of the work; intimations of future biological wars and racial holocausts abound. But the dreams of a "garden of delights," of "good sex on the morrow," to be brought about by "speaking out against the powers that be, telling the truth and promising enjoyment"—all this is dismissed as fatuous utopianism. In fact, Foucault argues, such dreams confirm, when they are not complicit in, a "discourse of sexuality" that exercises control and contributes to the massive process of "normalization," precisely insofar as they credit the myth of "repression" promoted by that discourse itself. Whence the twofold purpose of the proposed history of sexuality: to dissipate the myth of the repressive nature of modern society and to expose the operations of the *dispositif du pouvoir* in the very "knowledge" that claims to liberate us from the effects of this repression.

The paradoxical opening that we have come to expect in Foucault's discourse is not lacking in *La Volonté du savoir*. It consists of the argument that far from being sexually repressive, modern Western society, even in its Victorian golden age of repression, was anything but that. On the contrary, modern Western society has not only promoted more talk about sex, more study of it, more classifications of its forms, more theories of its processes than any culture known to human history, it has promoted as well the radical diversification of sexual practices, refined the forms that sexual desire and gratification may take, and accorded to "sex" a greater metaphysical function than has any other culture we know. The true originality of Western society in world culture, we might conclude, consists in its recognition that the promotion and control of the various forms of sexuality offers the best means of "policing" society, of "disciplining" human beings, and even of turning their "perversions" to socially useful, that is, power-serving, purposes.

Although the origins of this attitude towards sex are to be found in the Middle Ages, the "break" in a generally healthy attitude towards the body and its functions occurs in the eighteenth century. At this time, sex becomes subject to causal and quantitative analyses, a matter of concern to the state, and a resource to be "policed"—because sexual practices are perceived as the key to population control and therewith to "wealth." For the first time, at least in a significant way, "how people use sex becomes a concern of society" (37). In the nineteenth century, the control of sex is effected by means of a movement both political and scientific in which a sexual norm ("heterosexual monogamy") is constituted, and any form of sexuality that threatens that norm can be designated as "against nature" (52). Thus is created—and this is what is more important for an understanding of modern society than "repression"—"le monde de la perversion" (50–55).

This world is the place where "unnatural acts" are performed, and it is populated by a host of "antisocial" types whose activities threaten the purity and health of the species: the sodomite, the onanist, the necrophiliac, the homosexual, the sadist, the masochist, and so on (54–55). But while being exiled to the confines of "proper society," the inhabitants of this world are simultaneously discovered—by doctors, psychiatrists, preachers, teachers, and moralists in general—to reside also within the "normal" family as well, as a threat to its "health" and to the family's proper service to the "race." "Perversion" is now included within the body of the "normal" person as *potentia* that must be identified, treated, disciplined, guarded against—in a ceaseless exercise of self-examination, confession, (psycho)analysis, regimentation, and general vigilance that ceases only with death. In fact, not surprisingly, the modern *scientia sexualis,* which takes shape over against general medicine on the one side and the ancient *ars erotica* on the other, even succeeds in finding death, in the form of the "death wish," to underlie sexuality in general (72–73).

The great invention of this "science" is nothing other than sexuality itself (91). It discovers, before sex and beneath it, the play of a "force" that is "everywhere" and nowhere," a process that is pathological in essence and a "field of significations calling for decipherment," and a mechanism that, while localizable, is yet governed by indefinite causal connections (92). And the "science of sex" makes of this force the "secret," not only of life, but of the "individual subject" as well (93). By its success in making the individual and the group seek their "essence" and "impurity" in real or imagined "perversions," this "science" (which includes even that "liberating" discipline, psychoanalysis) serves a power that is only temporarily identifiable in class terms. Ultimately, Foucault predicts, it will serve to organize the wars of the races, each of which will see in sex a capital resource to be used in the "bio-politics" of the future.

But the theory, or rather the myth, of repression has its golden age and perfect ground of cultivation in the era of the bourgeois family; for during this era "science" identifies, and in the process brings into being, four specific social types which are generalized into the possible types that "normal" humanity may incarnate: the hysterical woman, the masturbatory child, the perverse adult, and the Malthusian couple. The family is simultaneously defined as the "normal" human unit and as the battleground (between men and women, young and old, parents and children, and, by extension, teachers and students, priests and lay-men, rulers and ruled) where the prize to be won and the weapons to be used in the battle consist of the same thing: sexuality (136). "Sci-ence," in seeking to control this battle, evolves four great strategies: the transformation of the body of the "hysterical" woman into a medical object; of the sex of the infant into an educational object; of perverse pleasures into a psychiatric phenomenon; and of procreative conduct into an object for social control (137–39). These strategies have the effect of "producing sexuality" and bringing under general social con-trol the unit in which sexuality has its greatest play: the family. A whole apparatus is created for dealing with nothing but the problems that sexuality, now generalized and deemed eminently effective in the long run, creates in the family (139–46, 148–49). "Love" in the family is always under the threat of falling into "perversion"; perversion in turn is linked to "degeneracy," and degeneracy to loss of "racial" power, wealth, status (157, 160).

What Foucault purports to show, then, is that the "theory of repression," far from being an instrument of liberation, is in fact a weapon used in the extension of social disciplining over every indi-vidual and group (169). And why this "will to discipline"? Modern society apparently knows clearly what the individual only dimly grasps: that "l'homme moderne est un animal dans la politique duquel sa vie d'être vivant est en question" (188). The "disciplines" not only know this, they "prove" it; they provide the theory of an "anatomo-politique du corps humain" and of a "bio-politique de la population" (183). In modern global warfare, Foucault concludes, the matter at issue is no longer one of "rights" but one of "life" itself (191). Since sex provides access to the "life of the body and the life of the species," it functions in these sciences as both "unique signifier" and "universal signified" (204)—so convincingly that these sciences have succeeded, more completely than any *ars erotica* could ever do, in making "sex itself desirable" (207).

Thus, the discourse on sexuality is shown simultaneously to reveal and to conceal the play of power in modern society and culture. Measured against the enormity of the power of this discourse, Foucault tells us, the manifestly "political" discourses of the traditional ideologies pale to insignificance. Even the Nazis look tame in com-parison with the "bio-politics" that Foucault sees taking shape on the horizon (197). He foresees an era of racial wars made more virulent than anything previously known in the degree to which "knowledge" will have succeeded in internalizing, within the individual and the group, the play of a "sexuality" intended solely to discipline "bodies and pleasures."

Thus, Foucault's coming books promise to be even more apocalyptical than his earlier ones, in part because he has now come upon his true subject: power. And power has been hypostatized and given the status that spirit once enjoyed in an earlier, humanistic dispensation. Of course, his real subject had always been power, but power specified, located in particular exchanges between words and things. Now the "void" out of which language was originally conceived to have spun its fictions has been filled. No void, but a plenum of force; not divine, but demonic. And the whole of culture, far from being that exercise of endless sublimation that humanism conceives to be the essence of our humanity, is revealed as nothing but repression. More or less killing, to be sure, but in the end nothing but destructive.

Summarized in this way, Foucault must seem to be little more than a continuation of a tradition of pessimistic, even decadent, thought of which Schopenhauer, Gobineau, Nordau, and Spengler are representative. And it is true that Foucault not only finds little to lament in the passing of Western civilization but offers less hope for its replacement by anything better. But philosophers are under no obligation to be optimists, and neither are cultural commentators. The issue is not whether a thinker is an optimist or a pessimist but the grounds for his point of view.

Foucault's grounds are difficult to specify, because he rejects most of the strategies of explanation that analysts of culture and history have honored as legitimate bases for praising or condemning social practices in the past. At the center of his thought is a theory of discourse based upon a rather conventional conception of the relation between language and experience, a theory originating in the now discredited discipline of rhetoric. Foucault uses rhetorical notions of language to project a conception of culture as magical, spectral, delusory. Strangely enough, this idea of language remains unexamined by him. In fact, although his thought is based primarily on a theory of language, he has not elaborated such a theory systematically. And as long as he fails to elaborate it, his thought remains captive of that very power that it has been his aim to dissipate.

*   *   *   *

This chapter was written some eight years ago. Since that time Foucault has died, but just before his death in 1984 he issued two volumes of his projected *History of Sexuality* and left another in sufficiently finished form to permit hope of its publication in the near future. The two volumes in hand, *L'Usage des plaisirs* and *Le Souci de soi,* represent a considerable departure from the original plan of the project, which was to have concentrated on the development of that *scientia sexualis* which he considered to be a creation unique to modern Western society. Instead, he turned to the study of the ancient *ars erotica* as it had developed from its putative invention in fourth-century Greece to its transformation into an "ethics of pleasure" in second-century Rome. The promised fourth volume, entitled *Les Aveux de la chair,* will deal with the elaboration of Christian "sexual ethics" during the patristic period.

These studies are not intended to provide a historical background for the understanding of the modern "science of sex" that had originally engaged Foucault's attention. On the contrary, he continued to insist on the discontinuities and differences between the three great traditions of the discourse of sexuality in the West. He denied, for example, that the ethical theories of the Roman Stoics had anything in common with Christian asceticism. On the contrary, he argued, the "ethics of pleasure" that took shape in Roman culture during the period of the Empire was the last phase of a development begun in Greece centuries earlier rather than a prefiguration of the "confessions of the flesh" that would triumph with Christianity in the fourth century A.D. Why, then, we must ask, did Foucault turn his attention to the study of what he might well have considered to be a purely antiquarian topic?

In the last interview given before his death, Foucault offered two reasons for his attention to the Classical period. One was his desire to study the phenomena of "individual conduct"; and the other was his interest in the relation of "the question of style" to ethics and morality. In his earlier studies of madness, health, the human sciences, and prisons, he said: "Many things that were implicit therein were never able to be rendered explicit because of the way I posed problems. I wished to pin down [*repérer*] three great types of problems: that of truth, that of power, and that of individual conduct." These three areas of experience, he continued, could be adequately comprehended "only in their interrelationships, and no one of them can be understood without the others." What bothered him about his earlier books was that he had "considered the first two experiences without taking into account the third." It was in the interest of taking into account "individual conduct" that he had been forced to elaborate the notion of style and especially the notion of a "style of life." The "question of style," he averred, was "central to the ancient experience: stylization of the relation with one's self, style of conduct, stylization of one's relations with others." The ancient world

> never ceased to pose the question of knowing whether it might be possible to define a style common to different areas of conduct. Effectively the discovery of this style would have permitted the definition of the subject. The unity of a "morality of style" began to be conceptualized only under the Roman Empire, in the second and third centuries, and immediately in terms of a code and of truth.

Not that Greek and Roman thought were to be held up as more enlightened or nobler alternatives to either Christian thought or its modern "scientific" counterparts. Quite the contrary: Foucault purported to have found nothing "admirable" or "exemplary" in ancient thought about sex, love, or pleasures. Ancient thought on these matters, in his view, consisted of little more than a "profound error." In fact, ancient thought was shot through with a massive contradiction: between the search for a "certain style of life" and "the effort to render it common to everybody." In other words, the very notion of a style of life was thinkable only against the notion of a style common to everybody. To have style, to live with style, was to live in contrast to what "everybody" else believed, thought, or practiced.

Style, then, is set in opposition to ethics, in the manner in which the individual is to be set in opposition to that "subject" that is always the presumption of every "system" of morality. What was admirable and original about Classical thought was its search for an adequate concept of style; what was less than admirable was its consistent confusion of style with a code that could be applied to all as a rule of ethical comportment. The transformation of the quest for a style of living into the project of constructing "a form of ethics that would be acceptable to everyone—in the sense that everyone would have been obliged to submit to it—seemed to me catastrophic."

The dynamics of this long, slow process of transformation is the subject of *L'Usage des plaisirs* and *Le Souci de soi*. In a sense, then, these volumes tell the story of the failure of Classical thought to escape the lure of ethics. What began as little more than a search for an aesthetics of pleasures, the means of heightening the gratifications of sexual desire, ends as an ethics of pleasures that defines gratification as abstinence from sexual activity or the confinement of it to the exigencies of a "spiritual matrimony." In the process, the individual is reduced to the status of a "subject" whose principal obligation to his "self" is to deny, repress, or sublimate his pleasures to his duties.

The irony of this story is contained in the fact that among the Greeks and Romans the pursuit of sexual pleasures was not regulated by the established centers of public power, the state and religion. Here was an area of individual freedom, at least for that small elite of nobles that made up the only group that counted in ancient times. Sex, Foucault insists, was regarded as a perfectly "natural" activity, carrying with it no imputation of being either evil in itself or harmful in its effects. At least, such was the case prior to the identification of sexual activity as an object of systematic study and cultivation in the fourth century B.C. This identification of sex as an object of study was tantamount to the Fall of Adam in the Garden of Eden, because once sex became fixed as an object of study, its "problematization" followed as a matter of course. And once it had been problematized, it was inevitably transformed into an object of moral concern and ethical regulation. Thus, the folly displayed in every "will to know" returns as the subject under discussion, as it had been in every one of Foucault's earlier books. And the plot of the story he has to tell is substantially the same also. Through a series of condensations and displacements, effected by discourse itself, what had once been conceived as simply a fact of life becomes first an object of systematic study, then a chaos of differences that must be reduced to an order, next a hierarchy of activities sharing more or less in the essence that is presumed to underlie them all, and finally a set of practices regulated by a code of comportment that prescribes abstinence as the means to gratification. The greater irony is contained in the fact that none of this was prescribed by the powers that governed society. It was all a consequence of that human fatality, the "will to know."

So L'Usage des plaisirs and Le Souci de soi are ironic titles, inasmuch as the former indicates a practice that leads to the disuse of pleasures and the latter indicates the mistake contained in the notion that there is a self to care for. The Greek search for an aesthetics of sexual pleasures ends in a conceptualization of "true love" (le véritable amour) in which the fixation on the desire of the adult male for the adolescent boy is sublimated into "the love of truth." The quest for "true love," that is, the essence of love, eventuates in a doctrine that makes the "access to truth" dependent upon "sexual austerity." And so, too, with respect to "the care of the self" as cultivated especially by Roman theorists of desire under the high Empire. Here too it is what might be called "the fetishism of truth" that triumphs over the desire to "know" about the self and to analyze its potentialities for the living of a "good life." By way of an account of how Roman thinkers conceptualized the topics of body, woman, and boys, Foucault's story culminates in his representation of the "new erotics" which resembles Christian asceticism in the rules it lays down for the living of the good life. But the orientation differs from the Greek project of aestheticizing sexual pleasures. "The care of the self" orients thought and practice differently from "the use of pleasures." These differences are reflected in the distances that separate "use" and "care," on the one side, and "pleasures" and "selves," on the other. The "new erotics" that crystallizes in the Roman Empire and is centered on the care of the self features as its ironic inversion the substitution of virginity for sex as the highest style of life.

At the center of the Roman ideal was a profound concern for that self that had been invented precisely to serve as the object of the "care" that now took the place of the pursuit of pleasures. This self was conceptualized in ways radically different from the Christian version thereof that would serve as the object of Christian regulation. But far from being the liberating discovery that modern humanists conceive it to have been, this self was nothing but another instrumentality for cultivating the concern that had generated its invention.

Foucault's analyses of Greek and Roman ethics are of a piece with his attacks elsewhere upon the illusions of humanism. At the base of these attacks is his refusal to credit the idea of a human subject. The idea that there resides within the individual a subjectivity—an essential self—that it is the duty of the individual to cultivate, at the expense of the pleasures available for enjoyment, is for Foucault the error shared by Christianity, Classical humanism, and the modern human sciences alike. Thus, volumes 2 and 3 of the *History of Sexuality* must be seen as parts of his more general project of contributing to that "death of Man" that he announced at the end of *The Order of Things*. But it is significant, I would say, that in these last works Foucault turned once more to reflection on the question of style and its relation to the play of the discourse of truth, on the one side, and that of desire, on the other. For in this turn we see a return to the one idea that, as I wrote in my original version of this essay, "appears to escape Foucault's critical ire," the idea of style.

I noted earlier that Foucault praised Roussel for his "reversed style," a manner of writing that effectively canceled itself out in its very articulation. In his account of the Classical discourse of sexuality, he appears to fault the ancients for their failure to develop a similarly reversed style in the cultivation of their pleasures. It was not, apparently, a matter of holding fast to an aesthetic attitude in this domain of experience, because insofar as a given experience is "problematized" by being made into an object of systematic inquiry, it is already on the way to becoming an object of moral concern—so intimately is morality related to any "will to know." A generally aesthetic attitude is no more intrinsically liberating than a purely cognitive one; in fact, it is repressive insofar as it involves a cognitive moment in its elaboration. What is required, it would seem, is an aesthetic attitude in which the cultivation of a style takes precedence over any curiosity about the true nature of the experience being stylized. A liberatory style would be one improvised solely for heightening pleasures on the occasion of their possibility but dissolved at the moment of gratification. Any attempt to extend the stylization improvised for one occasion to another, any attempt to generalize a style of comportment and to make of it a code applicable to all occasions, would represent a slippage from an aesthetic into an ethical attitude.

Needless to say, Foucault's attack on ethics—a project he inherited from Nietzsche—required that he practice a kind of scholarship or a manner of philosophizing that would not itself represent a distinct ethical stance or a merely aesthetic attitude, lacking any claim to cognitive authority. Apparently, he came to regard the notion of style or stylization as a third alternative to these two dangers. Not, to be sure, style understood as fine writing but rather style conceived as "a certain constant manner of speaking" that claimed authority to illuminate only the specific topic under study. In his last interview, Foucault opined that all of his early works featured "a certain use of specialized terms [*vocabulaire*], of play, and of philosophical experiment" as well as "methods slightly rhetorical." All this he characterized as a "refus du style." But, he continued, he had "abruptly broken" with these practices" around 1975–76 "when he had undertaken to "write a history of the subject . . . and of which it would be necessary to recount its genesis and dissolution." The development of a new style of presentation was necessitated by the desire to liberate himself from that earlier way of philosophizing ("de me deprendre de cette form—là de philosophie"). And while this turn to what appeared a purely historical interest might seem to some to mark a passage to a "radical non-philosophy" but that would be in reality a way of "thinking more radically the philosophical experience"—would this not be the equivalent in the human sciences of that *style renversé* that Foucault claimed to have found in Roussel's experiments in aleatory writing? And would not such a reverse style be appropriate for a scholar who wished to save his own individuality from the "subjection" that adherence to a consistent stylistic practice would signify? Would it not be the height of irony for a scholar known for his idiosyncratic style in his early works to end his career by the composition of at least two books in which what was written was "straight" history, in which the method used was the most conventional kind of philological analysis, and in which the manner of composition was so pedantic as to make of sex the most boring of subjects?

BOOKS BY FOUCAULT

Maladie mentale et psychologie. Paris, 1954.

Histoire de la folie. Paris, 1961. English translation, *Madness and Civilization: A History of Insanity in the Age of Reason,* trans. Richard Howard. New York, 1965.

Naissance de la clinique. Paris, 1963. English translation, *The Birth of the Clinic: An Archeology of Medical Perception,* trans. A. M. Sheridan Smith. New York, 1973.

Raymond Roussel. Paris, 1963.

Les Mots et les choses: Une archéologie des sciences humaines. Paris, 1966. English translation, *The Order of Things: An Archeology of the Human Sciences.* New York, 1970.

L'Archéologie du savoir. Paris, 1969. English translation, *The Archeology of Knowledge,* trans. A. M. Sheridan Smith. New York, 1976.

L'Ordre du discours. Paris, 1971. English translation, *The Discourse on Language,* trans. Rupert Sawyer for *Social Science Information* and reprinted as an appendix to *The Archeology of Knowledge,* cited above.

"Moi, Pierre Rivière, ayant égorgé ma mère, ma soeur, et mon frère . . .": Un Cas de parricide au XIXe siècle. Paris, 1973. With Claudine Barret-Kriegel et al. English translation, *"I, Pierre Rivière, Having Slaughtered My Mother, My Sister, and my Brother . . .,"* trans. F. Jellineck. Lincoln and London, 1982.

Surveiller et punir: Naissance de la prison. Paris, 1975. English translation, *Discipline and Punish: The Birth of the Prison,* trans. A. Sheridan. New York, 1977.

Histoire de la sexualité. Vol. 1, *La Volonté de savoir.* Paris, 1976.

Vol. 2, *L'Usage des plaisirs*. Paris, 1984.
Vol. 3, *Le Souci de soi*. Paris, 1984.

Foucault's last interview is printed as "Le Retour de la morale," in *Les Nouvelles*, 28 June–5 July 1984, 37–41.

6. Getting Out of History: Jameson's Redemption of Narrative

As we say of certain careers, history may lead to anything, provided you get out of it. —Lévi-Strauss

Marxists do not study the past in order to construct what happened in it, in the sense of determining what events occurred at specific times and places. They study history in order to derive the laws of historical dynamics. It is these laws that preside over the systemic changes in social formations, and it is knowledge of these laws (rather than those of structure) that permits Marxists to predict changes likely to occur in any given current social system. Knowledge of these laws of process makes it possible for us to distinguish between realistic and delusory programs for effecting social change. Only insofar as we have succeeded in accurately mapping what history has been down to the present are we permitted to know what is possible, and what impossible, in the way of any social program in the present designed for the future.

Marxism was never intended to be merely a reactive social philosophy, but it can be innovative and constitutive of a new life for humankind only to the extent that it has actually divined the laws of history and used them to uncover the "plot" of the whole human drama which renders its surface phenomena not only retrospectively understandable but prospectively meaningful as well. Many modern Marxists, embarrassed by the similarities between this notion of history and its religious, specifically Judaeo-Christian prototypes, have tended to play down this prophetic aspect and given themselves to the study of discrete, concrete historical and social phenomena. This allows them to appear more scientific, after the manner of their counterparts in the bourgeois social sciences, but it also deprives their discourse of that moral coloration that Marx derived from his

Hegelian, utopian, and religious forebears. Insofar as Marxist thought achieves the kind of respectability that comes with the aping of methods or techniques of contemporary social science, it loses in its power to inspire a visionary politics. Take the vision out of Marxism, and what remains is a timid historicism of the kind favored by liberals and the kind of accommodationist politics that utilitarians identify as the essence of politics itself.

The visionary side of Marxism has been left to the cultivation of literary artists and students of their work in the twentieth century. This conforms to the conditions of a larger split within the human sciences in general between practitioners who wish to contrive a knowledge that will be therapeutic, accommodationist, or adaptive in its effects and those who envision one that will be transformative, reconstitutive, radically revisionary in its aims. One can observe the crystallization of this split condition in the debates that occurred within Marxism in the 1920s and 1930s, in the thought of Lukács, Brecht, Benjamin, the members of the Frankfurt school, and so on. The more Marxism attained to (or claimed) the authority of a science, the more the stewardship of its "visionary" side fell to the literary artist and critic. The more it succeeded in becoming the theoretical orthodoxy of a specific political practice, as in the Soviet Union, the more its "utopian" element was progressively sublimated into a vague commitment to "planning." And the more that vision gave way to planning, the more the literary artist's and critic's efforts to defend the utopian moment in the Marxian legacy became suspect, on both epistemic and political grounds.

For how can a vision, especially a vision of human liberation and redemption from "society" itself, ever be authorized either on practical or on scientific grounds? Even if "history" attests to the fact that all men everywhere have always desired liberation from their condition as merely social beings, it also attests to the fact that they have never been able to satisfy that desire. Neither any practice actually established anywhere in history nor any science could ever direct us to what we ought to desire. Could Darwin instruct those turtles on the Galapagos to desire to be different from what "natural history" had made them? The fact of humanity's failure everywhere finally to redeem itself from the condition of sociality argues more for the delusory nature of this desire and for an accommodation to that condition, after the manner of Freud's argument in *Civilization and Its Discontents,* rather than for continued efforts to achieve what, in the nature of things, seems impossible.

It is at this point that the authority of art and literature, considered not only as documents attesting to the reality of the desire for redemption, but as also providing justification for the vision of its possible realization, enters into contention with practice, common sense, and science alike. Insofar as art and literature, across whatever local differences in their contents occasioned by their production in concrete historical conditions, not only instantiate the human capacity for imagining a better world but also, in the universality of the forms that they utilize for the representation of vision itself, actually provide us with models or paradigms of all creative productivity of a specifically human sort, they claim an authority different in kind from that claimed by both science and politics. It is the authority of "culture" that is to be distinguished from that of "society" precisely by the universal translatability of the forms of its products. Enjoying a special place amongst these forms by virtue of its power to master the dispiriting effects of the corrosive force of temporal processes is narrative. And it is to narrative, conceived as a "socially symbolic act" that by its form alone, rather than by the specific "contents" with which it is filled in its various concrete actualizations, endows events with meaning, that Jameson consigns the authority to justify the utopian moment both in human thought in general and in Marxism considered as the liberating science of that thought in particular.

Jameson is a genuinely dialectical, and not merely antithetical, critic. He seriously entertains the theories of other critics, and not only those who in general share his own Marxist perspective. On the contrary, he is especially interested in the work of those critics who are non- or anti-Marxist, because he knows that any theory must be measured by its capacity, not to demolish its opponents, but to expropriate what is valid and insightful in its strongest critics. In his long theoretical introduction to *The Political Unconscious,* entitled "On Interpretation: Literature as a Socially Symbolic Act," we have what is surely the most ambitious attempt at a synthesis of critical conventions since Frye's *Anatomy of Criticism.* Indeed, this introduction can be viewed as an attempt to compose a Marxist version of Frye's great work. As Marx claimed to have done with Hegel, Jameson wishes to stand Frye "on his feet" and plant him firmly in the hardened clay of "history." "The greatness of Frye," Jameson remarks, "and the radical difference between his work and that of the great bulk of garden-variety myth criticism lies in his willingness to raise the issue of community and to draw basic, essentially social consequences from the nature of religion as collective enterprise" (69). Jameson salutes Frye for reminding us that Marxist hermeneutics cannot do without the kind of attention to "symbolism" and the impulse to "libidinal trans-formation" that informs his approach to the study of literature (73). And what Jameson calls the political unconscious will be revealed in the course of his exposition as nothing less than the equivalent of the "vision" attained to on the level of what Frye, following the church fathers, called the anagogic moment of literary expression (74). The kind of "social hermeneutic" (he also calls it social poetics) envisaged by Jameson promises "to keep faith with its medieval precursor . . . and . . . restore a perspective in which the imagery of libidinal revolution and bodily transfiguration once again becomes a figure for the perfected community. The unity of the body must once again pre-figure the renewed organic identity of associative or collective life, rather than, as for Frye, the reverse" (74).

Now, it is in the nature of Jameson's project that rather than merely assert the superiority of a Marxist method of reading literary works, he should take his stand on what he calls simply "Marxist criti-cal insights" conceived as "something like an ultimate *semantic* pre-condition for the intelligibility of literary and cultural texts" (75). This formulation is important for anyone wishing to penetrate Jameson's complex argument, for it indicates his intention to get be-yond the conventional Marxist notion of the literary (or cultural) text as primarily a reflection of structures more basic. The Marxist critical insights alluded to provide a way of comprehending how literary texts achieve a kind of cognitive authority by virtue of their capacity to work up a certain knowledge (not merely a certain intuition) of the condi-tions of their own production and render those conditions intelligible thereby.

The text, it seems, is to be apprehended as a "symbolization" of what Jameson refers to as three concentric frameworks which function as "distinct semantic horizons." These are (1) political history, (2) the relevant social context, and (3) "history now conceived in its vastest sense of the sequence of modes of production and the succession and destiny of the various social formations, from prehistoric life to what-ever far future history has in store for us" (75). When embedded in the first framework, the literary text becomes apprehensible as a "symbolic act" itself "political" in nature. At the second level it is graspable as a manifestation of a general "ideologeme" of the social formation in which it arose or in which it is read—an ideologeme being "the smallest intelligible unit of the essentially collective discourses of social classes" (76). Finally, at the third level the text and its ideologemes must be read together, in terms of what Jameson calls "the *ideology* of form, that is, the symbolic messages transmitted to us by the coexistence of various sign-systems which are themselves traces or anticipations of modes of production" (76).

This notion of the way in which "Marxist insights" can be used as "something like an ultimate semantic precondition for the intelligibility of literary and cultural texts" turns, then, upon the conceptual efficacy of "the ideology of form" which, for its part, derives its authority as an organon of interpretation from its quest for the text's intelligibility (not from its effort to "explain" the text in any scientific sense or to "understand" it in the way of traditional hermeneutics). Texts are rendered intelligible—or rather their intelligibility is accounted for—by their systematic insertion into a "history" that is conceived to be not only sequenced but also layered in such a way as to require different methods of analysis at the different levels on which it achieves the integrity of what is normally thought of as the "style" of a "period."

Any analysis aspiring to more than an impressionistic reading, the authority of which resides in the "sensibility" of the reader alone, must confront the problem of causation. But when it comes to literary works, there are as many notions of causality as there are notions of what literature consists of. It is especially important for Jameson to consider the question of causality, because as a Marxist critic, he cannot fail to confront the problem of the production of texts. The production of literary texts must be regarded as a process no more and no less mysterious than other processes of cultural production. And the production of literary texts can be demystified only to the extent that the causes operative in that productive process are identified. Jameson surveys the various notions of causality (mechanical, expressive, and structural) that critics have used, implicitly or explicitly, in their consideration of the text viewed as an effect of causes more basic. While granting the appropriateness of these notions to any full account of a text's conditions of production, Jameson regards them as insufficient to a full account insofar as they fail to ascend to the consideration of history itself as a cause. But history is here to be understood in a special sense, that is to say, as an *"absent* cause" of effects in which we are permitted to espy the operations of the machinery moving the stage props of "history, . . . in its vastest sense of the sequence of modes of production and destiny of the various social formations, from prehistoric life to whatever far future history has in store for us." This machinery is comprised of nothing more consequent that Desire in conflict with Necessity.

The confusion to the reader that is likely to result from the effort to follow Jameson in his many uses of the term *history* will be more than justified. In part the confusion is inevitable, given the diversity of meanings that the term *history* covers in current usage. It applies to past events, to the record of those events, to the chain of events that make up a temporal process comprising the events of the past and present as well as those of the future, to systematically ordered accounts of the events attested by the record, to explanations of such systematically ordered accounts, and so forth. Throughout all of these possible usages of the term *history*, however, runs the thread of the distinction, drawn by Aristotle in the *Poetics,* between what can possibly happen and what actually did happen, between what can be known because it happened and what can only be imagined, and what, therefore, the historian can legitimately assert as a truth of experience and what the poet might wish to entertain as a truth of thought or conceptualization. The difficulty with the notion of a truth of past experience is that it can no longer be experienced, and this throws a specifically historical knowledge open to the charge that it is a construction as much of imagination as of thought and that its authority is no greater than the power of the historian to persuade his readers that his account is true. This puts historical discourse on the same level as any rhetorical performance and consigns it to the status of a textualization neither more nor less authoritative than literature itself can lay claim to.

Jameson is at pains to insist that he does not regard history as a text: "History is *not* a text, not a narrative, master or otherwise," he writes. Although "it is inaccessible to us except in textual form," history (in the sense of an account of the past) has a referent that is real and not merely imagined. But the ultimate referent of history (in the sense of the knowledge we can have of it as a process) can be approached only by "passing through its prior textualizations" to the apperception of its function as what Althusser calls the "absent cause" of present social effects that we experience as "Necessity" (35). Jameson's response to those who "draw the fashionable conclusion that because history is a text, the 'referent' does not exist" is simply to sweep aside the theoretical relevance of such a conclusion. Thus he writes: "History as ground and untranscendable horizon needs no particular theoretical justification: we may be sure that its alienating necessities will not forget us, however much we might prefer to ignore them" (102). For him, the question is not whether history exists but whether and to what extent we can make sense of that "Necessity" which our present experience requires us to acknowledge to be a product, not of our own, but rather of the actions of past human agents.

The formulation is Sartrean, of course; and like Sartre, Jameson regards the task of making sense of Necessity as too important to be consigned to the faculty of reason alone. It is rather to the imagination that this task is to be consigned, more specifically to the narrative capacities of the imagination, and even more specifically to the master narrative of history contrived by Marx himself. It is the Marxist master narrative of history that succeeds in dissolving what Jameson calls the mystery of the cultural past. It is the amplitude of that narrative structure, its capacity to unite all of the individual stories of societies, groups, and cultures into a single great story, that commends it to us in the first instance. But it is also to be commended to us by virtue of the narrativity of that structure. For the Marxist master narrative of history serves as the key to the only "anagoge" that a merely immanent life can have. Indeed, our conviction that the great artifacts of world culture can be "returned to life and warmth and allowed to speak once more" makes sense only on the basis of the presupposition that "the human adventure is one" and that those artifacts have a place

> within the unity of a single great collective *story;* only if, in however disguised and symbolic a form, they are seen as sharing a single fundamental *theme* — for Marxism, the collective struggle to wrest a realm of Freedom from a realm of Necessity; only if they are grasped as vital episodes in a single vast unfinished *plot:* "The history of all hitherto existing society is the history of class struggle. . . ." It is in detecting the traces of that uninterrupted *narrative,* in restoring to the surface of the text the repressed and buried reality of this fundamental history, that the doctrine of the political unconscious finds its function and its necessity. (19–20)

Thus, it should be recognized that the cognitive authority that Jameson consigns to narrative as a "socially symbolic act" derives from his conviction of the narrativity of the historical process itself. The master narrative of that process contrived by Marx derives its claim to realism and truthfulness by virtue of its adequacy to the representation of the structure (or what amounts to the same thing, the "plot") of that process. And this circumstance of the adequacy of narrative to the representation of history provides Jameson with a touchstone for distinguishing less between ideology and truth (because all representations of reality are ideological in nature) than between ideologies that conduce to the effort to liberate man from history and those that condemn him to an "eternal return" of its "alienating necessities." In those works of literature in which narrativity is either refused or breaks down, we are met with the traces of a despair that is to be assigned, not to the moral weakness or lack of knowledge of their authors, but rather to the apperception of a shape of social life grown old. The breakdown of narrativity in a culture, group, or social class is a symptom of its having entered into a state of crisis. For with any weakening of narrativizing capacity, the group loses its power to locate itself in history, to come to grips with the Necessity that its past represents for it, and to imagine a creative, if only provisional, transcendence of its "fate."

As I understand him, Jameson goes so far as to conceive of narrative as a mode of consciousness that renders possible a kind of action specifically historical in nature. To Althusser's list of three kinds of causality operative in history Jameson adds a fourth which might be called narratological causality. This would be a mode of causality that consists in a seizing of a past by consciousness in such a way as to make of the present a fulfillment of the former's promise rather than merely an effect of some prior (mechanistic, expressive, or structural) cause. The seizure by consciousness of a past in such a way as to define the present as a fulfillment rather than as an effect is precisely what is represented in a narrativization of a sequence of historical events so as to reveal every thing early in it as a prefiguration of a project to be realized in some future. Considered as a basis for a specific kind of human agency, narrativization sublimates necessity into a symbol of possible freedom.

The narrativization of history, for example, transforms every present into a "past future," on the one side, and a "future past," on the other. Considered as a transition between a past and a future, every present is at once a realization of projects performed by past human agents and a determination of a field of possible projects to be realized by living human agents in their future. Such a notion is "genealogical" in the Nietzschean sense of the possibility of substituting "a past from which one would wish to have descended" for that genetic past from which one actually had descended. It is human culture that provides human beings with this opportunity to choose a past, retrospectively and as a manner of negating whatever it was from which they had actually descended, and to act as if they were a self-fashioning community rather than epiphenomena of impersonal "forces."

Thus, for Jameson, there is a hierarchy of modes of causality operating across the distance between a humanity considered as a natural phenomenon, at the mercy of physical forces, and a humanity considered as a producer of meanings and a distinctively human culture. Physical and biological necessity predominate on the lower levels, where causality is experienced as mechanistic and expressive forces; social constraints and freedoms prevail on the next level; and cultural values and their transformations predominate on the highest level. "The collective struggle to wrest a realm of Freedom from a realm of Necessity," which in the Marxist formulation as given by Jameson forms the content of the plot of world history, serves as the subject matter of all of the master narratives available to Western man for making sense out of what otherwise has to be viewed as nothing but a blind play of chance and contingency.

We usually think of historical agents' freedom as being manifested in the launching of projects into a future, with the past serving as a repository of a certain knowledge about human actions, and the present, as the base from which the project into the future is to be launched. Actually, however, human beings can will backward as well as forward in time; willing backward occurs when we rearrange accounts of events in the past that have been emplotted in a given way, in order to endow them with a different meaning or to draw from the new emplotment reasons for acting differently in the future from the way we have become accustomed to acting in our present. Something like this occurs in religious conversion of the sort described by Augustine, who threw off a cultural ancestry pagan in nature and adopted one Christian in nature. It happens in political conversions as well, for example, when a person who counts himself a liberal suddenly sees the light and embraces a conservative or radical ideology. Such conversions may be seen as simply adopting a stance towards one's personal and social past that does not affect the historical past, the past as it really was, at all; but insofar as the new stance opens out a prospect that makes (or seems to make) a new kind of action possible in one's future, the historical past is affected as well. It is manifestly affected when, in the process of revolutionary political change, a whole society may decide to rewrite its history, so that events formerly regarded as unimportant are now redescribed as anticipations or prefigurations of the new society to be created by revolutionary action. Insofar as we can regard this change of perspective as a causal force in history, it can be seen as effecting changes in past ages' conceptions of their natures as given in the records they produced.

This notion of causation might be called narratological in that it takes the form of agents acting as if they were characters in a story charged with the task of realizing the possibilities inherent within the "plot" that links a beginning of a process to its conclusion. In Jameson's notion, this conception of causality resembles what Auerbach

called figural realism, based on the interpretation of historical processes informing medieval conceptions of the relations among events
in the Old Testament and those in the New. Just as for Dante the after-
life was a fulfillment of a figure of a given worldly existence, in history
every age or epoch was regarded as a fulfillment of a figure of some
earlier age or epoch. The meaning of every present was its completion
of what had been prefigured in the past. The secular version of this
same notion, translated into a specific kind of time-consciousness
between the Renaissance and the late Enlightenment, was, in Auerbach's interpretation, that "historism" that provided the matrix of
Western culture's conception of itself in nineteenth century. To grasp
the present as history was to comprehend it as a realization of forces
originating in a past but still active in such a way as both to give form
to social life and to effect the transformation of society into something
different. Thus, every later phase of a society's life is viewed as a fulfillment of possibilities of development laid down in the past, but this fulfillment itself determines new possibilities of development in the
future. Jameson, consistent with the visionary politics that inspires his
work, places emphasis on the actions of living human beings in choosing a past as the particular set of possibilities that they will labor to
realize or fulfill in their own future. This choice consists, among other
things, in identifying themselves with the characters in one or another
of the master narratives (myths?) and acting in such way as to make
the future projected by it a reality.

The master narratives from among which Western man may
choose are those of Greek fatalism, Christian redemptionism, bourgeois progressivism, and Marxist utopianism. Each of these ways of
construing the meaning of human history is still a possible option for
contemporary Western society insofar as the modes of production of
which these narratives are symbolic projections (slave, feudal, capitalist, and socialist) are still present, dominant, or emergent in Western
society. But for Jameson, the Marxist master narrative commends itself
as the only one whose promise remains to be fulfilled. Greek fatalism,
Christian redemptionism, and bourgeois progressivism have effectively
served their historical purpose in bringing us to that pass in history at
which we must now choose between a neurotic repetition of the past
and a heroic effort to realize the kind of community envisioned by
Marxist socialism as the promise of our future.

How narratological causation works can best be seen in such
areas of high cultural activity as the history of literature. Here the
interpretation of modernism is a crucial instance, because modernism

itself is, according to Jameson, both a symbolization of the experience of late capitalism, with all of its contradictions and anomalies, and a fulfillment of the possibilities of the representation of reality provided by the capitalist mode of production.

Jameson's story of modernism begins with the Romanticist break with Enlightenment rationalism and neoclassicism. It proceeds through representations of realism and naturalism to that point (represented by Conrad) at which the lineaments of modernism can be discerned, especially as it seeks to come to terms with its Romanticist origins. For Jameson this succession of styles has a logic exactly like that which informs the dialectical unfolding of the phases through which capitalism passes from an original struggle with feudalism, to a position of dominance and imperialist expansion, to the first stirrings of nativist movements against colonialism and the great economic crises that attend the movement of contraction.

But Romanticism is related to modernism as a figure to its fulfillment. Romanticism, born of the awareness of both the creative and the demonic aspects of capitalist society, prefigures the schizophrenic condition of life reflected in modernism's style. Realism and naturalism, in turn, are phases in the realization of the symbolizing possibilities of bourgeois consciousness first expressed in Romanticism. Modernism, however, is not related to Romanticism as effect to cause — in either a mechanistic, expressive, or structuralist mode. That this is so can be seen in Jameson's account of Conrad, who is considered as a writer trying to represent the reality of capitalist imperialism in a way that employs the "codes" of both Romanticism and modernism. Here Jameson reconceptualizes the notion of genre in such a way as to credit our apprehension of the extent to which it must be seen as a purely conventional representational strategy (a form with a content all its own) and the creative uses to which such a genre as the romance can be put by artists as different as Guillaume de Lorris, Manzoni, Balzac, and Conrad himself. The romance plot of Conrad's *Lord Jim* can be seen as continuing to emit the same kinds of messages about honor, love, and fidelity that served as its conceptual content in feudal society. At the same time, it is filled with a new content or used to indicate the new referent provided by the historical experience of imperialistic capitalism.

Here Jameson utilizes the modern linguistician's version of the four levels of discourse developed by medieval exegetes to revise the traditional problem of the relation between the form and the content of the literary work. Following Louis Hjelmslev's suggestion, a form (such as the genre of the romance) is seen to have its own content, which can be distinguished from any content of events, characters, and situations with which it might be filled in a given writer's adaptation of it for representing a reality historically different from that for which the genre was invented. Thus, in place of the conventional distinction between

Form = genre, style, formulas, rhetoric, etc.

Content = referent, characters, plots, myths, etc.

Jameson utilizes Hjelmslev's model, in which

$$\text{Form} = \frac{\text{EXPRESSION of the form}}{\text{SUBSTANCE of the form}}$$

$$\text{Content} = \frac{\text{EXPRESSION of the content}}{\text{SUBSTANCE of the content,}}$$

in order to explicate the relations between the levels of the discourse that are equivalent to the medieval fourfold distinctions among literal, figurative, moral, and anagogical (mystical) *meanings*. He then identifies the literal level *with* historical referentiality; the figurative level with codes: linguistic, rhetorical, logical, etc.; the moral level with psychology, of both authors and their characters; and the anagogical level with the political consciousness of the text.

Jameson's purpose, he tells us, is to transcend any impulse towards an ethical criticism in the direction of a criticism that recognizes the content of all morality as a sublimation of concerns and interests that are ultimately political in nature. It is politics—political values, interests, institutions, and practices—that is the ultimate content (equivalent to the medieval *anagoge* and Hjelmslev's "substance of the content") of those symbolic acts of which literature is a privileged instance because it is the most self-consciously symbolizing activity of culture.

Thus, a given cultural formation, such as modernism, when considered as a structure, can be seen to possess levels of signification ranging from characteristic linguistic and stylistic features, through preferred generic forms or patterns (the romance, the anatomy, the Gothic tale), through specific psychological obsessions, anxieties, and modes of sublimation (reflected, for example, in the famous "disociation of sensibility"), to a characteristic projection of a particular kind of politics (anarchic-totalitarian). At the same time, when viewed as a structure in the process of elaboration, this same formation can be seen as a fulfillment of that consciousness that first appears as Romanticism (with its combination of disgust with and fear of capitalist industrialist society and its nostalgia for an idealized past) and also a prefiguration of that post-modernist culture that succeeds it as a structure of consciousness dominant in post-industrial, multinational, and consumer society.

It is within the context of considerations such as these that Jameson attempts to rethink the crucial analytical concept of ideology. This begins with his revision of the Althusserian-Lacanian notion of ideology, conceived not as "false consciousness" or vague "system of values" but rather as an "imaginary relationship" to "transpersonal realities such as the social structure or the collective logic of history" (30). Ideology is not, for Jameson, a lie, a deception, or a distortion of a perceivable reality but rather an attempt to come to terms with and to transcend the unbearable relationships of social life. "To come to terms with" indicates the accommodationist, the conventionally conceived ideological moment in every world-view, while "to transcend" indicates its utopian moment. Unlike Mannheim and even such older Marxists as Lukács and Marcuse, Jameson does not work with the dichotomy of science and ideology. For him, any world-view that even can appear minimally realistic must contain both of these elements, one that apprehends clearly the divided nature of the human condition and another that seeks, more or less successfully, to imagine a world in which that divided condition will have been healed. The important point is whether our transportation into this imagined world returns us to our own ready to do political battle for its transformation or deepens our alienation by adding the sadness of "what might have been" to its dispiriting effects.

And this critical criterion holds for various versions of Marxism, no less than for liberalism and social democratism. It is not only a matter of divining the fact that history has a plot; it is also a matter of what kind of plot you find in it. In fact, in a bold reversal, Jameson turns the conventional critique of Marxism, namely, that it is only a kind of redemptive creed, a secular religion, a "romantic" or "comic" myth, back on those who make it. "The association of Marxism with romance," he writes, "does not discredit the former so much as it explains the persistence and vitality of the latter, which Frye takes to be the ultimate source and paradigm of all storytelling" (105). Indeed, he suggests, it is only the short-sightedness of a bourgeois-secularist perspective that fails to recognize the validity of the socially liberating impulse of both romance and the myths of the redemptive religions since time immemorial. If Marxism looks, sounds, and feels like a traditional religion, it is because it shares the desire for redemption that motivates the latter, even if it translates this desire into social terms and locates it in the domain of history as its proper field of possible cathexes. And in his conclusion, in which he meditates on the work of Benjamin, Bloch, and Durkheim, he suggests that far from negating religious ideals, Marxism discloses their true ground and points us to the only place in creation where they can be actualized, that is, in a history that has to be hated as much as comprehended if we are to escape from it.

At the same time, Marxism must be recognized for the "historicism" it is and in its own turn "historicized" if we are to escape the limitations of its original, nineteenth-century formulation. To historicize means to show the extent to which any ideal, Marxist or otherwise, must come to terms with the sedimented residues of past "forms of life" that went into any given formulation of its principles. Foucault remarks somewhere that Marxism swims in the nineteenth century like a fish in water, suggesting thereby that its authority as a discourse is weakened to the extent that our age is no longer that of Marx. Jameson's tack is to grant that Marxism can never be a finished creed, but always a system in evolution, the vitality of which consists in its capacity to "narrativize" its own development, to "situate" its successive incarnations within the context of their formulations, and to uncover the "plot" in which they play their parts and contribute to the articulation of their unifying "theme."

But if I read him aright, he is suggesting that the story of the development of Marxism, if correctly read, reveals two scandals which must be directly confronted and set right. One has to do with the ill-treatment by "scientific" (or rather "scientistic") Marxists of their anarchico-utopian comrades. The other is the incapacity of conventional or orthodox Marxism to deal with what Jameson calls the paradox of art. Jameson's allusions to "libidinal revolution" and "bodily transformation" indicate his affinities with the anarchist wing of nineteenth-century Marxism, although this brand of utopianism has been brought up to date in the light of post-Freudian theories of the sort promised by N. O. Brown and Marcuse. These theories appear in the guise of Lacanian-Deleuzean categories in the present work. Not that Jameson is an uncritical admirer of the current celebration of *le schizo*. His rule, good historicist that he is, is "contextualize, always contextualize"; and he sees the importance of Deleuze's twist on Lacan as residing in the radical critique that it offers to a domesticating psychoanalytical interpretative practice. He wants to justify interpretation against those who, in a fury of Schopenhauerian pessimism, want to throw out bathwater, baby, and bathtub alike. The *furioso* note is not lacking in Jameson's own mental set, but it is tempered by an old-fashioned respect for manual labor which channels his fury into the kind of anarchism that one associates with the older guild tradition of the nineteenth century.

The scandal in Marxism occasioned by its notion of the paradox of art is another matter. This paradox consists of nothing more than the fact that the artwork "reflects" the conditions of the time and place of its production and is therefore to be regarded as purely "timebound" as to its content, while it will manifestly transcend those conditions and speak meaningfully to the problems and concerns of other ages, times, and places, thereby escaping the kind of "determinism" Marxism must assign to it. How is this possible?

It is possible, Jameson argues, because historical epochs are not monolithically integrated social formations but, on the contrary, complex overlays of different modes of production that serve as the bases of different social groups and classes and, consequently, of their world-views. It is because there are a number of different modes of production in any given historical epoch that different classes can exist in a variety of kinds of antagonism with one another. This accounts for the absence of a fundamental schism in social life, in which the social field polarizes into opposed camps, in all periods of history except the principal axial ones, such as the late Classical period, the late medieval period, and our own late capitalist period. Even in such crisis periods, however, older modes of production are less wiped out than simply relegated to an inferior position in the hierarchy of modes of production. In any event, the forms of consciousness of older modes of production — the slave and feudal, for example — continue to persist within the later one of capitalism, and this gives them an aspect of realism insofar as they provide codes adequate to the representations of "conflicts" experienced as "contradictions" inherent in social life in general. Insofar as a given literary work produced under the conditions of a mode of production still present in a much later age grasps a kind of social contradiction as its subject matter and goes on to project a vision of a condition in which this mode of contradiction has been transcended, it remains relevant to any social formation similarly "contra-dicted." The literary classic does not appeal to later ages by virtue of some timeless wisdom of the sort that can be distilled into a "syntopicon" or digests of the hundred "great books." What the classic achieves is an instantiation of the human capacity to endow lived contradictions with intimations of their possible transcendence. The classic does this by giving the ideality of form to what otherwise would be a chaotic condition made more unbearable by the awareness, constantly suppressed, that this condition is a product of only human contrivance.

Among the various form-giving devices available to the imagination in this transcendentalizing work, narrative enjoys a privileged position. It is privileged because it permits a representation of both synchrony and diachrony, of structural continuities and of the processes by which those continuities are dissolved and reconstituted in the kind of meaning production met with in such forms of narrative as the novel. Narrativity not only represents but justifies, by virtue of its universality, a dream of how ideal community might be achieved. Not exactly a dream, rather more of a daydream, a wish-fulfilling fantasy that, like all such fantasies, is grounded in the real conditions of the dreamer's life but goes beyond these to the imagining of how, in spite of these conditions, things might be otherwise. Moreover, in its purely formal properties, the dialectical movement by which a unity of plot is imposed upon the superficial chaos of story elements, narrative serves as a paradigm of the kind of social movement by which a unity of meaning can be imposed upon the chaos of history. This is the burden of *The Political Unconscious* conceived as a study of *Narrative as a Socially Symbolic Act*. In many respects, the burden falls on the ontologically significant status given to narrativity itself. This is why the fate of narrative in the modern novel is presented as an evidence of the decline of the culture that produced it. In this book, the thesis outlined in an early article by Jameson, "Metacommentary," which won a prize from the Modern Language Association some years ago, is fleshed out and documented with a weight of evidence hard to deny.

Jameson knows that contradiction is a fact of consciousness of culture, not of nature. There are no oppositions in nature; things are simply similar or different. It is the encoding of things as opposites, an encoding that reenacts within culture, the conception of the opposition of things human to things animal, that gives to culture in general both its repressive and its liberating aspects. At the third — or "moral" — level of cultural productivity, where things, practices, and relationships are marked with the signs of positive and negative, presence and absence, fullness and lack, anteriority and posteriority, high and low, and so on, a social formation marks out the "conditions of possibility" for its members' attainment of a full humanity. In this respect, a society narrativizes itself, constructing a cast of social "characters" or "roles" for its members to play, if they are to play its game; a "plot" or ideal course of development for the relations presumed to exist among its recognized character types; and appropriate sanctions for those who deviate from the norms of social being and comportment adequate to the reinforcement of the values the society takes to be its own. This is the conservative side of symbolic action, which takes for granted the contradictions inherent in the relegation of a certain portion of is members to the obloquy of mere nature while reserving for itself the title of a full humanity. This denial of the rights of a full humanity to certain members of society, who become the "lower classes," is the fundamental contradiction inherent in any group that falls short of realizing a true community. Contradiction, then, belongs only to culture, and its simultaneous apprehension and denial constitute the basis of the dialectics of culture that is replicated in those productions and reproductions of meaning that we apprehend in the operation of high culture, in philosophy, literature, the visual and plastic arts, religion, morality, legal and political theory.

In a brilliant expropriation of Greimas's reworking of the medieval "semiotic square," Jameson uncovers the operations of "the political unconscious" which translates the original opposition between nature and culture into an ideology that permeates — and sustains — a specific social formation. According to Greimas, cultural meaning is produced by a complex elaboration of the logical possibilities contained in the relation between a binary opposition and its structures of negation and affirmation. Thus, for example, any simple opposition, such as "male vs. female," generates a field of possible relationships produced by what is implied by the marking of these with positive and negative signs, on the one side, and the contraries of these originary terms, on the other. Thus, for example, the putatively opposition pair "male" and "female" generates the following field of signification:

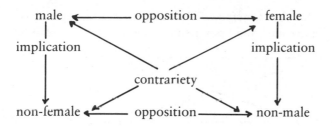

The category implied by the category of "male," when set in opposition to "female," is comprised of everything that is "contrary" to "female." That implied by the category "female," when set in opposition to "male," is comprised of everything contrary to "male." The category implied by "male" is everything that while seeming "male" is the contrary of "female" and the opposite of "non-male." The opposite of "non-male" is "*not* non-male" and the contrary of "female," which is the very structure of male homosexuality; while the opposite of "non-female" is the "non-male" and the contrary of "male," which is the very structure of female homosexuality.

This structure of the possible modalities of sexuality can then be superimposed upon another, comprised of class or social polarities, such that the opposition "white vs. black" or "noble vs. mean" can be represented as recapitulating the meaning of the original opposition of "male vs. female." And this yields a palimpsest of meaning produced by cultural cross-coding that generates the "ideologies" of class, racist, and sexist discourses.

Whether the Greimasian version of the semiotic rectangle is valid or not, Jameson's use of it as a meaning-production machine is original and illuminative of how narrative works both to reinforce and dissolve the "ideologies" of social formations in different epochs of their evolution. He regards a narrative, not as a simple elaboration of the Greimasian machine, but as setting down the "conditions of possibility" of the narratives that a culture will tell of itself. The characters of a novel derive their depth and interest from their status as "mediators" between "the conditions of possibility" laid down by dominant dual-binary structures of the sort postulated by Greimas as the basis of all signification. Thus, for example, in Conrad's *Lord Jim,* the meaningful characters function as mediators between the relations postulated by the presumed opposition between "activity" (or "work") and "value," the crucial "contradiction" created by the antinomies of the modern capitalist mode of production.

This opposition generates—by implication and contrariety—the categories "nonvalue" and "nonactivity," yielding the model:

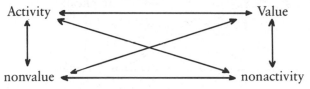

Activity ⟷ Value

nonvalue ⟷ nonactivity

"Lord" Jim himself mediates the primary opposition; the Pilgrims that come aboard Jim's ship mediate the difference implied by the category "value" (i.e., nonactivity); the "Deck-chair sailors" mediate the opposition between nonvalue and nonactivity; and the Buccaneers mediate the difference implied between activity and nonvalue.

Here "plot" is analyzed synchronically rather than diachronically—that is, as setting down the "conditions of possibility" of what can possibly happen in a world construed in these terms. What the problematic ending of *Lord Jim* suggests to Jameson is that Conrad's resolution of the contradictions he perceived to exist between "activity" and "value" (under the conditions of imperialistic capitalism) could only be an "imaginary" resolution (256 n.42), product of an "imaginary" relation to the "real" conditions of existence apprehended as "contradictory" in their essence. Conrad's narrative is to be regarded, then, not as an unrealistic representation of the world he inhabited but as one that is both "realistic" in its apprehension of the actual, contradictory nature of his society and "ideological" in its symbolic handling of the resolutions of these contradictions in the novel. Its ideology is contained in its "metaphysical" representation of "nature" as a dark, malicious force bent on man's destruction and in its "melodramatic" handling of "culture" as a place where the themes of honor, sacrifice, and duty in the face of fate are worked out.

Jameson is preeminently concerned with the current cultural moment, but his whole enterprise depends on his effort to rethink the cultural moment just preceding our own, the period of the triumph and decline of realism, extending from the French Revolution to just before World War I. This period marks the transition to high capitalism in the domain of production and to modernism in literature, art, and thought. His consideration of what we used to call Romanticism, realism, and naturalism in modern literature requires that we view these stylistic changes as phases in the rise and entrance into crisis of the bourgeois world-view. He plots this process as a movement in which the class antagonisms and contradictions of social life in the capitalist age are, first, apprehended (Romanticism); second, affirmed as a "referent" of an objective vision of the world (realism); and third, systematically repressed or sublimated by a combination of what he calls "metaphysics" and "melodrama" (naturalism). In this last phase, we witness the cultivation of the very *ressentiment* that the modern novel wished to account for. Needless to say, modernism, the fourth phase of this process, the phase in which we now live, is that in which this *ressentiment* reappears as the reality that can no longer be denied. Jameson does not deal with this modernist phase in *The Political Unconscious,* having accounted for it in his study of Wyndham Lewis, *Fables of Aggression,* published in 1979, a work subtitled *The Modernist as Fascist.*

I do not know why the book on Lewis, originally conceived as a part of *The Political Unconscious,* was published separately. It may have something to do with the ambivalence that any Marxist must feel about modernism. After all, modernism has to appear as decadent, the form in literature and art that reflects the crisis into which late capitalism has entered (modernism as literary fascism, and so on). At the same time, as a historical phenomenon, modernism must be presumed to carry within itself the potentialities for its own transcendence, especially since in Jameson's reformulation of the Base-Superstructural relationship culture is to be viewed less as a reflection of the modes of production than as simply another aspect of these modes. In Jameson's own emplotment of modern Western literature from Romanticism to the present, modernism appears as the final form of a problematic that begins with Romanticism and achieves its own ironic reversal and decomposition through a working out of its potentialities across the movements conventionally called realism and naturalism. Modernism thus envisaged is nothing but this reversal and decomposition (see the last chapter of *Fables of Aggression* [California, 1979], esp. 171–77). The penultimate chapter of *The Political Unconscious,* entitled "Romance and Reification," ends with the words:

> The perfected poetic apparatus of high modernism represses History just as successfully as the perfected narrative apparatus of high realism did the random heterogeneity of the as yet uncentered subject. At that point, however, the political, no longer visible in the high modernist texts, any more than in the everyday world of appearance of bourgeois life, and relentlessly driven underground by accumulated reification, has at last become a genuine Unconscious. (280)

Since modernism is the end of a story that begins with Romanticism, the conceptualization of the latter is of crucial importance for the understanding of the "plot" that this story describes. It is in Romanticism that the contradictions (and not merely the conflicts) between feudal and capitalist modes of production are clearly apprehended for the first time, and the price that will have to be paid for the triumph of the latter first dimly perceived. These contradictions are, as it were, sublimated and subjected to artistic "working through" in the peculiar hesitancies, exhilarations and depressions, combinations of Promethean bombast and *Welschmerz,* of Romanticism. The dimensions of this schismatic condition are manifested in the combination of archaic longing for an older, seemingly richer and more humane way of life nostalgically recuperated in idealized images of the Middle Ages, on the one hand, and the genuinely utopian, futuristic, and science-fictional kinds of visionary literature produced by that movement, on the other.

The novel, with its heavy baggage of reconfiscated genres, its license to experiment with different modes of articulation, its authorization to fiddle with conventional notions of plot, character, and point of view, appears especially well-suited to the needs of a schizophrenic consciousness that will, over the course of the nineteenth century, be symbolically elaborated—from Stendhal, Manzoni, and Austin, through Balzac, Flaubert, and Dickens, down to Gissing, Zola, Dreiser, and Conrad—and the realism that marks them all will be finally played out. This prepares the way for the advent of modernism, in which Romanticist notions, now revived as an even more sublimated longing for meaning and coherency in human affairs, enjoy a second life as elements of a paradigm of what cultural creativity can aspire to amongst both writers and critics alike. This sublimated Romanticism is the true content of those forms of exacerbated subjectivity that appear in modernist literature as a rejection of history, and in modernist criticism as a denial that meaning is "determinable," not only for texts but also, and especially, for human consciousness in general.

Jameson's explication of this "plot" of nineteenth-century cultural history and its relation to social reality is itself elaborated across a systematic analysis of works by three writers. Balzac, Gissing, and Conrad, who are treated as emblemata of the stages of classical realism, naturalism, and proto-modernism, respectively. Jameson does not claim that his treatment of these writers constitutes a true and proper history of nineteenth-century literature or even an outline of such a history. They are used to illustrate and substantiate a critical stance or *prise de conscience* of the literary artifact in its function as a social document. He does not even claim that his book should be taken as providing a method for reading all novels, although he accords to the novel a crucial role for the understanding of the bourgeois writer's attempts to deal with and transcend the condition of *ressentiment* which he regards as the "ideologeme" or "class fantasy" of the bourgeoisie in general (88).

What interests him about the novel is the fact that, in his (Bakhtinian) estimation, it uses older genres as its "raw material" every bit as much as it uses the detritus of "everyday life" which is supposed to be its principal subject matter (151). Because the novel enjoys the freedom that a free mixture of generic conventions provides, it is ideally suited to reflect the numerous "codes" for endowing events with meaning that arise from the various social classes' different functions in the multiple modes of production present in every age or social formation. Because the novel uses a host of older generic conventions for its representation of a reality that is apprehended as multiple, complex, internally antagonistic, historical, and ultimately threatening to our humanity, it provides the ideal instrument for the examination of what Jameson calls the ideology of form. The use that Jameson makes of this concept signals his acceptance of the formalist heresy appropriately revised for Marxist purposes. What constitutes the literary work's ideology is its form, not its putative contents, whether conceived à la Auerbach, as the activities of a given class, or as certain everyday phenomena formerly excluded from representation in "serious" literatures. Where he differs from most formalists and Structuralists is in his conviction that the form of the literary work is where not only technical writing problems but also specifically political ones are worked out. What modern Western literature achieves in the course of its development from Romanticism on is a sublimation of *ressentiment,* its endowment with a form so perfect as to make of it an object of Desire. The modernist writer not only writes about or reflects *ressentiment,* he (or she) positively wills it, seeks it, and celebrates it—and does so, moreover, by draining every representation of life of any concrete content whatsoever. This is what the celebration of form in modern culture signals. This celebration is not only a political act but the form politics assumes in everyday life under the conditions of late capitalism.

This is not the place to recapitulate the many insights into the work of the writers dealt with by Jameson. His are "strong" readings, not made easier to follow by the Greimasian apparatus he uses to earn them. Nor is this the place to subject these readings to any kind of "empirical" test. In spite of the fact that Jameson indicates his willingness to let his theory stand or fall on its capacity to generate insights into the structures of literary works, any objection to a given reading would simply indicate the presence of an alternative theory or presuppose a reading of the text in question that was simply more "valid" than Jameson's account of it. On the matter of Jameson's readings of specific texts, I will simply reiterate a remark made to me once by an eminent anti-Marxist critic: that he had never read anything by Jameson that was not illuminative of the texts under discussion. Suffice it to say, then, that the readings of Manzoni, Balzac, Gissing, Conrad, Dreiser, and so forth, are well worth the effort it takes to assimilate the theory that enables them as a price of admission.

The theory itself is another matter. Not everyone feels the need for a theory, especially a theory of literature. This is true even of some ethical critics who wish to relate literature to its social contexts and to write its "history." For such critics as these, Jameson's work will be as alienating as the alienation his theory wishes to account for. But an ethical critic who thinks that history comprises a body of facts that are easier to understand than the literary texts he or she wishes to insert into it, in whatever manner, is proceeding under a delusion. Whatever one may think of Marxism as a social philosophy, it has succeeded in placing under question the concept of history inherited from the early nineteenth century and ensconsed as an orthodoxy of belief amongst professional, academic historians. It is not a matter of appealing to history as a way of deciding between conflicting interpretations of a literary text, as if this history were a seamless web and told only one story which could be invoked as a way of defining what is only fictive and what is real in a given literary representation of a form of life. For Jameson is surely right when he argues that ethical criticism must choose between a version of history that makes sense in its totality as a universal human experience and one that does so only with respect to finite parts of that totality.

If one is going to "go to history," one had better have an address in mind rather than go wandering around the streets of the past like a *flaneur*. Historical *flaneurisme* is undeniably enjoyable, but the history we are living today is no place for tourists. If you are going to "go to history," you had better have a clear idea of which history, and you had better have a pretty good notion as to whether it is hospitable to the values you carry into it. This is the function of theory in general— that is to say, to provide justification of a stance vis-à-vis the materials being dealt with that can render it plausible. Indeed, the function of theory is to justify a notion of plausibility itself. Without such a justification, criticism especially is left with nothing but "common sense" to fall back on.

In literary theory in particular, the aim is to define—for primarily heuristic purposes and not as a matter of constituting some Platonic absolute—what will be permitted to count as a specifically literary work and what kinds of relationships the work thus defined can be conceived to bear to other kinds of cultural artifacts, on the one side, and to whatever passes for a noncultural artifact, on the other. At this level of inquiry, it can be seen how far Jameson has rejected the currently fashionable Structuralist and Post-Structuralist notion of textuality which has been extended to cover every aspect of culture. In this respect, Jameson continues to honor the concept of the literary artifact as a work rather than as a text. The notion of text has served to authorize a manner of reading that celebrates the "undecidability" of the literary artifact and, by extension, all cultural artifacts. The closure to which the nineteenth-century novel, in its classical form, aspired is not regarded by Jameson, as it is for a certain current convention of interpretation, as prima facie evidence of its contamination by an idealizing and therefore duplicitous (bourgeois) ideology. The aspiration to closure may be what characterizes narrative, in the same way that it characterizes every "constative" sentence, but this aspiration is not to be written off as another evidence of a dominant class's desire to hide its privileges and to feed the masses with the opiate of teleology. And it is certainly not to be written off as the "ideological" alternative to the genuinely "utopian" vision supposedly reflected in the more "open" form of a hypostatized (lyrical) "poetry" (after the manner of Julia Kristeva in "The Novel as Polylogue" and the later Barthes). For Jameson, the closure to which every narrative aspires is justified, as it were, "ontologically" insofar as it conforms to a vision of a humanity finally reconciled with nature and with itself, of a society finally delivered into the kind of community that both traditional religion and the Marxist master narrative of history envision as a moral necessity.

It was this larger version of history as a story of redemption that got lost to Marxists who failed to win power in the West and who, having won it in the Soviet Union, forgot about it. The substitution of pragmatic or reformist programs for the revolutionary vision of Marx seemed justified by the work of Marxist historians themselves, who, in their contemplation of the "failure" of every concrete program of revolutionary transformation, tended to produce "visions of historical Necessity . . . in the form of the inexorable logic involved in the determinate failure of all revolutions that have taken place in human history" (101–2). Such a "realistic" notion of historical reality is fully justified on the basis of the "facts" alone, but in Jameson's view, such a perspective only tells us what it is that hurts us, not how to cure it or heal the pain. This "cure" is not so much given by art as the search for it is authorized therein. Precisely because all art is ideology, refined, fully elaborated, worked out, as Goldmann used to say, to the "limits of possibility," it reveals the utopian impulse inherent in culture itself. And this is as true of fascist art as it is of liberal, conservative, and radical art, because "*all* class consciousness, . . . all ideology in the strongest sense, including the most exclusive forms of ruling-class consciousness just as much as that of opposition or oppressed classes — is in its very nature Utopian" (289).

Consequently, for Jameson, "Marxist analysis of culture . . . must . . . seek, through and beyond a demonstration of the instrumental function of a given cultural object, to project its simultaneously Utopian power as the symbolic affirmation of a specific historical and class form of collective unity" (291). If, then, Jameson's work indicts any "positive hermeneutic" that, like Frye's, "relaxes into the religious or theological, the edifying and the moralistic," insofar as 'it is not informed by a sense of the class dynamics of social life and cultural production" (292), it also indicts a "Marxian 'negative hermeneutics'" which "fully justifies complaints about the 'mechanical' or purely instrumental nature of certain Marxian cultural analyses" (291). If it were ever to happen that in cultural analysis in general "the opposition of the ideological to the Utopian, or the functional-instrumental to the collective" were transcended, we could be sure that we were on the verge of "the end of what Marx calls prehistory" (293). Need it be said that in *The Political Unconscious* Jameson purports to have laid the basis for such a theoretical transcendence?

If an "empirical" test of Jameson's theory is not called for on this occasion, neither is a critical reading of it that, from within a certitude of its own adequacy, would simply "unpack" the congeries of presuppositions that inform it. I could, for example, read Jameson's account of the career of the nineteenth-century novel, with its four-stage development, as merely another rehearsal of the Marxian four-stage dialectic which all significant social and cultural processes undergo. And I could do a similar job on his analysis of the four kinds of causality he thinks are at work in the production of the literary work. But his would be only to make manifest the commitment to Marxist "dialectics" that Jameson openly admits to. It is Jameson's own refinements on the use of this dialectic and his identification of it with narrative in general—and especially with the Marxist master narrative of world history—that are at issue.

It is significant, I think, that when, in his introduction, Jameson is arguing for the adequacy of the Marxist master narrative to account for the "essential *mystery* of the cultural past," he lapses into the conditional mood: "Only *if* the human adventure is one . . ." (19). In the end, he must leave it to individual judgment to decide whether the Marxist master narrative of world history is the best story that can be told about it. We are left in much the same situation as Orestes in Sartre's *The Flies* or Hugo at the end of *Dirty Hands,* that is to say, with the option of either choosing the Marxist story or not, but still choosing even by our refusal to choose. Like Sartre, Jameson seems to think that a life makes sense only insofar as it is worked up into a story, this story is embedded in another story of greater, transpersonal scope, and this in another, and so on. This may well be the case from a conventional psychoanalytical perspective, and even from the perspective of common sense, but the crucial problem from the perspective of political struggle is not whose story is the best or truest but who has the power to make his story stick as the one that others will choose to live by or in. It may well be that the decline of narrative reflects less a condition of decadence than sickness unto death with the stories that representatives of official culture are always invoking to justify the sacrifices and sufferings of the citizenry. One alternative to "collective unity" is enforced upon us by a combination of master narratives and instruments of control backed by weapons.

This raises an even more crucial theoretical problem, namely, that of Jameson's identification of the "anagogic" dimension of art with a meaning that is specifically political. He is no doubt right in arguing that modern high culture reflects a repression of politics, but it may well be that the politics it has repressed is one that is no longer possible. I mean, of course, politics in the classical formulation, the last vestige of which is to be observed in the workings of the parliamentary regimes of the nineteenth century, which featured "representative" parties, debate, a willingness to abide by the rules of the game, faith in the workings of a "hidden hand" that would mysteriously conduce to the "greatest good for the greatest number" over the long run, and so forth. On the face of it, our age has witnessed a transformation of what since the Renaissance was conceived as politics, a circumstance that fascism affirms as a condition of its possibility and old-fashioned humanists lament as the cause of our discontents. The death of this politics is surely of a piece with the death of a cultural endowment that takes the "timelessness" of the "classics" for granted. At the very end of his book, Jameson recalls Benjamin's "identification of culture and barbarism" in "The Theses on the Philosophy of History." Benjamin reminds us of the extent to which even "the greatest cultural monuments" are "stained with the guilt not merely of culture in particular but of History itself as one long nightmare" (299). And this reminder, Jameson says, is a salutary "rebuke" and "corrective" to "the doctrine of the political unconscious" itself. It recalls us to consciousness of the extent to which "within the symbolic power of art and culture the will to domination preserves intact."

And if this is true of "art and culture," is it not true also of those philosophies of art and culture, of which the Marxist master narrative is one? Is it not possibly true of narrative itself? Is it not possible that the doctrine of history, so arduously cultivated by the Western tradition of thought since the Greeks as an instrument for releasing human consciousness from the constraints of the Archaic age, is ready for retirement along with the politics it helped to enable? And could not the death of "History," politics, and narrative all be aspects of another great transformation, similar in scope and effect to that which marked the break with Archaicism begun by the Greeks? Marx thought the communist revolution would release humankind from the conditions of pseudo-historical existence and usher in a genuinely historical one. The problem may be not how to get into history but how to get out of it. And in this respect, modernism in the arts may be less a regression to a pseudo-mythic condition of consciousness than an impulse to get beyond the myth-history distinction, which has served as the theoretical basis for a politics that has outlived its usefulness, and into a post-political age insofar as politics is conceived in its nineteenth-century incarnations.

7. The Metaphysics of Narrativity: Time and Symbol in Ricoeur's Philosophy of History

Recent debate over the nature of historical narrative has been carried out in terms of the adequacy of the story form of discourse to the representation of reality. Historical theorists such as the *Annalistes,* who were interested in transforming historiography into a science, could legitimately point out that the natural sciences had little interest in storytelling as an aim of their enterprise. And indeed, it could be argued with some pertinence that the transformation of a field of study into a genuine science has always been attended by an abandonment of anything like an interest in inventing a story to tell about its object of study in favor of the task of discovering the laws that governed its structures and functions. According to this view, the prevalence of any interest in storytelling within a discipline aspiring to the status of a science was prima facie evidence of its proto-scientific, not to mention its manifestly mythical or ideological, nature. Getting the "story" out of "history" was therefore a first step in the transformation of historical studies into a science.

The defense of narrative history by Anglo-American thinkers was based on a similar identification of narrative with the story form of discourse. For the principal defenders of narrative historiography in this tradition, the adequacy of the story form to the representation of historical events and processes was manifest, even if the theoretical justification of that adequacy remained to be provided. In their view, not only was a story a legitimate form of explanation for specifically historical events and processes but it was the *proper* way of representing historical events in discourse, inasmuch as such events could be established as displaying the kind of forms met with in traditional story types. Historical stories differed from fictional stories by virtue of the fact that they referred to real rather than to imaginary events. But "true" historical stories did not differ from historical events by virtue of their formal features, because history itself was a congeries of lived stories awaiting only the historian to transform them into prose equivalents.

Now, neither the attack on nor the defense of narrative history did justice to the variety of kinds of stories met with in literature, folklore, and myth; the differences between the techniques of the traditional novel and the modernist novel; or the complex relation between "literature" and the "real world," to which the former undeniably referred even if in the most indirect and allegorical manner. The notion that historical narratives were unrealistic because they were cast in the form of a story implied that literature could not illuminate the "real world" in any important way. But the idea that historical narratives illuminated the "real world" because the world displayed the form of a well-made story, with "characters" engaged in conflicts similar to those encountered in traditional kinds of stories, was similarly untenable. What was obviously called for was an analysis of narrative, narration, and narrativity that would take into account the many forms of story-telling met with in world literature, from ancient epics through the post-modernist novel, and a reconceptualization of the possible relations existing between the three principal kinds of narrative discourse—mythic, historical, and fictional—and the "real world" to which they undeniably referred. It was to these tasks that Paul Ricoeur turned in the late 1970s.

The results of Ricoeur's labors are now available in his magisterial *Temps et récit* (*Time and Narrative*), which must be accounted the most important synthesis of literary and historical theory produced in our century.[1] Although at the moment of this writing only two of the projected three volumes of *Time and Narrative* have been published, the plan of the whole is discernible. The analysis consists of four parts in three volumes. Volume 1 contains parts 1 and 2: "The Circle of Narrativity and Temporality" and "History and Narrative," respectively. Volume 2 contains part 3: "Configuration in Fictional Narrative." Volume 3, entitled *Temps raconté,* will present "the threefold testimony of phenomenology, history, and fiction" regarding the "power" of narrative to "refigure time" in such a way as to reveal the "secret relationship" of eternity to death (*TN,* preface and 101).

In his work, Ricoeur seeks to sort out the different notions of story, storytelling, and narrativity informing the principal theories of narrative discourse set forth in our time. In the process, he redefines historical narrative as a kind of allegory of temporality, but an allegory of a special kind, namely, a true allegory. This is not to say that he denies cognitive authority to other kinds of allegory, such as theological, mythical, and poetic allegory. On the contrary, he grants to fictional narrativity a capacity to represent a deeper insight into the "human experience of temporality" than does either its historical or its mythical counterpart. Nonetheless, historical narrative is assigned a specific task in the representation of a reality that presents itself to human consciousness, in one aspect at least, as an insoluble but ultimately "comprehensible" mystery. This mystery is nothing other than the enigma of being-in-time. Taken in conjunction with Ricoeur's earlier *The Rule of Metaphor* (*La metaphore vive*),[2] which forms what he calls a "pair" with *Time and Narrative* (*TN*, 2:ix), we will have, when the latter work is finished, a comprehensive theory of the relation between language, narrative discourse, and temporality by which to appreciate the degree of truth to be accorded to any representation of the world in the form of a narrative.

The overarching thesis of *Time and Narrative* is that temporality is "the structure of existence that reaches language in narrativity" and that narrativity is "the language structure that has temporality as its ultimate referent." This formulation appears in Ricoeur's 1980 essay, "Narrative Time," which plainly indicates that his study of the truth of narrative is based on a notion of the narrativistic nature of time itself.[3] The contention is not that historians impose a narrative form on sets or sequences of real events that might just as legitimately be represented in some other, nonnarrative discourse but that historical events possess the same structure as narrative discourse. It is their narrative structure that distinguishes historical events from natural events (which lack such a structure). It is because historical events possess a narrative structure that historians are justified in regarding stories as valid representations of such events and treating such representations as explanations of them.

Needless to say, Ricoeur's notion of story differs in important ways from that used by recent Anglo-American philosophers to account for the explanatory effect of narrative histories. It is not enough simply to tell the story of what happened in the past, in the manner of a sports journalist recounting the sequence of contingencies that resulted in the outcome of an athletic contest on a given day. A narrative history is not necessarily, Ricoeur insists, a "species" of the genus "story" (*TN*, 1:179, 228). Any number of different kinds of stories could be told about any given sequence of real events, and all of them might be equally plausible accounts thereof. We could follow such stories perfectly well and credit them all as possible ways of making sense of the events related in them but still not feel that we had been provided with a specifically "historical" account of the events in question—any more than we feel that we have been provided with a historical account of yesterday's political or economic events after we have read a newspaper account of them. Journalists tell stories about "what happened" yesterday or yesteryear and often explain what happened with greater or lesser adequacy, in the same way that detectives or lawyers in courts of law may do. But the stories they tell should not be confused with historical narratives—as theorists of historiography looking for an analogue of historical discourse in the world of everyday affairs so often do—because such stories typically lack the "secondary referentiality" of historical narratives, the indirect reference to the "structure of temporality" that gives to the events related in the story the aura of "historicality" (*Geschichtlichkeit*).[4] Without this particular secondary referent, the journalistic story, however interesting, insightful, informative, and even explanatory it may be, remains locked within the confines of the purview of the "chronicle."

By the same token, Ricoeur's notion of the historical narrative differs from that of certain formalist or rhetorical analysts of folktales, epics, and novels, for whom the essence of a story is contained in its disposition of "functional mechanisms," which can be put in any order as long as the conventions of the genre to which the story belongs are observed (or, conversely, systematically transgressed). What such notions of narrative miss, in Ricoeur's view, is the logic, or rather the poetics, that presides over the integration of such mechanisms into a discursive whole that means more, because it says more than the sum total of the sentences that it comprises. For him, a narrative discourse is not analyzable into the local meanings of the sentences that make it up. A discourse is not, as some would have it, a sentence writ large; any analysis of a discourse carried out on the analogy of a grammatical or rhetorical explication of the sentence will miss the larger structure of meaning, figurative or allegorical in nature, that the discourse as a whole produces.

In contrast, then, to both chronicles of events and what we may call "dissertative" discourses, the kinds of discursive stories that interest Ricoeur and that he takes to be the types told in narrative histories are characterized by their possession of plots. To "emplot" a sequence of events and thereby transform what would otherwise be only a chronicle of events into a story is to effect a mediation between events and certain universally human "experiences of temporality." And this goes for fictional stories no less than for historical stories. The meaning of stories is given in their "emplotment." By emplotment, a sequence of events is "configured" ("grasped together") in such a way as to represent "symbolically" what would otherwise be unutterable in language,[5] namely, the ineluctably "aporetic" nature of the human experience of time.[6]

Historical discourse is a privileged instantiation of the human capacity to endow the experience of time with meaning, because the immediate referent (the *Bedeutung*) of this discourse is real, rather than imaginary, events. The novelist can invent the events that his stories comprise, in the sense of imaginatively producing them, in response to the exigencies of emplotment or, for that matter, of disemplotment, after the manner of modernist, antinarrativist writers. But the historian cannot, in this sense, invent the events of his stories; he must (in that other, equally traditional sense of *invention*) "find" or "discover" them. This is because historical events have already been "invented" (in the sense of "created") by past human agents who, by their actions, produced lives worthy of having stories told about them.[7] This means that the intentionality informing human actions, as against mere motions, conduces to the creation of lives that have the coherency of emplotted stories. This is one reason why, I take it, the very notion of a modernist historiography, modeled on the modernist, antinarrativist novel, would be in Ricoeur's estimation a contradiction in terms.

The meaning of real human lives, whether of individuals or collectivities, is the meaning of the plots, quasiplots, paraplots, or failed plots by which the events that those lives comprise are endowed with the aspect of stories having a discernible beginning, middle, and end. A meaningful life is one that aspires to the coherency of a story with a plot. Historical agents prospectively prefigure their lives as stories with plots. This is why the historian's retrospective emplotment of historical events cannot be the product of the imaginative freedom enjoyed by the writer of fictions. Historiographical emplotment is, Ricoeur argues, a poetic activity, but it belongs to the (Kantian) "productive imagination" rather than to the "reproductive" or merely "associative" imagination of the writer of fictions, because it is the productive imagination that is at work in the making of distinctively historical events no less than in the activity of retrospectively emplotting, or refiguring, them which it is the historian's duty to carry out (*TN*, 1:68).

The creation of a historical narrative, then, is an action exactly like that by which historical events are created, but in the domain of "wording" rather than that of "working."[8] By discerning the plots "prefigured" in historical actions by the agents that produced them and "configuring" them as sequences of events having the coherency of stories with a beginning, middle, and end, historians make explicit the meaning implicit in historical events themselves. While this meaning is prefigured in the actions of historical agents, the agents themselves cannot foresee it, because human actions have consequences that extend beyond the purview of those who perform them. This is why it is wrong, from Ricoeur's point of view, for historians to limit them-selves to trying to see things from the position of past agents alone, to trying to think themselves back into the mind or consciousness of past actors in the historical drama. They are fully justified in availing them-selves of the advantages of hindsight. Moreover, they are fully justified in using the techniques of analysis developed by the social sciences of their own time to identify social forces at work in the agent's milieus, because these forces may have been only emergent in the agent's time and place and not perceivable to the latter.

Human actions have consequences that are both foreseeable and unforeseeable, that are informed by intentions both conscious and unconscious, and that are frustratable by contingent factors that are both knowable and unknowable. It is for this reason that narrative is necessary for the representation of "what actually happened" in a given domain of historical occurrences. A scientific (or scientistic) historiography of the sort envisioned by the *Annalistes*, which deals in large-scale, physical and social, anonymous "forces," is not so much wrong as simply able to tell only a part of the story of human beings at grips with their individual and collective destinies. It produces the historiographical equivalent of a drama that is all scene and no actors, or a novel that is all theme but lacking in characters. Such a histori-ography features all background and no foreground. The best it could provide would be "quasi-history," comprising "quasi-events," enacted by "quasi-characters," and displaying the form of a "quasi-plot" (*TN*, 1:206 ff.).

And, indeed, as Ricoeur shows in his analysis of Braudel's great book, *The Mediterranean*, once a human being is allowed to enter such a scene, inhabited only by forces, processes, and structures, it becomes impossible to resist the lure of the narrative mode of discourse for representing what is "happening" in that scene (*TN*, 1:25). Even Braudel must tell stories whenever human beings acting as agents are permitted to appear against the background of those "forces" that he would describe solely in quantitative and statistical terms. This even against his own conscious repudiation of narrativity as the principal impediment to the creation of a scientific historiography.

Historians, then, not only are justified in telling stories about the past but cannot do otherwise and still do justice to the full content of the historical past. The historical past is populated above all by human beings, who, besides being acted on by "forces," are acting with or against such forces for the realization of life projects that have all the drama and fascination, but also the meaning (*Sinn*), of the kinds of stories we encounter in myth, religious parable, and literary fiction. Ricoeur does not erase the distinction between literary fiction and historiography, as I have been accused of doing, but he does scumble the line between them by insisting that both belong to the category of symbolic discourses and share a single "ultimate referent." While freely granting that history and literature differ from one another in terms of their immediate referents (*Bedeutungen*), which are "real" and "imaginary" events, respectively, he stresses that insofar as both produce emplotted stories, their ultimate referent (*Sinn*) is the human experience of time or "the structures of temporality."[9]

Ricoeur's insistence that history and literature share a common "ultimate referent" represents a considerable advancement over previous discussions of the relations between history and literature based on the supposed opposition of "factual" to "fictional" discourse (*TN*, 1:64). Just by virtue of its narrative form, historical discourse resembles such literary fictions as epics, novels, short stories, and so on, and Barthes and the *Annalistes* are justified in stressing those resemblances. But instead of regarding this as a sign of narrative history's weakness, Ricoeur interprets it as a strength. If histories resemble novels, he points out, this may be because both are speaking indirectly, figuratively, or, what amounts to the same thing, "symbolically," about the same "ultimate referent." Speaking indirectly because that about which both history and literature speak, the aporias of temporality, cannot be spoken about directly without contradiction. The aporias of temporality must be spoken about in the idiom of symbolic discourse rather than in that of logical and technical discourse. But history and literature speak indirectly about the aporetic experiences of temporality by means of and through signifiers that belong to different orders of being, real events on the one side, imaginary events on the other.[10]

Ricoeur's conception of the symbolic nature of all discourses that feature temporality as an organizing principle also allows him to make a significant advance over many contemporary discussions of the relation between the history and the chronicle. For him, the chronicle of events out of which the historian makes his story is not an innocent representation of raw facts given by the documentary record and presenting itself, as it were, spontaneously to the eye of the historian, who then "explains" the events or identifies the story embedded within the sparse chronological account. Ricoeur points out that the chronicle is already a figurated representation of events, a first-order symbolization that, like the "history" made out of it, has a double referent: events on the one side and a "structure of temporality" on the other.

There is nothing natural about chronologically ordered registrations of events. Not only is the chronological code in terms of which the events are ordered culture-specific and conventional but the events included in the chronicle must be selected by the chronicler and placed there to the exclusion of other events that might have been included if the time of their occurrence had been the only operative consideration. A chronicle is not a narrative, by Ricoeur's reasoning, because it does not possess the kind of structure with which a plot alone could endow it. But that does not mean that it is not a mode of symbolic discourse, for neither its referentiality nor its meaning is exhausted by the truths of its several singular existential statements taken distributively, in the way that the truth value of a logical and technical discourse can be determined. While the value of the chronicle considered as a list of facts is undeniable, its value as an instance of proto-narrative discourse is equally great. In fact, Ricoeur argues, the chronicle is the symbolic mode in which the human experience of "within-time-ness" achieves expression in discourse.[11]

What the chronicle says, then, is not only that so-and-so happened at a given time and then something else happened at another time, but that "seriality" is a mode or level of organization of a life lived "within-time." This double saying of the chronicle provides a basis for distinguishing between well-made chronicles and those more crudely composed and, indeed, between artistic and everyday forms of chronicling, the "plotless" novel being an example of the former and the diary or register of business transactions being an example of the latter. There is a difference between giving expression to the experience of "within-time-ness" (as in a diary) and self-consciously affirming that this is the only experience of temporality human beings can know (as the modernist, antinarrative novel seems to do). This difference also appears in the distinction, often drawn by Ricoeur in his studies of religious myths, between those that locate the origin of evil in the physical cosmos and those that try to "take the origin back to man."[12] In the former kind of myth, we have the equivalent of the expression of the experience of "within-time-ness"; in the latter, that of the expression of the experience of "historicality." This difference marks a qualitative advance, within the general category of mythic thought in cognitive self-consciousness and human self-awareness. The difference between a chronicle and a history marks a similar kind of advance in the human effort to "make sense" of temporality.

If every chronicle is a first-order symbolization of temporality, awaiting the emplotting powers of the historian to transform it into a history, so, too "within-time-ness" is only a first-order experience of temporality, awaiting a deeper recognition of the level of temporality, which Ricoeur calls the "experience of historicality" (*Geschichtlichkeit*). Here the crucial difference is between the experience of time as mere seriality and an experience of temporality in which events take on the aspect of elements of lived stories, with a discernible beginning, middle, and end. In historicality, events appear not only to succeed one another in the regular order of the series but also to function as inaugurations, transitions, and terminations of processes that are meaningful because they manifest the structures of plots. Historians bear witness to the reality of this level of temporal organization by casting their accounts in the form of narrratives, because this mode of discourse alone is adequate to the representation of the experience of historicality in a way that is both literal in what it asserts about specific events and figurative in which it suggests about the meaning of this experience. What the historical narrative literally asserts about specific events is that they really happened, and what it figuratively suggests is that the whole sequence of events that really happened has the order and significance of well-made stories.

Here Ricoeur skates dangerously near to the formalism that he wishes to avoid, for when the notion of the well-made story, that is, the emplotted story, is applied to historical narrative, it appears to make historiography a matter of "style" and internal coherence rather than one of adequacy to what it represents. Ricoeur seeks to avoid this danger by reworking the notion of mimesis in order to account for the fact that historical stories both are "well-made" and correspond in their outlines to the sequences of events of which they are representations.

Ricoeur reworks the concept of mimesis in order to show how a discourse cast in the form of a narrative can be both symbolic and realistic at one and the same time. His exposition, drawing upon his earlier work on metaphor and myth, is too complex for a brief recapitulation here. His crucial point, however, is that insofar as historical representation is concerned, mimesis has less to do with "imitation" than with the kind of action (praxis) that properly serves as the subject matter of a history. He challenges the traditional, Aristotelian distinction between mimesis, considered as an imitation of an action in a discourse, and diegesis, considered as a description of events, on which the opposition of fictional to factual discourse conventionally has been based (*TN*, 2:36–37). For Ricoeur, this distinction is useful enough for the characterization of the kinds of representations met with in the drama. When used, however, to analyze the narrative mode of discourse, it obscures the fact that a narrative not only describes but actually imitates the events of which it speaks, because narrative, like discourse in general, is a product of the same kinds of actions as those that produce the kinds of events deemed worthy of being represented in a history.[13]

In Ricoeur's view, then, narrative discourse does not simply reflect or passively register a world already made; it works up the material given in perception and reflection, fashions it, and creates something new, in precisely the same way that human agents by their actions fashion distinctive forms of historical life out of the world they inherit as their past. Thus conceived, a historical narrative is not only an icon of the events, past or present, of which it speaks; it is also an index of the kind of actions that produce the kinds of events we wish to call historical. It is this indexical nature of historical narrative that assures the adequacy of its symbolic representations to the real events about which they speak. Historical events can be distinguished from natural events by virtue of the fact that they are products of the actions of human agents seeking, more or less self-consciously, to endow the world in which they live with symbolic meaning. Historical events can therefore be represented realistically in symbolic discourse, because such events are themselves symbolic in nature. So it is with the historian's composition of a narrative account of historical events: the narrativization of historical events effects a symbolic representation of the processes by which human life is endowed with symbolic meaning.

Narrative discourse, then, is as much "performative" as it is "constative," to use the terminology of early Austin, which Ricoeur favors at crucial junctures in his discussions of metaphoric language and symbolic discourse.[14] And historical narrative, which takes the events created by human actions as its immediate subject, does much more than merely describe those events; it also imitates them, that is, performs the same kind of creative act as those performed by historical agents. History has meaning because human actions produce meanings. These meanings are continuous over the generations of human time. This continuity, in turn, is felt in the human experience of time organized as future, past, and present rather than as mere serial consecution. To experience time as future, past, and present rather than as a series of instants in which every one has the same weight or significance as every other is to experience "historicality." This experience of historicality, finally, can be represented symbolically in narrative discourse, because such discourse is a product of the same kind of hypotactical figuration of events (as beginnings, middles, and ends) as that met with in the actions of historical agents who hypotactically figurate their lives as meaningful stories.

Obviously, any adequate criticism of Ricoeur's argument would have to examine in depth his whole theory of symbolic language and discourse, his revision of the concept of mimesis as it applies to representation in narrative, his conception of the nature of the distinctively historical event, his notion of the different levels of temporality and the ways in which these attain to expression in language, his ideas of emplotment as the key to the understanding of a distinctively historical mode of consciousness, his characterization of the kind of knowledge we derive from our reflection on history, and a host of other issues. His conceptualization of each of these matters constitutes an important contribution to literary theory, the philosophy of history, social theory, and metaphysics alike. It is difficult, however, to detach any one conceptualization from the others for purposes of analysis, because each is a part of a whole argument that is more "symbolical" than either "logical" or "technical" (to use his own categories for classifying kinds of discourses) in structure.[15] To be sure, Ricoeur's work is always cast on the manifest level as a technical, philosophical discourse presided over by the protocols of literal speech and traditional logic. But as he has said of those mythic and religious texts that he himself has analyzed so perspicuously as examples of symbolic speech, Ricoeur's own discourse always says something "more" and "other" than what it appears to be asserting on the literal level of its articulation. It is fair to ask, then, What is the something "more" and "other" that Ricoeur is saying about historical narrative?

One thing he is saying is that narrative historians need feel no embarrassment about resemblances between the stories they tell and those told by writers of fiction. Historical stories and fictional stories resemble one another because whatever the differences between their immediate contents (real events and imaginary events, respectively), their ultimate content is the same: the structures of human time. Their shared form, narrative, is a function of this shared content. There is nothing more real for human beings than the experience of temporality—and nothing more fateful, either for individuals or for whole civilizations. Thus, any narrative representation of human events is an enterprise of profound philosophical—one could even say anthropological—seriousness. It does not matter whether the events that serve as the immediate referents of a narrative are considered to be real or only imaginary; what matters is whether these events are considered to be typically human.

Historical narratives may, therefore, resemble fictional narratives, but this tells us more about such fictions than about such histories. Far from being an antithetical opposite of historical narrative, fictional narrative is its complement and ally in the universal human effort to reflect on the mystery of temporality. Indeed, narrative fiction permits historians to perceive clearly the metaphysical interest motivating their traditional effort to tell "what really happened" in the past in the form of a story. There, in narrative fiction, the experiences of both "within-time-ness" and "historicality" can be dissolved in the apprehension of the relation of "eternity" to "death," which is the content of the form of temporality itself.

Thus conceived, narrative fiction provides glimpses of the deep structure of historical consciousness and, by implication, of both historical reflection and historical discourse. This resemblance between historical narrative and fictional narrative, which is a function of their shared interest in the mystery of time, would account, I surmise, for the appeal of those great classics of historical narrative—from Herodotus's *Persian Wars* through Augustine's *City of God,* Gibbon's *Decline and Fall of the Roman Empire,* Michelet's *History of France,* and Burckhardt's *Civilization of the Renaissance in Italy* down to, yes, even Spengler's *Decline of the West*—that makes them worthy of study and reflection long after their scholarship has become outmoded and their arguments have been consigned to the status of commonplaces of the culture moments of their composition. It is true, as the conventional opinion has it, that such classics continue to appeal to us because of their "literary" quality; but this quality should not be identified with verbal style or rhetorical eloquence, as if style could be dissociated from meaning, or rhetorical form from semantic content. On the basis of Ricoeur's theory of historical discourse, we are permitted to attribute the timeless fascination of the historiographical classic to the content that it shares with every poetic utterance cast in the mode of a narrative. This content is allegorical: every great historical narrative is an allegory of temporality. Thus, long after its scholarship has been superseded and its arguments exploded as prejudices of the cultural moment of its production (as in Gibbon's contention that the fall of Rome was caused by the solvent effects of Christianity on pagan manly virtues), the classic historical narrative continues to fascinate as the product of a universal human need to reflect on the insoluble mystery of time.

But in suggesting that historical narratives are, in the final analysis, allegories of temporality, what something "more" and "other" is Ricoeur saying about allegory itself? As I understand him, he is saying that histories are not *mere* allegories, in the sense of being nothing but plays of analogy or "extended metaphors," for it is clear on the basis of what Ricoeur has to say about *allegoresis* in other contexts that there are for him different kinds of allegorization, different ways of "speaking otherwise," and different degrees of responsibility to those aspects of reality about which we can speak in only an indirect or symbolic manner.[16] For Ricoeur, the problem presented by both historical discourse and the interpretation thereof is false allegorization, a speaking otherwise about history that suggests either that it is a timeless, mechanical structure of functions without meaning or that it is a temporal process the meaning of which can be provided by metaphysical speculation of religious dogma. For Ricoeur, the meaning of history resides in its aspect as a drama of the human effort to endow life with meaning. This universal, human quest for meaning is carried out in the awareness of the corrosive power of time, but it is also made possible and given its distinctively human pathos by this very awareness. In this respect, that manner of being-in-the-world that we call "historical" is paradoxical and cannot be apprehended by human thought except in the form of an enigma. If this enigma cannot be resolved by pure reason and scientific explanation, it can be grasped in all its complexity and multilayeredness in symbolic thought and given a real, if only provisional, comprehensibility in those true allegories of temporality that we call narrative histories. Their truth resides not only in their fidelity to the facts of given individual or collective lives but also, and most importantly, in their faithfulness to that vision of human life informing the poetic genre of tragedy. In this respect, the symbolic content of narrative history, the content of its form, is the tragic vision itself.[17]

Historical narratives are true allegories, then, when they display the facts of human existence under their temporal aspect and symbolically suggest that the human experience of time is tragic in nature. But what is the nature of this narrative truth, which is not literal but yet is not merely figurative either? What is being indirectly asserted about historical narrative in Ricoeur's own symbolic speech?

In trying to identify the allegorical meaning of Ricoeur's discourse on historical discourse, I cast about for a way of characterizing a manner of speaking that would be allegorical in its structure but more than allegorical in its meaning. My friend and colleague Norman O. Brown directed me to the late Charles Singleton's commentary on Dante's discussion of the distinction between poetic allegory and scriptural allegory in the *Convivio*. The distinction is different from that offered in *The Letter to Can Grande,* wherein the topic discussed is the relation between the literal and the figurative senses of the language used in the *Commedia*. In the *Convivio,* Dante wishes to distinguish between the "allegory of poets" and the "allegory of Holy Scripture." The difference between the two kinds of allegory, he maintains, stems not from the distinction between the literal and the figurative levels of the two kinds of discourse but rather from the nature of the uses to which the *literal* sense is put in each. Singleton explicates Dante's thought in the following way:

> The "allegory of poets," which is that of fable, of parable (and hence is also to be found in Scriptures), is a mode in which the first and literal sense is one devised, fashioned (*fictio* in its original meaning) in order to conceal, and in concealing to convey, a truth. Not so in the other (scriptural allegorical) mode. . . . There the first sense is historical, as Dante says it is, and not "fiction." The children of Israel did depart from Egypt in the time of Moses. Whatever the other senses may be, this first sense abides, stands quite on its own, is not devised "for the sake of." Indeed it was generally recognized that in Holy Scripture the historical sense might at times be the only sense there. These things have been so; they have happened in time. This is the record of them.[18]

This means, Singleton goes on to explain, that although in Scripture "the historical . . . sense can and does yield another sense," in the same way that the literal sense in poetic allegory does, as when, for example, the Exodus can be read as a figure of "the movement of the soul on the way to salvation," the relation between the two senses should not be seen as that of a fiction to its moral or anagogical meaning.

The relation is, rather, that of a "fact" to its moral or anagogical significance. In scriptural allegory, events are portrayed, not in order to "conceal, and in concealing to convey, a truth," but rather to reveal, and in revealing to convey, yet another, deeper truth. For Dante, Singleton writes, "only God could use events as words, causing them to point beyond themselves" to meanings that must be construed as being literal truths on *all* of their multifold levels of significance. Thus conceived, history, considered as a sequence of events, is God's "poetry."[19] God writes in events as poets write in words. This is why any history considered as the human account of those events would be at best a translation of God's "poetry" into "prose," or what amounts to the same thing, a merely human "poetry." Since no poet or historian possesses God's power, the best either could do would be to "imitate God's way of writing"—which Dante purported to do in the *Commedia*. But since this writing will always be only an imitation of God's power to write in events, every history will always be something other than the events of which it speaks, both in its form and in its content. It will be a special kind of poetry which, in its intention to speak literally, is always frustrated, driven to speak poetically, that is to say, figuratively, and in so speaking to conceal what it wishes to reveal—but by concealing, conveying a much deeper truth.

Something like this, I take it, is what Ricoeur is saying in his reflections on historical narrative—although he is saying this indirectly, figuratively, allegorically. His is an allegory of allegorization, intended—if I understand him correctly—to save the moral dimension of historical consciousness from the fallacy of a false literalism and the dangers of a false objectivity.

But to reveal the allegorical nature of a discourse that does not know itself to be such is to de-allegorize it. To identify the referent of the figurative level of such discourse is to re-literalize it, even if on a level of signification different from that of its manifest or "first-order" level of signification. In Ricoeur's view, every historical discourse worthy of the name is not only a literal account of the past and a figuration of temporality but, beyond that, a literal representation of the content of a timeless drama, that of humanity at grips with the "experience of temporality." This content, in turn, is nothing other than the moral meaning of humanity's aspiration to redemption from history itself.

This seems right to me, for otherwise I cannot account for the ferocity of all those struggles, between human beings and whole societies, for the authority to decide what history means, what it teaches, and what obligations it lays upon us all. I am not surprised, therefore, that Ricoeur presses on to the discovery of yet another level of temporal experience, what he calls the experience of "deep temporality," which has as its content the enigma of death and eternity, the ultimate mystery figurated in every manifestation of human consciousness.[20] On this level, which would correspond to the anagogical level in the scholastic fourfold schema, not only discourse but speech itself reaches a limit. But the form in which the experience of deep temporality reaches expression in language is glimpsed in such disemplotted "fables about time" as *Mrs. Dalloway* and *The Remembrance of Things Past* (*TN*, 2:101).

The function of the notion of deep temporality in Ricoeur's thought about history, narrativity, and time seems clear. It saves historical thinking from its most common temptation, that of irony. In this work of redemption, Ricoeur joins the efforts of Hegel and Nietzsche, for both of whom the overcoming of irony was the central problem of a distinctively human thought. While arguing (or suggesting) that historical thinking is allegorical but not merely such, that is to say, that it has a secondary referentiality in its figurative dimension to a reality that lies beyond history itself, he has escaped the danger that philosophical reflection faces when confronted by any instance of symbolic discourse, the peril of a *merely* allegorical interpretation. But has he escaped the other peril, the one that, by his own account, threatens thought in its speculative aspect, the "temptation of gnosis," the inclination to repeat "the symbol in a mimic of rationality," to rationalize "symbols as such" and "thereby fix . . . them on the imaginative plane where they are born and take shape"?[21] The answer to his question must await the appearance of the projected third volume of Ricoeur's meditation on narrative. Whether he will escape the danger of "dogmatic mythology" that threatens the "gnostic" turn of mind, we shall have to wait and see. It would, however, be the supreme irony if, in his efforts to save historical reflection from irony, he were forced to collapse the distinction between myth and history, without which the very notion of fiction is difficult to imagine.

8. The Context in the Text: Method and Ideology in Intellectual History

Today we discern a wish to rethink the basic issues of intellectual historiography, to reexamine governing concepts and strategies of interpretation, not out of any feeling of beleaguredness, but on the contrary, in response to new methodologies that have arisen in philosophy, literary criticism, and linguistics and that offer new ways of conceiving the tasks of historical hermeneutics. The older authorities in the field—Hegel, Marx, Nietzsche, Dilthey, and Freud—are still present to the consciousness of the current generation of intellectual historians, but more as ancestral shades or sanctioning grandfathers than as models and guides to specific research tasks. New models, represented by Benjamin, Gadamer, and Ricoeur, by Habermas, Foucault, Derrida, Barthes, and possibly J. L. Austin, appear to have moved to the center of the scene. They authorize new ways of looking at texts, of inscribing texts within "discourses" (a new term for intellectual historians), and of linking both texts and discourses to their contexts. The social historiography of the past generation has, temporarily at least, reached a limit in its incapacity to speak meaningfully about what might be called consciousness, and the explanatory procedures of that historiography are giving way to hermeneutical procedures deriving from phenomenology, analytical philosophy and speech-act theory, deconstruction, and discourse analysis.

Clear evidence of these changes can be seen in the recent collection of essays edited by Dominick LaCapra and Steven L. Kaplan, *Modern European Intellectual History: Reappraisals and New Perspectives* (Cornell University Press, 1982). The themes that recur in this collection touch on the principal *topoi* of the field of intellectual history since its inception by Hegel. At the center of this set of themes is the crucial one, not only for intellectual historians but for historians of anything whatsoever, namely, that of the text-context relationship. What is this relationship? What, indeed, is a text—an entity that once had an assuring solidity and concreteness, indeed a kind of identity that allowed it to serve as a model of whatever was comprehensible in both culture and nature. What happened to that text that used to lay before the scholar in a comforting materiality and possessed an authority that the "context" in which it had arisen and to the existence of which it attested could never have? Where is this context which literary historians used to invoke as a matter of course to "explain" the distinctive features of the poetic text and to anchor it in an ambience more solid than words? What are the dimensions and levels of this context? Where does it begin and end? And what is its status as a component of the historically real which it is the historian's purpose to identify if not to explain? The text-context relationship, once an unexamined presupposition of historical investigation, has become a problem, not in the sense of being simply difficult to establish by the once vaunted "rules of evidence," but rather in the sense of becoming "undecidable," elusive, uncreditable—in the same way as the so-called rules of evidence. And yet this very undecidability of the question of where the text ends and the context begins and the nature of their relationship appears to be a cause for celebration, to provide a vista onto a new and more fruitful activity for the intellectual historian, to authorize a posture before the archive of history more dialogistic than analytic, more conversational than assertive and judgmental.

And if the text-context distinction is now problematized, so, too, is the distinction, within the domain of historical artifacts, between the so-called classic text and the common, or merely documentary, text. It used to be thought that certain texts, such as those produced by the great nineteenth-century theorists of civilization, were themselves less cultural artifacts than self-interpreting models for explanation in the human sciences. But now not even Hegel, Marx, Nietzsche, and Freud can escape the charge of ideological deformation that they once brought against their opponents in the methodological and theoretical disputes of their own times. They too must be "deconstructed," their "blindness" specified, and their places in the *épistèmes* of their epochs determined before they can enter the lists as possible models of historical reconstruction and analysis. And as it is with Marx and Freud, so it is with every other "classic" text that once served as a "representative" text of the best thought of an age: Homer and Plato, Tacitus and Augustine, Machiavelli and Erasmus, and so forth. Their very "representativeness" is brought under question, their status as both "evidence" of a "spirit of the age" and the privileged interpreters of their own time and place is placed in doubt, because representativeness and interpretation are no longer taken as unambiguous possibilities of texts. Or rather, since every text, grand or humble, is seen to be equally representative, equally interpretative of its proper milieu, the very notion of a text that might serve as an especially privileged interpretative model is set aside.

And if the classic text is problematized, so, too, is the distinction, which is of the same order, between reliably transparent texts or documents and "ideologically" distorted, unreliable, or opaque texts. Considered as historical evidence, all texts are regarded as being equally shot through with ideological elements or, what amounts to the same thing, as being equally transparent, reliable, or evidential in what they can tell us about the "mental climate" (here variously construed) in which they arose. To the historian equipped with the proper tools, it is suggested, any text or artifact can figure forth the thought-world and possibly even the world of emotional investment and praxis of its time and place of production. Not that any given text can alone call up the whole world of its origin or that any given set of texts can reveal its world completely. But in principle, it seems to be held that we today possess the tools to probe texts in ways only dimly perceived or, if perceived, not fully utilized by earlier intellectual or other historians. And these tools, it is suggested, are generally linguistic in nature.

This is not the uniform opinion, of course, and for obvious reasons. For some historians, a linguistically oriented approach to the study of history raises the specter of a Whorfian kind of relativism. A specifically Structuralist-linguistic approach to historical texts raises the threat of "ahistoricity" for which Structuralism is ritualistically denounced by many historians. A specifically Post-Structuralist–linguistic approach to historical texts holds out the prospect of an infinite "free play" of interpretative fantasy that takes one further and further from, rather than closer and closer to, the origin and subject of the texts studied. It is for reasons such as these, I surmise, that cultural critics divide rather evenly into those who (1) take their stand on one or more of the classical hermeneutics of the nineteenth century (Hegel, Dilthey, Marx, Freud) or their twentieth-century avatars; (2) adopt a neo-Humboldtian, philological theory of language lately revived and refined by Gadamer and Ricoeur; or (3) openly embrace the post-Saussurian theory of the linguistic sign, of which both Foucault and Derrida, though in different ways, are exponents.

Here arises a division between the historian who wishes primarily to "reconstruct" or "explain" the past and one who is interested either in "interpreting" it or using its detritus as an occasion for his own speculations on the present (and future). Nineteenth-century systematic hermeneutics — of the Comtian, Hegelian, Marxist, and so on, varieties — was concerned to "explain" the past; classical philological hermeneutics, to "reconstruct" it; and modern, post-Saussurian hermeneutics, usually laced with a good dose of Nietzsche, to "interpret" it. The differences between these notions of explanation, reconstruction, and interpretation are more specific than generic, since any one of them contains elements of the others; but they point to different degrees of interest in a "scientific" enterprise, an "object of study" (the past), or the investigator's own powers of composition and invention, respectively. And this question of the domain to which the historian is responsible is, of course, a crucial issue in any effort to determine what is an appropriate performance in the discipline of history. On this question turns what might be called the ethics and possibly the politics of the discipline. To what is the historian responsible, or rather, to what *should* one be responsible?

There can be no answer to this question, I should think, that is not value-laden and normative, prescriptive and judgmental, rather than obvious, self-evident, or objectively determinable. To be sure, the field of linguistics is, in the human sciences, the principal new field of investigation opened up in the twentieth century in the West, surpassing in its importance even the field of ethnography (which, in a way, has finally found its favored hermeneutical models in this very field of linguistics). And to expect that historians would not find linguistics at least as attractive as investigators in other fields have found it would be naïve. Historians have always had to draw upon theories from other fields in the humanities and social sciences, when they have not credited current common sense or traditional wisdom, for their analytical strategies. And indeed modern, historical method was, in its Rankean formulation, little more than the philological method carried over to the investigation of documents of a nonliterary sort. Historians have always used some version of a theory of language to assist them in their work of "translating" meaning across the historical continuum in order to "make sense" of their documents. It would appear, therefore, that the question confronting contemporary historians is not whether they will utilize a linguistic model to aid them in their work of translation but what kind of linguistic model they will use. And this is especially crucial for intellectual historians, who are concerned above all with the problem of meaning and that of translating between different meaning systems, whether as between past and present or between the documents and those readers of history books who wish to know what these documents "really mean."

But which linguistic theory will be used, or might be used, or even should be used to help us in this work of translation? There are at least four ways to construe the relation between language and the world of things. Language can be taken to be (1) a *manifestation* of causal relationships governing the world of things in which it arises, in the mode of an index; (2) a *representation* of that world, in the mode of an icon (or mimesis); (3) a *symbol* of that world, in the mode of an analogue, natural or culture-specific, as the case might be; (4) simply another among those things that populate the human world, but more specifically a *sign system,* that is, a code bearing no necessary, or "motivated," relation to that which it signifies.[1]

Marxists—and social determinists in general—tend to think of language as an index of the world (or rather its world), rather like a symptom or an effect of causal forces conceived to be more basic, residing in the "infrastructure" or at least in the "social relations of production." As one lives, so one speaks. A weaker version of the same idea, but usually unattended by the theoretical apparatus of the Marxist notion, holds that language does not so much "indicate" as "represent" a world, and does so as much in its grammar and syntax as in its lexicon, such that the kinds of meanings that a given cultural configuration can generate are reflected in the formal features of its modes of discourse, grammatically defined. This is the basis of the faith in the philological method espoused by an older generation of intellectual historians or historians of ideas, of whom Spitzer, Auerbach, Cassirer, and so on, were representative. The iconic fidelity of language, if not of texts, was taken for granted, and one had only to know the structure of the language to penetrate to the real meaning of texts or historical documents.

A third way of construing the nature of the relation of language to its world was to regard language in general as a symbol of that world, that is, a natural analogue of that of which it was a representation. This was the Hegelian view, and it underwrote the whole enterprise of *Geistesgeschichte* which presupposed a *Zeitgeist* manifested in all aspects of a culture but in language especially, such that a proper analysis of any artifact deriving from the culture would reveal the "essence" of the whole, "microcosmically," as it were, in the mode of a synecdoche.

All of these notions of language, then, presuppose some "natural" relation between it and the world it represents: causal, mimetic, or analogical, as the case may be. And one or another of these notions of language has underwritten different approaches to intellectual or cultural history in the modern period. What is notable at this moment in the evolution of language theory is that one or another of these versions of the nature of language still informs most intellectual historians' conceptualizations of the text, textuality, discourse, and evidence for their field of study. This is interesting because it reflects the extent to which even those intellectual historians enlivened to the implications of modern language studies for the field have not yet fully assimilated the Saussurian theory of language as a sign system, the theory that stands at the basis of both Structuralism and post-Structuralism and offers, in my view, the best immediate prospects for a fruitful revision of the central problem of intellectual history, the problem of ideology.

I call ideology the central problem of intellectual history because intellectual history has to do with meaning, its production, distribution, and consumption, so to speak, in different historical epochs. But in the West at least, the question of meaning—or more precisely that of the meaning of meaning—has evolved against the background of a conviction of the irreconcilable opposition between science (conceived as some kind of objective view of reality) and ideology (conceived as a distorted, fragmentary, or otherwise deformed view, produced to serve the interest of a specific social group or class).[2] This distinction regenerates most of the earlier epistemological conflicts of our culture, as between reason and faith, philosophy and theology, secular and sacred learning, and so forth, but with this difference: whereas earlier conflicts of this sort had envisioned a resolution in the form of the establishment of one or the other of these pairs as an organon of or propaedeutic to the other, the science-ideology conflict took on, in the course of the nineteenth century, the aspect of a Manichaean struggle that could end only with the extirpation of ideology and its replacement by a scientific view of reality.

The intellectual historian's own conception of his discipline required that he assume the role of arbitrator as to what counted as a more or less "objective," "realistic," or "reliable" representation of reality and what had to be identified as primarily "ideological" in nature. Underlying and authorizing this critical activity was—as I noted above—a tacit theory of language, of discourse, and of representation in general by which to sort out the distortions of reality present in any text under analysis and a presupposition of the concreteness and accessibility of a text's original historical context by which a given distortion could be verified. But once it was realized (or conceded) that this context was itself accessible only through the medium of verbal artifacts and that these were subject to the same distortions by virtue of their textuality as was the evidence of which the context was to serve as a control, the problem of identifying ideological elements in a given text was extended to the concept of the context as well. Therewith, the very enterprise not only of the intellectual historian but of other historians too was opened up to the dangers of ideologism. For if the context represented to one in the documents was subject to distortion, by virtue of its being represented or being accessible only by way of verbal artifacts, the same could be said of that "science" one invoked as organon for guiding one's own investigations.

Of course, one could still moot the whole question of language and continue to act as if the problem of its opacity did not exist, but this became increasingly difficult to do in the wake of Structuralism (Lévi-Strauss, Barthes, and so on) and post-Structuralism (Foucault, Derrida, Lacan) and especially the problematizing of the whole task of textual interpretation by literary scholars, hermeneuticists, and even such neo-Marxists as Althusser and Habermas under the press of a new sensitivity to the problem of language itself. And here it is possible to specify the nature of a crucial split, among not only intellectual historians but cultural analysts in general, between those who continue to use a linguistic theory of the text and those who embrace a specifically semiological conception of it.

By a linguistic theory of texts I mean one that takes specifically lexical and grammatical categories as elements in its analytical model and, on the basis of this model, seeks to establish rules for identifying a "proper," as against an "improper," instance of language use after the manner of Russell, Wittgenstein, Austin, or Chomsky. By a semiological conception of texts I mean the tradition of cultural analysis that builds upon the theory of language as a sign (rather than a word) system, after the manner of Saussure, Jakobson, and Benveniste, and distinguishes between those sign systems that are extrareferential and those that have as their referents some other sign system. This provides the basis for a methodologically significant distinction between a linguistic inquiry and a specifically semiological one that has important implications for the way we might conceptualize the problem of characterizing the ideological aspects of a given text, discourse, or artifact. As Paolo Valesio puts it, the ideological aspects of a text are specifically those "metalinguistic" gestures by which it substitutes another sign system for the putatively extralinguistic referent about which it pretends to speak or of which it pretends to be a straightforward, objective, or value-free description.[3] A semiological approach to the study of texts permits us to moot the question of the text's reliability as witness to events or phenomena extrinsic to it, to pass over the question of the text's "honesty," its objectivity, and to regard its ideological aspect less as a product (whether of self-interest or group interest, whether of conscious or unconscious impulses) than as a process. It permits us, more precisely, to regard ideology as a process by which different kinds of meaning are produced and reproduced by the establishment of a mental set towards the world in which certain sign systems are privileged as necessary, even natural, ways of recognizing a "meaning" in things and others are suppressed, ignored, or hidden in the very process of representing a world to consciousness. This process goes on in scientific discourse no less than in fictional or legal-political discourse. Indeed, a discourse could not appear scientific if it did not, in the process of its own elaboration, substitute a specific sign system (the "code" of science) for the referent ("nature," "atoms," "genes," and so forth) that is its manifest object of representation and analysis. This has implications not only for the way we read historical texts but for the ways we read the works of other historians as well.

When historians analyze and criticize the work of their colleagues or predecessors in order to identify the ideological elements in their work, they are inclined to present the points at issue in terms of "contents": "themes," "concepts," "arguments," "judgments," "values," or the like. The conventional procedure is then to characterize these contents as being either distortions of the facts or deviations from the truth — as these "facts" and "truths" are given in some other corpus of works, either the "documents" the investigator regards as having been correctly analyzed by himself or some interpretative canon, such as Marxism, the investigator regards as having been properly interpreted by himself and established as the ultimate court of appeal for the authority and rectitude of his own interpretations. What is offered as a description of the work under analysis, in this case the corpus of, say, Freud's or Marx's writings and the "facts" of their careers, usually turns out to be a set of quotations, paraphrases of passages in selected texts, or condensed summaries of positions that are themselves as distorted as the works in question are presumed to be. The question of why or in what manner Marx's or Freud's work has enjoyed the authority it has had among other historians is dealt with by simply assuming that historians appeal to other, ideologically mystified coprofessionals because they share common ideological biases. This amounts to a form of petitio principii, which assumes the existence and nature of that for which it is supposed to offer an analysis and explanation.

But we should take this as given: a bourgeois historian will of course make sense to other bourgeois historians and not to Marxist ones, just as the Marxist will make sense to other Marxist historians and not to bourgeois ones. This is less in the nature of a problem than an assumption that all ideologically oriented analysis must presuppose even to entitle its heuristic quest. The more interesting question would be to ask, not What do Freud, Foucault, and so on, assert, allege, argue? but How do they establish, through the articulation of their texts, the plausibility of their discourse by referring the "meaning" of these, not to other "facts" or "events," but rather to a complex sign system which is treated as "natural" rather than as a code specific to the praxis of a given social group, stratum, or class? This is to shift hermeneutic interest from the content of the texts being investigated to their formal properties, considered not in terms of the relatively vacuous notion of style but rather as a dynamic process of overt and covert code shifting by which a specific subjectivity is called up and established in the reader, who is supposed to entertain this representation of the world as a realistic one in virtue of its congeniality to the imaginary relationship the subject bears to his own social and cultural situation.[4]

All of this is, of course, highly abstract and would require not only a wealth of illustrative exemplifications but also considerably more theoretical exposition than space here permits to gain even minimal plausibility for its claims. Such a theoretical exposition would require, however, at least detailed reference to the work of Jakobson, Benveniste, Eco, Barthes, and so on, as well as to that of Lévi-Strauss, Althusser, Lacan, the neorhetoricians and theorists of discourse analysis, and so forth, on which its authority as a theory would in many ways depend. Moreover, it would itself be able to escape the charges of tautology and petitio principii that I have leveled against the "content" method of analysis only if it plainly displayed and drew explicit attention to the code shifts by which *it* provided a "meaning" for phenomena that it might pretend only to describe and objectively analyse.

More specifically, such an exposition would have to draw explicit attention to the problem of exemplification itself, the semiological significance both of the text it had chosen as a specimen for illustrative purposes and of those portions of the text on which it had chosen to lavish its hermeneutical attention. Nor could it obscure the fact that the very distinction on which the analysis is based, that between linguistic and semiological analysis, is hardly universally agreed upon; it is rather in the nature of an enabling presupposition the utility of which is to be assessed solely in terms of a quantitative criterion, namely, its capacity to account for more of the elements of any given text, of whatever length, than any contending, "content"-oriented method could match. Beyond that, this approach would demonstrate its "objectivity" above all in the methodological tolerance and patience it lavished on texts opposed to the investigator's own consciously held political, social, cultural, and scientific values, it being one of the universally agreed-upon criteria for assessing any hermeneutic its capacity to entertain sympathetically not only those texts the specific hermeneut values and regards as classic but also and especially those texts representing other, opposed positions, projects, and the like. But all this having been said, an example by way of illustration is called for.

Suppose we are interested in characterizing the ideological status, and thereby the historically evidentiary nature, of a work such as *The Education of Henry Adams*.[5] The conventional approach would be to try to identify certain generic elements of the text, themes, arguments, and so forth, in the interest of establishing what the text is about, what point of view its author represents, and its importance as evidence of some aspect of early twentieth-century American social and cultural history. We might say that the text sets forth views and arguments with respect to politics, society, culture, ethics and morality, epistemology, and so forth, and we would then proceed to assess the validity of the positions assigned to the author or the text, to determine the extent to which they were prophetic, prejudiced, foresighted, reflective, sapient, antiquated, and so forth, much in the way that D. W. Brogan did in his introduction to a 1961 edition of the *Education*. Here, for example, we find such statements as:

It is, indeed, on the surface, the story of one who failed.

For Adams is a child of Rousseau, of the romantic movement.

The *Education* . . . illuminat[es] . . . American history, seen sometimes from an exceptionally good position on the sidelines. . . .

And it is a statement of the predicament of modern man in the late 19th century.

The book can only be appreciated if it is realized how American the book is and yet what an exceptional American Adams, merely as an Adams, was bound to be.

The *Education,* briefly summed up, is the story of a lifelong apprenticeship to the fact that the world could ignore the standards, the ranks, the assumptions of Boston, that nothing was stable, not even the natural precedence of the Adams family.

From one point of view, this [the first twenty chapters, dealing with Adams's formal education and service in the American ministry in London during the Civil War] is the most successful part of the book.

It can be held (I hold this view) that the most important part of the *Education* is the record of disillusionment with the victorious Union.

Adams was an artist and an anarchist.

Adams was not a scientist or a philosopher but a historian, and he had shown in his writings a mastery of the techniques of historical scholarship.

Henry took a . . . pessimistic point of view . . . [but] this pessimism is partly "an act."

There was in his correspondence with [his brother Brooks] an unattractive and rather stupid strain of anti-Semitism.

For the background of our present perplexities, the *Education* is an indispensable document.
But it is more than that; it is a great work of art and in its first half, at any rate, a nearly perfect work of art.

Adams . . . fell more and more under the influence of French ways of thinking and writing. The stylistic effects are beneficial.

And finally:

He [Adams] speaks to us as mere Presidents and millionaires cannot and he speaks for an American attitude that we tend to ignore, for that critical side of American life that knows how much more the human heart needs than mere material goods and the vulgar success that Henry Adams, to our profit, escaped.

I want to stress that this kind of mixture of thematic description and assessment (the two are hardly distinguishable) is a perfectly legitimate kind of commentary, and when only impressionistic and unsystematic, as this example is, it can be illuminating to the reader when the commentator is a shrewd, knowledgeable, and eloquent impressionist, as Brogan was. But in no way can it serve as a model of analysis, for students to emulate and apply to other texts (unless they became versions of Brogan himself), and it provides absolutely no criterion for assessing the validity of the various generalizations offered in the commentary. We may intuitively credit certain of the generalizations and reject others (but this would be a matter of personal taste on our part), and we can imagine a commentary on this text that might take the negative of every one of Brogan's predications as the real truth about the text or Adams and, probably, find some passage in the text that would justify this reading rather than the one offered by Brogan (also on the basis of personal taste, inclination, or ideological commitment) and arrive at an utterly different account of what the text really means. The authority of Brogan's reading is simply assumed, rather than argued for, and the picture it gives of the text, not less than the assessments it makes of its various aspects, is utterly arbitrary, by which I mean a matter of the psychology of the commentator rather than the result of a theoretical position vis-à-vis the nature of texts and the problem of discriminating between what they say and what, in an ideological sense, they might mean or do.

From a semiological perspective, by contrast, we can provide a theoretically generated reading of this text, which would give an account for every element of it, whether as large as the book's gross organization (with editor's preface, author's preface, its thirty-five chapters with their curious pattern of entitlement, the concluding chapter's title, "Nunc Age" and so forth) or as small as a single paragraph, sentence, or phrase. Not an account in the sense of providing a causal explanation of why Adams says what he says wherever he says it but an account that would help identify the patterns of code shifting by which its ideological implications are substituted for the straightforward representation of a social life or meditation on a single life that the text pretends to be. Such an analysis would begin with a rhetorical characterization of the text's elements, after the manner of Barthes's *S/Z*,[6] by which to identify the nature of the authority claimed by the text as a perspective on the reality it purports to represent, and would proceed to the disclosure of the modality of code shifting by which a specific mental set is specified as necessary to the proper reception of the text by an ideal reader, and thence to a detailed analysis of the metalinguistic elements of specific passages where a particular kind of social code is invoked as the standard for assessing the validity of all social codes in the reader's purview.

Here the rule is to begin at the beginning, in this case with the title of the book, which does not feature reference to an author, except indirectly or inferentially: *The Education of Henry Adams [An Autobiography]*. The title appears to be nothing other than the product of an act of nomination, although on reflection the idiosyncrasy of the locution (why not: "The Autobiography of Henry Adams: An Education" or any number of other possibilities? Why "education" for "life?" And so on) should alert the hermeneut to other rhetorical moves having to do with the manipulation of the genre of autobiography specifically. One notices that although the author of the work is also its subject, the subject is featured at the expense of the reader's sense of the author. The work is not offered as being "by" Henry Adams. It is only by the device of labeling the genre to which the work belongs — the label was affixed by the Massachusetts Historical Society, not Adams — that we can infer that it was written by its subject. And it is "an" autobiography, not the "the" autobiography, which, as the text will confirm, is specifically the case: it is a version of a life that, because it can be said hardly to have existed at all, would presumably bear many more than only a single, definitive version. It does not matter that the title replicates a conventional formula of entitlement, for any of a number of alternative formulae might have been followed. The choice of this convention, along with its peculiar twists of locution, immediately locates us in a thought-world more like that of Henry James than that of Thoreau (compare *Walden or, Life in the Woods* "by" Henry David Thoreau) or Jean Jacques Rousseau (*The Confessions* "of" Jean Jacques Rousseau). With this title, the text already signals the reticence of the author, that denial of authorial ego that Adams himself justifies in his own preface and that "dissolution of the ego" that remains a theme throughout the book.

Next we would comment on the number, subject matter, and above all the titles of the thirty-five chapters given in the table of contents (titles with place names, proper nouns, and subjects indeterminable from the title alone) and the curious gap that the "Contents" indicates, that of the years 1871–1892, in which, it would appear, "nothing happened." This, we would learn from extratextual sources, comprises the period of Adams's marriage, the suicide of his wife, and other events that we would expect to be included in an "autobiography." The fact that they are not included suggests to us that we should be prepared for anything but an "ordinary" or "conventional" autobiography and that we should note with especial care what has been left out of the account and try to determine what other rules of exclusion systematically operated in the construction of the text.

We would next attend to the "Editor's Preface," which is signed "Henry Cabot Lodge," seemingly acting as the spokesman for the Massachusetts Historical Society, under whose auspices the text is being offered to the public. We would not realize, unless we had other evidence to substantiate it, that this "Editor's Preface" was written, not by Lodge, but by Adams himself for Lodge's signature — another example of the author's reticence, duplicity, humility, desire for control, or what? I am not sure. But what strikes our eye, especially once we have read the author's preface, is the seeming equivocation, deferral, or ambiguity with which the author viewed his own text and the pains he took to ensure that his readers (if they attended to these opening gestures especially) would read the work in the "proper" spirit or frame of mind. In both prefaces, the author seeks to characterize his own book, assign it to a genre and identify its specificity within the genre, and bracket, as it were, the whole problem of the sincerity, authenticity, veracity, or literalness of a text that, because it is an autobiography, should have all these qualities.

The "Editor's Preface," for example, likens the work to Augustine's *Confessions,* only to qualify the supposed similarity between them by stressing the differences between them and, implicitly, to suggest the superiority of Adams's work over that of his Christian prototype. In the author's preface, by contrast, the work is likened to the model provided by Rousseau's *Confessions* and, in an aside, Franklin's *Autobiography,* only, again, to stress the differences between them and, by implication, the superiority of Adams's work over theirs. We might, from a semiological perspective, regard all this as a working of the code of literary genres in such a way as to foreclose any impulse to compare Adams's work with similar examples of the genre, thereby establishing the author's originality, and locating the reader in the appropriate domain of critical response for assessing his product (in this case, the aesthetic domain rather than that of religion, psychology, or ethics).

In fact, this had already been explicitly suggested in the preface by "Lodge" when he stated that the author's dissatisfaction with his own work had been so strong that, according to "Lodge," he had decided never to have it published and that this dissatisfaction had to do, not with the content of the work, the matters of fact or judgments rendered in it, but what "Lodge" calls "the usual [problem] of literary form." This was "the point on which the author failed to please himself," and it was the one point on which he "could get no light from readers or friends"—all of which suggests the *topos* of the isolated artist struggling to express a truth too deep to be rendered in mere words and refers us not so much to an actual fact or condition (since Adams's sense of his own stylistic capability was as inflated as that of Henry James or any other mandarin writer of the time) as to a specific ideology of a certain kind of artist—not a Romantic one at all, as Brogan suggests, but rather more like Oscar Wilde, to whom Brogan does liken Adams, but only to dismiss the comparison as inappropriate.

The location of the artist's persona in the precious, however serious, world of Oscar Wilde and Swinburne (whom Adams professes to admire) is further effected by a passage in the author's preface that turns upon a reworking of another literary *topos,* that of the "philosophy of clothes" which was dominantly present in nineteenth-century Anglo-American literary culture in Carlyle's influential *Sartor Resartus*. This passage is crucial for the semiologist because it is one in which the author comments on his own work, less in a metalinguistic than in a metageneric intervention, and ironically, almost to the point of malign satire, signals the literal "emptiness" of his text as a fit vehicle for the representation of the emptiness of his own ego and then sketches what might be called a "mannikin" theory of the literary work, which makes of it not a product of a dialectic between form and content, but rather a relationship between two forms equally evanescent: the clothes in which the tailor's dummy is garbed and the surface of the dummy's body which feigns the form of a man but has no interior.

But no sooner is the mannikin model invoked than it too is distanced and brought into question by being characterized in the sense in which the term is conventionally used, that is, as a model only, which "must be taken for real, must be treated as though it had life," in order to serve as a "measure of motion, of proportion, of human condition." But this new characterization is itself dissolved in the rhetorical question that forms the last thought of the preface. This question is, Did the mannikin ever have any life? And the answer given is, "Who knows? Possibly it had!" A rhetorical question followed by an ambiguous answer—which might very well serve as an emblem of the "style" of Henry Adams.

But alongside the rhetoric of aestheticism and evasion by which Adams locates his work within a specific domain of the writer's code of his time and place is another important *topos* that is more social-class-specific and surfaces right at the beginning of the pseudonymous preface signed "Henry Cabot Lodge." The first words of this preface are: "This volume, written in 1905, as a sequel to the same author's 'Mont-Saint-Michel and Chartres,' was privately printed, to the number of one hundred copies, in 1906, and sent to the persons interested, for their assent, correction, and suggestion." Not only does this passage attest to the author's scrupulousness concerning the factual "content" of his text but the phrase "privately printed" summons up a specific kind of writerly condition and a notion of this writer's potential public that is at once patrician or aristocratic and seemingly solvent of any aspiration to the attention of the general public. This *topos* of privacy-publicity recurs in the third paragraph of "Lodge"'s preface when he mentions that "the 'Chartres' was finished and privately printed in 1904." The publicizing of both of these texts, their projection into the public domain, is explicitly characterized by "Lodge" as having happened beyond the author's "control." "In 1913," "Lodge" reports, "the Institute of American Architects published the 'Mont-Saint-Michel and Chartres'"—a phrase that leaves unspecified how the institute claimed the right to do so (it is almost as if Adams had had nothing to say about the matter). But the placement of the text under the auspices of a professional institution has the effect of signaling the kind of authority as a scholarly work to which it can lay claim, as well as suggesting that the book was, as it were, "fated" to see the light of day, whatever the author's "private" wishes on the matter.

This motif is repeated in the next sentence, where "Lodge" reports that "already, the 'Education' had become almost as well known as the 'Chartres,' and was freely quoted by every book whose author requested it." So much for "privacy"—quality will out! But so will fate: "The author," we are told, "could no longer withdraw either volume; he could no longer rewrite either, and he could not publish that which he thought unprepared and unfinished, although in his opinion the other was historically purposeless without its sequel." In the end, therefore, he preferred to leave the "Education" unpublished, "avowedly incomplete, trusting that it might quietly fade from memory," thereby confirming a precept he had long believed, namely, that "silence next to good-temper was the mark of sense." Since this was made an "absolute" rule after midsummer 1914, the intervention of the Massachusetts Historical Society alone was able to overcome the author's express wishes to ignore his book, and so, as "Lodge" tells us: "The Massachusetts Historical Society now publishes the 'Education' . . . not in opposition to the author's judgment, but only to put both volumes equally within reach of students who have occasion to consult them."

Now, a preface is, by its very nature, an instruction on how to read the text that follows it and, by the same token, an attempt to guard against certain misreadings of the text, in other words, an attempt at control. In his masterful meditation on the preface as genre in Western writing, Derrida notes that the preface is always a narcissistic enterprise, but a special kind, that in which a proud parent looks upon and praises, excuses, or otherwise prepares the way for his child, the text that he has at once sired and given birth to. If we might consider the matter in this way for a moment, what do we make of an autobiographical text that has two prefaces (both written by the author but one offered over the name of a friend who is a representative not only of the Boston patriciate but also of the Massachusetts Historical Society)?

The double preface is at best redundant and, as such, symptomatic of an excessive solicitude for the future of the progeny for whom it obviously wishes to prepare and smooth the way. The shadow of the author casts itself over the work not only as one presence seeking to guide the reader's approach to the text but as two, the first of which wishes to guide the reader's approach to the text and the author. The repetitiveness of the pretextual gesture already puts it in the domain of obsessive concern which, from a psychoanalytical perspective, we might refer to some traumatic experience in the life of the text's author. Not only does the double preface suggest an especial concern about the fate of the text (a concern explicitly stated in "Lodge"'s account of the reluctant "birth" of the text) but it suggests a kind of fear of being muffled by prejudicial misreading which is repeated in the text proper by the theme of the burden of an inherited tradition that misfitted the author for a proper "life" in the twentieth century.

All this is, I believe, clear enough, but from what perspective(s)? From a psychoanalytical perspective, concerned as it would be with moving from the text to a determination of the author's unconscious and conscious intentions in writing the text (and the conflicts between them), this excessive concern is to be regarded as a symptom, that is, an index of the writer's state of mind and stance vis-à-vis his world as he perceives it. This state of mind is to be referred, in turn, to the sociodynamics of the author's family experiences as the cause of the neurotic fixations in response to which both the text and the activity of writing are to be regarded as sublimations. The typicality of the text, then, its status as evidence of the social world in which it takes its rise, resides in the extent to which it reveals something about the psychoeconomics of a particular kind of family structure. And this is one way to proceed, as long as it is recognized that in order to carry out the analytical operation, one must presume the adequacy of some version of Freudian doctrine to such an analysis.

From a Marxist perspective, the text will also be treated as an index of a structure (a contradictory one by definition), that of a specific class consciousness and practice and, to the extent that it is self-consciously a representation of that consciousness and practice, an icon as well. If, beyond that, the text is treated as an especially apt manifestation of this class consciousness, one that systematically offers itself to its public in such a way as both to mask its class nature and surreptitiously to defend it, it will be elevated to the status of a symbol. This leads the investigator from the text through the postulated consciousness of the author to the social context, of which the text is then supposed to be a highly complex but still perfectly decodable reflection. And this too is a way to proceed, as long, however—as with the Freudian tactic—as it is recognized that one must simply presume the adequacy of the Marxist doctrine to explicate the double relation between the text and the author, and between the author and the "superstructure."

A semiological perspective, on the other hand, treats the text less as an effect of causes more basic or as a reflection, however, refracted, of a structure more fundamental than as a complex mediation between various codes by which reality is to be assigned possible meanings. It seeks, first of all, to identify the hierarchy of codes that is established in the process of the text's elaboration, in which one or more emerge as seemingly self-evident, obvious, natural ways of making sense of the world.

In the dynamics of a complex text such as that represented by the *Education,* various codes are "tried on," rather in the way that one tries on various sizes and styles of suits, before finding the one that "fits" more or less adequately—one that appears to have been especially tailored for the thing it is meant to clothe, adorn, warm, and protect from the elements. In the *Education,* the codes of history, science, philosophy, law, art, and so on, as well as various social codes, cultural codes, etiquettes, protocols, and so forth, are all "tried on" only to be rejected as "unsuited" to the needs of a "sensitive" intelligence asked to come to terms with the "real" forces governing life in the twentieth century. These are systematically reduced to the status of a "patchwork" or "motley," of dispersed "fragments" or "sherds," to harlequinade — the utility of which for life is adjudged to be nil. What is revealed to be operative in the new world is power, or rather brute force, represented as an "energy" that has no end or purpose beyond pure process itself (in the animal world the symbol of this force is represented by the shark *Pteraspis,* in the physical world by the "dynamo," and in the cultural world by the "Virgin"). Standing over against this impersonal, blind, undirected force, as a last refuge of sensitivity (itself seen as a kind of "sport" of nature) that is itself rapidly disappearing in response to powers it can not begin to resist, is the "personal" gesture of the exemplary autobiography, whose "authority" as a meaningful gesture is contained in its status as mere "literature" and whose "integrity" is confirmed by its aspiration to a stylistic consistency which the author himself adjudges not to have been achieved.

The code switching involved here is, on the level of formal argument, from a postulated social consciousness inherited from the eighteenth century to a putatively more "realistic" perception of "the way things really are" in the nineteenth century and, on the level of affect or valuation, from a putative historical and scientific knowledge to a hypostatized, but purely local or personal, aesthetic consciousness The form of the discourse, that of the autobiography, enacts a similar switching of codes. Its manifest message is that it is impossible to write an autobiography like any of the traditional types (religious, psychological, ethical) on the basis of the modern experience. Second, by virtue of the stated incompleteness of the effort on Adams's own part, it is asserted to be impossible to write an autobiography at all (this in evidence of the dissolution of the "ego" which modern society and culture are seen to have effected). And third, it is suggested that the only possible justification of even the effort to write an autobiography would be the consistency of style with which the enterprise was undertaken by a person like Adams — a purely aesthetic criterion, although it is represented in the text as having moral implications.

The strategy suggested in all this is that of taking what one considers to be the defects of one's own culture or historical moment (in this case its dissolution of the "ego") and turning them into first, a method of observation, representation, and assessment and, second, a protocol for orchestrating the introduction of the text in which they are given so as to limit the kind of audience it will find — that complex ballet of approach-avoidance that we have seen manifested in the two prefaces of the work. In the two prefaces, the triple irony that pervades the text is given direct embodiment. And the form of the whole text can be seen to figure forth the precise nature of the value attached to the messages contained in the text proper.

Indeed, in a way quite different from Augustine and Rousseau, not to mention Franklin, the form of this work can be seen, from a semiological perspective, as the specifically ideological content of the text as a whole. And our assent to the form of the text as something given, in the interest of entertaining, assessing, and otherwise responding to the thematic content, representations, judgments, and so forth, contained in the narrative levels of the text, is the sign of the power of this text considered as an exercise in ideological mystification.

Once we are enlivened to the extent to which the form of the text is the place where it does its ideologically significant work, aspects of the text that a criticism unsensitized to the operations of a form-as-message will find bewildering, surprising, inconsistent, or simply offensive (such as the "gap" in the account of the years 1871–92 or the shift from a narrative account in the early years [which Brogan and most modern commentators like] to the so-called speculative discourses of the last fourteen chapters [especially offensive to historians by virtue of their supposedly abstract or a priori or deductive method]) themselves become meaningful as message. In fact, the formal differences between the account of the earlier years and that of the later ones involve a code switch from a putatively empirical record of social and political events, of which the author was more or less a witness, to a manifestly speculative and deductive meditation on processes, a switch required by the supposedly different "natures" of the matters dealt with. But since this change of scale, scope, and content is not mediated by any theoretical necessity that the author can envisage (he has rejected Hegel, Marx, Darwin, and so on), and since it is authorized by a canon of "taste" and "sensitivity" rather than of method or formal thought, the "gap" in the account of the years 1871–92 is not only fully justified from an aesthetic standpoint but a necessary element of the message of the text as a whole.

To say that Adams left this hole in his text, this rupture in his account, because of the pain he suffered during those years, that these experiences were too personal for recounting, given the fastidiousness of his patrician nature, is to acquiesce in the fiction of "taste" as epistemic criterion which informs the work and is consistently invoked to validate its judgments. All of this talk about Adams's suffering may be true, but how could we be sure? The textual fact is the gap in the chronicle of the narrative. The reasons for or causes of this gap we can only speculate about. But the textual function of the gap is clear enough. As message, it reinforces the thesis of the emptiness of life that Adams adumbrates in the figure of the mannikin throughout the book. Adams cannot account for this emptiness, ontological in nature as he envisions it, either by historical-empirical-narrative methods (the methods of the first part) or by aprioristic, deductive, and speculative methods (those used in the second part). It is like the gap between the pseudo-editor's preface and the author's preface. These may reflect a kind of schizophrenic condition in Adams's psyche, but to explain or interpret a rupture in a text by referring it to a rupture in the author's psyche is merely to double the problem and to pass off this doubling operation as a solution to it.

The two parts of the text are manifestly not intended to be viewed as phases of a continuous narrative or as stages in the elaboration of a comprehensive argument. They are, as Adams himself suggests at the opening of his penultimate chapter, to be apprehended as aspects of a complex image: "Images are not arguments, rarely even lead to proof, but the mind craves them, and, of late more than ever, the keenest experimenters find twenty images better than one, especially if contradictory; since the human mind has already learned to deal in contradictions" (489). But this image — as we can expect from reading almost any other part of the text — has a hole in its center, conformable to the text's explicit assertions that the depths of the individual personality are as unplummable as the mysteries of history and nature. This sense of an unplummable mystery more than adequately justifies, within the terms of the text itself, the structure of the last chapter, ironically entitled "Nunc Age" (meaning both "Now, depart" and "Now act") and ending with a meditation on Hamlet's last words: "The rest is silence." Before the enormity of the mystery of death, Adams suggests, we are capable only of either commonplace or silence. And, as he says in the "Editor's Preface," "silence next to good-temper was the mark of sense."

All of this places the reader firmly within a social domain specifically literary in nature, in a society inhabited by such figures as Henry James, Swinburne, Wilde, Carlyle, and so forth, but also in a world in which meaning is conferred upon experience, not by reference to some empirically discernible reality, social or natural, but rather by reference to other literary works, artistic monuments, and similarly

encoded "texts." It was, Barthes has argued, the supreme achievement
of nineteenth-century realism, whether in literature or in social
commentary, to substitute surreptitiously an already textualized image
of the world for the concrete reality it feigned iconically to represent.
We can locate Adams within this tradition—along with James, Proust,
Virginia Woolf, Joyce, and other heralds of modernism—as another
representative of realism's imminent unmasking and the writer's sur-
render to the free play of language itself as the true function of literature as John Carlos Rowe has persuasively argued. But Rowe's suggestion that Adams's art, which "uses its artifice to question the nature
of all signification," summons us to return once again "to the human
dialogue that we ought to be renewing" seems more a pious hope on
Rowe's part than a conclusion justified by either the explicit messages
of the text or that implicit message given in its form. Rowe's concluding suggestion returns Adams to that favored domain of the traditional
humanist, the realm of the timeless "classic" which always shows us
that "some beauty and nobility lurk in the anguished burden of human
consciousness."[7]

For an antidote to the arbitrarily hopeful reading of the *Education,* let us look at the last sentence of the text, which reports a fantasy
in which Adams imagines himself returning to the world in 1938, the
centenary of his own birth, with his two best friends, John Hay and
Clarence King (not, be it noted, with his wife), "for a holiday, to see
their own mistakes made clear in the light of the mistakes of their suc-
cessors." "Perhaps then," the wish continues, "for the first time since
man began his education among the carnivores, they would find a
world that sensitive and timid natures could regard without a shudder"
(505). "THE END."

It is possible, of course, to read any text as a meditation, more or
less explicit, on the impossibility of representation and the aporias of
signification just by virtue of the fact that any text attempting to grasp
any reality through the medium of language or to represent it in that
medium raises the specter of the impossibility of the task undertaken.
But Adams's text is anything but an invitation, explicit or implicit, to
a renewal of any dialogue. Its suppression of the expected "voice" of
the dialogistic mode of discourse, that "I" that implies the existence of
a "you" to participate in the verbal exchange by which meaning is to
be dialectically teased out of the words used as a medium, is enough
to suggest as much. This alone is enough to establish its essential
difference from a work such as Thoreau's *Walden,* with which it might
be profitably compared in semiological terms, and show that it was

intended implicitly to be dialogistic in spite of its manifestly egoistic form. Adams's autobiography is a monologue, and if we can speculatively summon up the elements of dialogue in it, we must insist that the other party in the exchange can only be imagined to be some fragment or sherd of Adams's own fractured persona. He speaks of himself in the third person singular—as "he," "Adams," and so forth—splitting himself into both the speaker who is hidden behind the anonymity of the narrative form and the referent or subject of the narrative, who occupies center stage, around which (and in the fiction of the book, for which) the events of both nature and history occur, just as, in the prefatorial matter, he splits himself into two speakers, "Lodge" and "Adams," and assigns them slightly different things to say about his book.

This splitting, unraveling, or doubling of the persona of the author is, to be sure, a function of authorship itself, in which every writer is both the producer and consumer of his own discourse. The narcissistic—or onanistic—nature of this function is manifest. And on one level at least, texts differ by virtue of their respective efforts to transcend the narcissism inherent in the author function and move to what a Freudian might call that anaclitic relationship that sociality presupposes as its basis. Not that we would follow Freud in regarding this as a qualitatively (morally) superior condition to the narcissistic one, for we could do that only by moving outside the text and affirming another ideology that regards the anaclitic form of love as more human, that is, more natural, than its narcissistic counterpart. Far from being an "egoless" text, the *Education* is, in spite of the suppression of the authorial "I," or perhaps because of it—a supremely egoistic one—moreover, an egoistic one that is explicitly class-based. Thus, in the second paragraph of the *Education,* in which Adams likens his "christening" to a "brand" as burdensome as that laid upon any Jew in the synagogue, he writes:

> To his life as a whole he was a consenting, contracting party and partner from the moment he was born to the moment he died. Only with that understanding—as a consciously assenting member in full partnership with the society of his age—had his education an interest to himself or to others.
>
> As it happened, he never got to the point of playing the game at all; he lost himself in the study of it, watching the errors of the players; but this is the only interest in the story, which otherwise has no moral and little incident. (4)

The *Education*'s manifest announcement and demonstration of the end of the ego in the modern age has to be viewed as a message not only personal and subjective but social and historical as well. Insofar as Adams identifies his own ego with that of his class, the announcement of the dissolution of one is also the announcement of the dissolution of the other.

The seeming depersonalization of Adams's autobiography, the use of the objectivizing voice of the third-person narrative, of an author who distances himself from himself and writes the history of his (mis)education, is another sign of the fusion of the subjective ego with that of a specific social class. And the theme of (mis)education provides simply another way of speaking about the (mis)fortunes of the latter in terms of those of the former. As for the further identification of "Henry Brooks Adams" with world history, which is also explicitly made, however much on its surface it is ironically made, means that far from being a mannikinlike counterpart of Augustine's *Confessions,* the *Education* is intended to provide a superior alternative to the former. Its superiority consists, it is suggested, not so much in its worldliness (in contrast to the Christian mythology of Augustine's *Confessions*) as in its egotism (a quality Augustine seeks to erode in his own text as much by precept as by discursive example).

I could go on indefinitely this way, seeking to identify the various codes — psychological, social, metaphysical, ethical, and artistic — by which the complex fabric of the text could be said to emit messages more phatic and optative, to use Jakobson's terminology, than referential or predicative. The aim would be not to reduce all of these messages to a single, seemingly monolithic position that could be neatly condensed into an emblematic paraphrase, but rather to show the myriad different messages and different kinds of messages that the text emits. The aim would also be, however, to characterize the types of messages emitted in terms of the several codes in which they are cast and to map the relationships among the codes thus identified both as a hierarchy of codes and as a sequence of their elaboration, which would locate the text within a certain domain of the culture of the time of its production.

How, then, does a semiological approach to intellectual history contribute to the resolution of the specific problems arising in that field of inquiry? How does it help to resolve the problem of the text-context relationship, the classic text–documentary text relationship, the interpreter text–interpreted text relationship, and so on? Crucial to any historical investigation is the evidential status of any given artifact, or, more precisely, its referential status. Of what is the artifact evidence? to what does it refer? Or put another way, what referent does it permit us, however indirectly, to perceive? As long as the object to which an artifact gives access is conceived to exist outside the artifact, these questions are irresolvable, at least when it is a matter of historical perception, because by definition, we might say, a datum is past only to the extent that it is no longer something to which I can be referred as a possible object of living perception.

The historically real, the past real, is that to which I can be referred only by way of an artifact that is textual in nature. The indexical, iconic, and symbolic notions of language, and therefore of texts, obscure the nature of this indirect referentiality and hold out the possibility of (feign) direct referentiality, create the illusion that there is a past out there that is directly reflected in the texts. But even if we grant this, what we see is the reflection, not the thing reflected. By directing our attention to the reflection of things that appear in the text, a semiological approach to intellectual history fixes us directly before the process of meaning production that is the special subject of intellectual history conceived as a subfield of historical inquiry in general.

It goes without saying that not all historical inquiry is concerned with the production of meanings. In fact, most historical inquiry is concerned less with the production of meanings than with the effects of such productive processes—what we might wish to call the exchange and consumption of meanings within a given sociocultural configuration. Wars, alliances, economic activity, exercises of political power and authority, anything involving intentional creation and destruction, aim-oriented activities entered into by individuals and groups—these are what I have in mind. If intellectual history, which takes as its special subject matter the ideas, *mentalités,* thought systems, systems of values and ideals of particular societies in the past, simply treats these as data that reflect processes in some way more "basic" (such as economic, social, political, or even psychological processes), then intellectual history is supererogatory in relation to the historical reconstruction of these other processes, for in that case it can only double the accounts provided by specialists in these other fields of study, tell the same story, with slightly different material and in a slightly different register, as the story told about these other fields.

Manifestly, however, the data of the intellectual historian are different from those with which political and economic historians work, and their differentness consists in the fact that these data show us directly the processes by which cultures produce the kinds of meaning systems that give to their practical activities the aspect of meaningfulness, or value. Groups engage in political activities for political purposes, to be sure, but these activities are meaningful to them only by reference to some other, extrapolitical aim, purpose, or value. This is what permits them to imagine that their political activities are qualitatively different from those of their opponents or represent a higher value than those of their enemies—who are enemies or opponents precisely to the extent that they envision other aims, purposes, values, specifically different from their own though generically similar to them. This is also true of economic, religious, or social activities. Historical events differ from natural events in that they are meaningful for their agents and variously meaningful to the different groups that carry them out.

Economic activity no doubt has to do with economic aims—the production, exchange, and consumption of goods—but different modalities of economic activity (feudal, capitalist, socialist, and all mixtures thereof) exist because this activity is regarded as serving other ends than those of mere production, exchange, and consumption of goods. Food, clothing, and shelter may be basic "economic" necessities, but what is considered the proper kind of food, appropriate clothing, and humanly adequate shelter varies from culture to culture. Moreover, the provision of these necessities in any given culture is governed by rules and laws that have their justification in an extraeconomic domain, specifically that in which the meaning of what is to be considered proper, appropriate, and adequate is produced.

Put this way, it immediately becomes obvious why intellectual historians take their inspiration from Hegel, Marx, Freud, and Nietzsche—and their modern avatars, Lévi-Strauss, Habermas, Foucault, Derrida, Ricoeur, Gadamer, J. L. Austin, and so on. Every one of these is concerned with the problem of mediation, which we can construe as the deflection of basic impulses (economic, social, sexual, aesthetic, intellectual, whatever) from their putatively immediate aims by considerations that are culture-specific in nature. And here *culture-specific* means specific to a historically determinate system of meaning.

The intellectual historical artifact viewed semiologically permits us to see the system of meaning production operating directly in a way that other kinds of historical artifacts do not—because these other kinds of artifacts (weapons, treaties, contracts, account books) inevitably appear to us more as the effects of such operations, or at best as instruments of them, rather than as causes of them. This is why a content-oriented, history-of-ideas approach to intellectual history is perfectly appropriate for the analysis of certain kinds of documents in those situations in which we are interested more in the effects of culture on its members than in the ways that culture produces those effects. And this way of formulating the matter points to a way of resolving the classic text–documentary text relationship.

The classic text seems to command our attention because it not only contains ideas and insights about "the human condition" in general but provides an interpretative model by which to carry further our investigations in our own time or, indeed, any time. In reality, however, the classic text, the master text, intrigues us, not because (or not only because) its meaning-content is universally valid or authoritative (for that is manifestly impossible; in any event, it is a profoundly unhistorical way of looking at anything), but because it gives us insight into a process that is universal and definitive of human species-being in general, the process of meaning production. To be sure, even the most banal comic strip can yield some insight into this process, especially when submitted to semiological analysis — and in a way that it could not do, incidentally, under investment by a conventional history-of-ideas approach. And in the interest of a scientific responsibility that must inform our work if it is to claim an authority any larger than that of virtuoso performance, we must be prepared to grant that the comic strip cannot be treated as qualitatively inferior to a Shakespeare play or any other classic text. From a semiological perspective, the difference is not qualitative but only quantitative, a difference of degree of complexity in the meaning-production process (complexity, I assume it will be granted, marks a qualitative difference between two objects only for those for whom complexity itself is a value). The difference in degree of complexity has to do with the extent to which the classic text reveals, indeed actively draws attention to, its own processes of meaning production and makes of these processes its own subject matter, its own "content."

Thus, to return by way of conclusion to *The Education of Henry Adams,* the text serves us especially well as an intellectual historical document, in a way that Adams's diaries, letters, and other documents relating his daily life would not, precisely to the extent that it contains all of those evidences of self-concern and fear of failure that we have indicated as aspects of its ideologizing function. What might be regarded as its flaws from the standpoint of a naïve expositor, that is, anyone wishing to assess its logical consistency or to assign points for its stylistic proprieties in its various parts, becomes for the semiologically oriented commentator its very virtue as a "document" of intellectual history. The differences between the first part of the *Education,* so beloved by diplomatic historians for its observations of the diplomatic scene and by those with a conventional notion of what a "narrative" should be, and the second part, with its metahistorical speculations and tone of pessimism (which offends those who have a conventional notion of what a proper "autobiography" should be), the mandarinlike pickiness and preciosity of the diction of the whole work, its hesitancies and duplicities, the thematic obsessions, the pervasive irony—all become equally valuable for the analyst concerned with meaning production rather than with meaning produced, with processes of the text rather than with the text as product. It is precisely these "flaws" that point us to what makes the *Education* a classic work, an example of a self-conscious and self-celebrating creativity, poiesis.

As for the text-context problem—the extent to which the *Education* was a product of causal forces more basic, whether these are regarded as social, psychological, economic, or what have you, the extent to which Adams's work either "reflects" his own time or "reflects on" it perspicuously, as Brogan praises it for doing—I have suggested that this problem becomes resolvable from the semiological perspective to the extent that what conventional historians call the context is already in the text in the specific modalities of code shifting by which Adams's discourse produces its meanings. For surely, when we inquire into the context of a work such as the *Education,* we are interested above all in the extent to which that context provided resources for the production of the kinds of meanings that this text displays to us. To have information about this aspect of the text's context would not illuminate the operations of Adams's work in their specificity, in their details as we follow or track the text's narrative. On the contrary, it is the other way around: the context is illuminated in its detailed operations by the moves made in Adams's text.

Of course, Adams drew upon his society and his culture for the kinds of operations he carries out in his text, by which to endow his experiences, his "life," with a meaning, even if the meaning provided is only the judgment that life itself is meaningless. What Adams does is show us one example of how the cultural resources of his historical moment and place could be fashioned into a plausible justification for this kind of nihilistic judgment. In wedding the general notion of nihilism with the particularities of his life, Adams produces an individual version of the nihilistic credo, which is to say, a type of this credo (*type* being defined as a mediation between particulars and real or merely feigned universals). It is the typicality of Adams's discourse that makes it translatable as evidence of his own age that a reader in our age can comprehend, receive as message, understand.

Typicality is produced by the imposition of a specific form on an otherwise wild content. The imposition of this form is carried out in the discourse materialized in Adams's text. It is the enactment of this discourse that attests to Adams's status as a representative of the culture of his age. And it is the product of that enactment, the text entitled *The Education of Henry Adams,* considered as a finished form, that gives us insight into the type of meaning production available in the culture of Adams's time and place.

This notion of the typicality of the text permits us to deal with the problem of the hated "reduction" of the complex text which hermeneuticists lament endlessly. In saying that a given text represents a type of meaning production, we are not reducing the text to the status of an effect of some causal force conceived to be more basic than that of meaning production in general. We are pointing, rather, to what is both obvious and undeniable, namely, that Adams himself has "condensed" his life into the form that it displays in the *Education* and, moreover, transformed that life into a symbol of the sociocultural processes of his own time and place as he perceived them thereby. This is not a reduction but a sublimation or transumption of meaning which is a possible response of human consciousness to its world everywhere and at all times. By unpacking the rich symbolic content of Adams's work, we de-sublimate it and return it to its status as an immanent product of the culture in which it arose. Far from reducing the work, we have, on the contrary, enflowered it, permitted it to bloom and caused it to display its richness and power as a symbolizing process.

Notes

1. The Value of Narrativity in the Representation of Reality

1. Roland Barthes, "Introduction to the Structural Analysis of Narratives," *Image, Music, Text*, trans. Stephen Heath (New York, 1977), 79.

2. The words *narrative, narration, to narrate,* etc., derive via the Latin *gnārus* ("knowing," "acquainted with," "expert," "skilful," etc) and *narrō* ("relate," "tell") from the Sanskrit root *gnâ* ("know"). The same root yields γνώριμος ("knowable," "known"). See Emile Boisacq, *Dictionnaire étymologique de la langue grecque* (Heidelberg, 1950), s v γνώριμος. My thanks to Ted Morris, of Cornell, one of our great etymologists.

3. See Alexis de Tocqueville, *Democracy in America,* trans. Henry Reeve (London, 1838); Jakob Christoph Burckhardt, *The Civilization of the Renaissance in Italy,* trans. S. G. C. Middlemore (London, 1878); Johan Huizinga, *The Waning of the Middle Ages: A Study of the Forms of Life, Thought, and Art in France and the Netherlands in the Dawn of the Renaissance,* trans. F. Hopman (London, 1924); and Fernand Braudel, *The Mediterranean and the Mediterranean World in the Age of Philip II,* trans. Siân Reynolds (New York, 1972). See also Hayden White, *Metahistory: The Historical Imagination in Nineteenth-Century Europe* (Baltimore, 1973); and Hans Kellner, "Disorderly Conduct: Braudel's Mediterranean Satire," *History and Thought* 18, no. 2 (1979): 197–222.

4. Gerard Genette, "Boundaries of Narrative," *New Literary History* 8, no. 1 (1978): 11. See also Jonathan Culler, *Structuralist Poetics: Structuralism, Linguistics, and the Study of Literature* (Ithaca, 1975), chap. 9; Philip Pettit, *The Concept of Structuralism: A Critical Analysis* (Berkeley and Los Angeles, 1977); Tel Quel [Group], *Théorie d'ensemble* (Paris, 1968), articles by Jean-Louis Baudry, Philippe Sollers, and Julia Kristeva; Robert Scholes, *Structuralism in Literature: An Introduction* (New Haven and London, 1974), chaps. 4–5; Tzvetan Todorov, *Poétique de la prose* (Paris, 1971), chap. 9; and Paul

Zumthor, *Langue, texte, énigme* (Paris, 1975), pt. 4.

5. Genette, "Boundaries of Narrative," 8–9.

6. Ibid., 9. Cf. Emile Benveniste, *Problems in General Linguistics,* trans. Mary Elizabeth Meek (Coral Gables, Fla., 1971), 208.

7. See Louis O. Mink, "Narrative Form as a Cognitive Instrument," and Lionel Gossman, "History and Literature," both in *The Writing of History: Literary Form and Historical Understanding,* ed. Robert H. Canary and Henry Kozicki (Madison, Wis., 1978), with complete bibliography on the problem of narrative form in historical writing.

8. For purposes of economy, I use as representative of the conventional view of the history of historical writing Harry Elmer Barnes, *A History of Historical Writing* (New York, 1963), chap. 3, which deals with medieval historiography in the West. Cf. Robert Scholes and Robert Kellogg, *The Nature of Narrative* (Oxford, 1976), 64, 211.

9. White, *Metahistory,* 318–85.

10. Peter Gay, *Style in History* (New York, 1974), 189.

11. *Annales Sangallenses Maiores, dicti Hepidanni,* ed. Ildefonsus ab Arx, in *Monumenta Germaniae Historica,* series *Scriptores,* ed. George Heinrich Pertz, 32 vols. (Hanover, 1826; reprint, Stuttgart, 1963]), 1:72 ff.

12. Oswald Ducrot and Tzvetan Todorov, *Encyclopedic Dictionary of the Sciences of Language,* trans. Catherine Porter (Baltimore, 1979), 297–99.

13. Barnes, *History of Historical Writing,* 65.

14. G. W. F. Hegel, *The Philosophy of History,* trans. J. Sibree (New York, 1956), 60–63.

15. Roman Jakobson and Morris Halle, *Fundamentals of Language* (The Hague, 1971), 85–86.

16. Barnes, *History of Historical Writing,* 65. ff.

17. Richer, *Histoire de France, 888–995,* ed. and trans. Robert Latouche, 2 vols. (Paris, 1930–37), 1:3; further references to this work are cited parenthetically in the text (my translations).

18. *La cronica di Dino Compagni delle cose occorrenti ne'tempi suoi e La canzone morale Del Pregio dello stesso autore,* ed. Isidoro Del Lungo, 4th ed., rev. (Florence, 1902); cf. Barnes, *History of Historical Writing,* 80–81.

19. Ibid., 5.

20. Frank Kermode, *The Sense of an Ending: Studies in the Theory of Fiction* (Oxford, 1967), chap. 1.

21. Compagni, *La cronica,* 209–10.

2. The Question of Narrative in Contemporary Historical Theory

1. As Roland Barthes remarks, "Narrative is international, transhistorical, transcultural: it is simply there, like life itself" ("Introduction to the Structural Analysis of Narratives," in *Image, Music, Text,* trans. Stephen Heath [New York, 1977], 79). The narrative mode of representation is, of course, no more "natural" than any other mode of discourse, although whether it is a

primary mode, against which other discursive modes are to be contrasted, is a matter of interest to historical linguistics (see Emile Benveniste, *Problèmes de linguistique générale* [Paris, 1966]; and Gérard Genette, "Frontières du récit," *Figures II* [Paris, 49-69). E. H. Gombrich has suggested the importance of the relation between the narrative mode of representation, a distinctively historical (as against a mythical) consciousness, and "realism" in Western art (*Art and Illusion: A Study in the Psychology of Pictorial Representation* [New York, 1960], 116-46).

2. Thus, for example, Maurice Mandelbaum denies the propriety of calling the kinds of accounts produced by historians *narratives,* if this term is to be regarded as synonymous with *stories* (*The Anatomy of Historical Knowledge* [Baltimore, 1977], 25-26). In the physical sciences, narratives have no place at all, except as prefatory anecdotes to the presentation of findings; a physicist or biologist would find it strange to tell a story about his data *rather than* to analyze them. Biology became a science when it ceased to be practiced as "natural history," i.e., when scientists of organic nature ceased trying to construct the "true story" of "what happened" and began looking for the laws, purely causal and nonteleological, that could account for the evidence given by the fossil record, results of breeding practices, and so on. To be sure, as Mandelbaum stresses, a *sequential* account of a set of events is not the same as a narrative account thereof. And the difference between them is the absence of any interest in teleology as an explanatory principle in the former. Any narrative account of anything whatsoever is a teleological account, and it is for this reason as much as any other that narrativity is suspect in the physical sciences. But Mandelbaum's remarks miss the point of the conventional distinction between a chronicle and a history based on the difference between a *merely* sequential account and a narrative account. The difference is reflected in the extent to which the history thus conceived approaches the formal coherence of a story (see Hayden White, "The Value of Narrativity in the Representation of Reality," chap. 1 in this volume).

3. See Geoffrey Elton, *The Practice of History* (New York, 1967), 118-41; and J. H. Hexter, *Reappraisals in History* (New York, 1961), 8 ff. These two works may be taken as indicative of the view of the profession in the 1960s concerning the adequacy of "storytelling" to the aims and purposes of historical studies. For both, narrative representations are an option of the historian, which he may choose or not according to his purposes. The same view was expressed by Georges Lefebvre in *La Naissance de l'historiographie moderne* (lectures delivered originally in 1945-46) (Paris, 1971), 321-26.

4. The distinction between dissertation and narrative was a commonplace of eighteenth-century rhetorical theories of historical composition (See Hugh Blair, *Lectures on Rhetoric and Belles Lettres* [London, 1783], ed. Harold F. Harding [Carbondale, Ill., 1965], 259-310; see also Johann Gustav Droysen, *Historik,* ed. Peter Leyh [Stuttgart, 1977], 222-80). For a more recent statement of the distinction see Peter Gay, who writes: "Historical narration without analysis is trivial, historical analysis without narration is

incomplete" (*Style in History* [New York, 1974], 189); see also the survey by Stephan Bann, "Towards a Critical Historiography: Recent Works in Philosophy of History," *Philosophy* 56 (1981): 365–85.

5. This was Croce's earliest position on the matter. See "La storia ridotta sotto il concetto generale dell'arte" (1893), in *Primi saggi* (Bari, 1951), 3–41. Croce wrote: "Prima condizione per avere storia vera (e insième opera d'arte) è che sia possibile costruire una narrazione" (38). And: "Ma si può, in conclusione, negare che tutto il lavoro di preparazione tenda a produrre narrzioni di cio ch'è accaduto?" (40). Which was not to say, in Croce's view, that narration was in itself history. Obviously, it was the connection with facts attested by "documenti vivi" that made a historical narrative "historical." See the discussion in *Teoria e storia della storiografia* (1917) (Bari, 1966), 3–17, where Croce dilates on the difference between *chronicle* and *history*. Here it is the distinction between a "dead" and a "living" account of the past that is stressed, rather than the absence or presence of "narrative" in the account. Here, too, Croce stresses that one cannot write a genuine history on the basis of "narrations" *about* "documents" that no longer exist, and defines *chronicle* as "narrazione vuota" (11–15).

6. "Es ist eine innerliche gemeinsame Grundlage, welche sie zusammen hervortreibt" (G. W. F. Hegel, *Vorlesungen über die Philosophie der Geschichte* [Frankfurt am Main, 1970], 83; further references to this work are cited parenthetically in the text).

7. This is not to say, of course, that certain historians were not averse to the notion of a scientific politics to which historiography might contribute, as the example of Tocqueville and the whole "Machiavellian" tradition, which includes Treitschke and Weber, makes clear enough. But it is important to recognize that the notion of the science to which historiography was to contribute was always distinguished from the kind of science cultivated in the study of natural phenomena. Whence the long debate over the presumed differences between the *Geisteswissenschaften* and *Naturwissenschaften* throughout the nineteenth century, in which "historical studies" played the role of paradigm of the former kind of science. Insofar as certain thinkers, such as Comte and Marx, envisioned a science of politics based on a science of history, they were regarded less as historians than as philosophers of history and therefore not as contributors to historical studies at all.

As for the "science of politics" itself, professional historians have generally held that attempts to construct such a science on the basis of historical studies give rise to "totalitarian" ideologies of the sort represented by Nazism and Stalinism. The literature on this topic is vast, but the thrust of the argument that sustains it is admirably articulated in the work of the late Hannah Arendt. For example:

In any consideration of the modern concept of history one of the crucial problems is to explain its sudden rise during the last third of the eighteenth century and the concomitant decrease of interest in purely political thinking. . . . Where a genuine interest in political theory still survived it ended in despair, as in Tocqueville, or in the confusion of politics with history, as in Marx. For what else but despair could have inspired Tocqueville's assertion that "since the past has ceased to throw its light upon the future the mind of man wanders in obscurity"? This is actually the conclusion of the great work in which he had "delineated the society of the modern world" and in the introduction to which he had proclaimed that "a new science of politics is needed for a new world." And what else but confusion . . . could have led to Marx's identification of action with "the making of history"? ("The Concept of History," in *Between Past and Future* [London, 1961], 77)

Obviously, Arendt was lamenting, not the dissociation of historical studies from political thinking, but rather the degradation of historical studies into the "philosophy of history." Since, in her view, political thinking moves in the domain of human wisdom, a knowledge of history was certainly necessary for its "realistic" cultivation. It followed that both political thinking and historical studies ceased to be "realistic" when they began to aspire to the status of (positive) sciences.

The view was given another formulation in Karl R. Popper's influential *The Poverty of Historicism* 1944–45) (London, 1957):

I wish to defend the view, so often attacked as old-fashioned by historicists, that *history is characterized by its interest in actual, singular, or specific events, rather than in laws or generalizations.* . . . In the sense of this analysis, *all* causal explanations of a singular event can be said to be historical in so far as "cause" is always described by singular initial conditions. And this agrees entirely with the popular idea that to explain a thing causally is to explain how and why it happened, that is to say, to tell its "story." But it is only in history that we are really interested in the causal explanation of a singular event. In the theoretical sciences, such causal explanations are mainly means to a different end — the testing of universal laws. (143–44)

Popper's work was directed against all forms of social planning based on the pretension of a discovery of laws of history or, what amounted to the same thing in his view, laws of society. I have no quarrel with this point of view. My point here is merely that Popper's defense of "old-fashioned" historiography, which equates an "explanation" with the telling of a story, is a conventional way of both asserting the cognitive authority of this "old-fashioned" historiography and denying the possibility of any productive relationship between the study of history and a prospective "science of politics." See also Jörn Rüsen and Hans Süssmith, eds., *Theorien in der Geschichtswissenschaft* (Düsseldorf, 1980), 29–31.

8. The arguments set forth by this group are varied in detail, since

different philosophers give different accounts of the grounds on which a narrative account can be *considered* to be an explanation at all; and they run in diversity from the position that narrative is a "porous," "partial," or "sketchy" version of the nomological-deductive explanations given in the sciences (this is Carl Hempel's later view) to the notion that narratives "explain" by techniques such as "colligation" or "configuration," for which there are no counterparts in scientific explanations (see the anthologies of writings on the subject collected by Patrick Gardiner, ed., *Theories of History* [London, 1959]; and William H. Dray, *Philosophical Analysis and History* [New York, 1966]. See also the surveys of the subject by Dray, *Philosophy of History* [Englewood Cliffs, 1964]; and, more recently, R. F. Atkinson, *Knowledge and Explanation in History* [Ithaca, 1978]. For an early response in France to the Anglo-American debate see Paul Veyne, *Comment on écrit l'histoire: Essai d'épistémologie* [Paris, 1971], 194–209. And in Germany, Reinhart Koselleck and Wolf-Dieter Stempel, eds., *Geschichte-Ereignis und Erzählung* [Munich, 1973]).

9. The basic text is Fernand Braudel, *Ecrits sur l'histoire* (Paris, 1969), but see also, among many other works in a similarly polemical vein, François Furet, "Quantitative History," in *Historical Studies Today,* ed. F. Gilbert and S. R. Graubard (New York, 1972), 54–60; and Jerome Dumoulin and Dominique Moisie, eds., *The Historian between the Ethnologist and the Futurologist* (Paris and The Hague, 1973), proceedings of a congress held in Venice in 1971, in which the statements of Furet and Le Goff especially should be noted.

10. I stress the term *semiological* as a way of gathering under a single label a group of thinkers who, whatever their differences, have had a special interest in narrative, narration, and narrativity, have addressed the problem of historical narrative from the standpoint of a more general interest in theory of discourse, and have in common only a tendency to start from a *semiological theory of language* in their analyses. A basic, explicative text is Roland Barthes, *Elements of Semiology,* trans. Annette Lavers and Colin Smith (New York, 1968); but see also Tel Quel [Group], *Théorie d'ensemble* (Paris, 1968). And for a comprehensive theory of "semiohistory" see Paolo Valesio, *The Practice of Literary Semiotics: A Theoretical Proposal,* Centro Internazionale di Semiotica e di Linguistica, Universita di Urbino, no. 71, series D (Urbino, 1978); and idem, *Novantiqua: Rhetorics as a Contemporary Theory* (Bloomington, Ind., 1980).

A generally semiological approach to the study of narrative has engendered a new field of studies called narratology. The current state and interests of scholars working in this field can be glimpsed by a perusal of three volumes of papers collected in *Poetics Today: Narratology I, II, III,* 2 vols. (Tel Aviv, 1980–81). See also *New Literary History* 6 (1975) and 11 (1980), two volumes devoted to contemporary theories of *Narrative and Narratives;* and *On Narrative,* the special edition of *Critical Inquiry,* 6, no. 1 (1980).

11. The positions are set forth in Hans-Georg Gadamer, *Le problème de la conscience historique* (Louvain, 1963); and Paul Ricoeur, *History and Truth,*

trans. C. A. Kelbley (Evanston, Ill., 1965), idem, "The Model of the Text: Meaningful Action Considered as a Text," *Social Research* 38, no. 3 (1971); idem, "Expliquer et comprendre," *Revue philosophique de Louvain* 55 (1977); and idem, "Narrative Time," *Critical Inquiry* 7, no. 1 (1980).

12. J. H. Hexter, *Doing History* (Bloomington, Ind., 1971), 1–14, 77–106. A philosopher who holds a similar "craft" notion of historical studies is Isaiah Berlin ("The Concept of Scientific History," *History and Theory* 1, no. 1 [1960]: 11).

13. The defense of historiography as an empirical enterprise continues and is often manifested in an open suspicion of "theory" (see, for example, E. P. Thompson, *The Poverty of Theory* [London, 1978]; and the discussion of this work by Perry Anderson, *Arguments within English Marxism* [London, 1980]).

14. Fernand Braudel, "The Situation of History in 1950," trans. Sarah Matthews, in *On History* (Chicago, 1980), 11.

15. Furet's position varies according to the occasion. Compare his remarks in his "Introduction" to *In the Workshop of History*, trans. Jonathan Mandelbaum (Chicago, 1984), with those in his essay "Quantitative History," where he criticizes "histoire événementielle," not because it is concerned with "political facts" or because it is "made up of a mere narrative of certain selected 'events' along the time axis," but because "it is based on the idea that these events are unique and cannot be set out statistically, and that the unique is the material par excellence of history." He concludes: "That is why this kind of history paradoxically deals at one and the same time in the short term and in a finalistic ideology" (54).

16. Cf. Jacques Le Goff: "The *Annales* school loathed the trio formed by political history, narrative history, and chronicle or episodic (*événementielle*) history. All this, for them, was mere pseudohistory, history on the cheap, a superficial affair" ("Is Politics Still the Backbone of History?" trans. Barbara Bray, in Gilbert and Graubard, *History Studies Today*, 340).

17. According to Furet, "Traditional historical explanation obeys the logic of the narrative," which he glosses as "What comes first explains what follows." The selection of the facts is governed, he continues, by "the same implicit logic: the period takes precedence over the object being analyzed; events are chosen according to their place in a narrative, defined by a beginning and an end." He then goes on to characterize "political history" as "the model of this type of history," because "politics, in a wide sense, constitutes the prime repertoire of change," and this in turn allows the presentation of history in terms of the categories of "human freedom." Since "politics is the quintessential realm of chance, and so of freedom," history can be represented as having "the structure of a novel" (Furet, *In the Workshop of History*, 8–9).

18. Thus, Furet observes that "historians have been led to give up not only the major form of their discipline—narrative—but also its favorite subject matter—politics" because "the language of the social sciences is founded on

the search for the determinants and limits of action" rather than on the study of chance and freedom in human affairs (ibid., 9–10).

19. Some of the better expositions are: Oswald Ducrot et al., *Qu'est-ce que le structuralisme?* (Paris, 1968); Richard Macksey and Eugenio Donato, eds., *The Languages of Criticism and the Sciences of Man: The Structuralist Controversy* (Baltimore, 1970); Josué Harari, ed., *Textual Strategies: Perspectives in Post-Structuralist Criticism* (Ithaca, 1979); and John Sturrock, ed., *Structuralism and Since* (Oxford, 1979). On Structuralism and historical theory see Alfred Schmidt, *Geschichte und Struktur: Fragen einer marxistischen Historik* (Munich, 1971). I have dealt with some of the issues in two books: *Metahistory: The Historical Imagination in Nineteenth-Century Europe* (Baltimore, 1973); and *Tropics of Discourse* (Baltimore, 1978). For a fascinating example of the application of Structuralist–Post-Structuralist ideas to problems of historical inquiry and exposition see Tzvetan Todorov, *La Conquête de l'Amérique: La Question de l'autre* (Paris, 1982).

20. Claude Lévi-Strauss, *The Savage Mind* (London, 1966), chap. 9, "History and Dialectic." Lévi-Strauss writes: "In Sartre's system, history plays exactly the part of myth" (254–55). Again: "It suffices for history to move away from us in time or for us to move away from it in thought, for it to cease to be internalizable and to lose its intelligibility, a spurious intelligibility attaching to a temporary internality" (255). And again: "As we say of certain careers, history may lead to anything, provided you get out of it" (262).

21. "We need only recognize that history is a method with no distinct object corresponding to it to reject the equivalence between the notion of history and the notion of humanity" (Ibid.; see also 248–50 and 254).

22. "In fact history is tied neither to man nor to any particular object. It consists wholly in its method, which experience proves to be indispensable for cataloguing the elements of any structure whatever, human or non-human, in their entirety" (ibid., 262).

23. Ibid., 261n.

24. Claude Lévi-Strauss, *L'Origine des manières de table* (Paris, 1968), pt. 2, chap. 2.

25. See Rosalind Coward and John Ellis, *Language and Materialism: Developments in Semiology and the Theory of the Subject* (London and Boston, 1977), 81–82; and Hayden White, "Foucault's Discourse," chap. 5 in this volume.

26. Jacques Derrida, "The Law of Genre," *Critical Inquiry* 7, no. 1 (1980): 55–82; idem, "La Structure, le signe et le jeu dans le discours des sciences humaines," chap. 10 in *L'Ecriture et la différence* (Paris, 1967). Julia Kristeva writes: "In the narrative, the speaking subject constitutes itself as the subject of a family, a clan, or state group; it has been shown that the syntactically normative sentence develops within the context of prosaic and, later, historic narration. The simultaneous appearance of narrative genre and sentence limits the signifying process to an attitude of request and communica-

tion" ("The Novel as Polylogue," in Kristeva, *Desire in Language: A Semiotic Approach to Literature and Art,* ed. Leon S. Roudiez [New York, 1980], 174; see also Jean-François Lyotard, "Petite économie libidinale d'un dispositif narratif," in *Des dispositifs pulsionnels* [Paris, 1973], 180–84).

27. Roland Barthes, "Le Discours de l'histoire," *Social Science Information* (Paris, 1967), in English, "The Discourse of History," trans. Stephen Bann, in *Comparative Criticism: A Year book,* vol. 3, ed. E. S. Schaffer (Cambridge, 1981), 7.

28. Roland Barthes, *Mythologies,* trans. Annette Lavers (New York, 1972), 148–59.

29. Barthes, "The Discourse of History," 16–17.

30. Ibid., 18.

31. "Beyond the narrational level begins the world" (Barthes, "Introduction to the Structural Analysis of Narratives," 115).

32. Ibid., 124.

33. Barthes, "The Discourse of History," 17.

34. Cf. Anderson, *Arguments within English Marxism,* 14, 98, 162.

35. See the remarks of Daniel Bell and Peter Wiles in Dumoulin and Moisi, *The Historian,* 64–71, 89–90.

36. Roman Jakobson, "Linguistics and Poetics," in *Style in Language,* ed. Thomas A. Sebeok (Cambridge, 1960), 352–58. This essay by Jakobson is absolutely essential for the understanding of theory of discourse as it has developed within a generally semiological orientation since the 1960s. It should be stressed that whereas many of the Post-Structuralists have taken their stand on the arbitrariness of the sign and *a fortiori* the arbitrariness of the constitution of discourses in general, Jakobson continued to insist on the possibility of intrinsic meaning's residing even in the phoneme. Hence, whereas discursive referentiality was regarded as an illusion by the more radical Post-Structuralists, such as Derrida, Kristeva, Sollers, and the later Barthes, it was not so regarded by Jakobson. Referentiality was simply one of the "six basic functions of verbal communication" (Ibid., 357).

37. As Paolo Valesio puts it, "Every discourse in its functional aspect is based on a relatively limited set of mechanisms . . . that reduce every referential choice to a formal choice" (*Novantiqua,* 21). Hence,

it is never a question . . . of pointing to referents in the "real" world, of distinguishing true from false, right from wrong, beautiful from ugly, and so forth. The choice is only between what mechanisms to employ, and these mechanisms already condition every discourse since they are simplified representations of reality, inevitably and intrinsically slanted in a partisan direction. The mechanisms always appear . . . to to be gnoseological, but in reality they are *eristic:* they give a positive or a negative connotation to the *image* of the entity they describe in the very moment in which they start describing it. (21–22)

38. The example is from Arthur C. Danto, *Analytical Philosophy of History* (Cambridge, 1965).

39. See Dray, *Philosophy of History,* 43–47, 19.

40. Juri Lotman, *The Structure of the Artistic Text,* trans. Ronald Vroon (Ann Arbor, 1977), 9–20, 280–84.

41. Ibid., 35–38.

42. See Hayden White, "Introduction: The Poetics of History," in *Metahistory,* 1–38; and idem, *Tropics of Discourse,* chaps. 2–5.

43. Louis O. Mink, "Narrative Form as a Cognitive Instrument," in *The Writing of History: Literary Form and Historical Understanding,* ed. Robert H. Canary and Henry Kozicki (Madison, Wis., 1978), 143–44.

44. "Hegel remarks somewhere that all facts and personages of great importance in world history occur, as it were, twice. He forgot to add: the first time as tragedy, the second as farce. Caussidière for Danton, Louis Blanc for Robespierre, the *Montagne* of 1848 to 1851 for the *Montagne* of 1793 to 1795, the Nephew for the Uncle. And the same caricature occurs in the circumstances attending the second edition of the eighteenth Brumaire" (Karl Marx, "The Eighteenth Brumaire of Louis Buonaparte," in Karl Marx and Friedrich Engels, *Selected Works* [New York, 1969], 97). This is not merely an aphorism; the whole work is composed as a farce (see White, *Metahistory,* 320–27; and idem, "The Problem of Style in Realistic Representation: Marx and Flaubert," in *The Concept of Style,* ed. Berel Lang [Philadelphia, 1979], 213–29).

45. Hans-Georg Gadamer, "The Problem of Historical Consciousness," in *Interpretive Social Science: A Reader,* ed. Paul Rabinow and William Sullivan (Berkeley, 1979), 106–7, 134; Paul Ricoeur, "Du conflit à la convergence des méthodes en exégèse biblique," in *Exégèse et herméneutique,* ed. Roland Barthes et al. (Paris, 1971), 47–51.

46. Paul Ricoeur, "Explanation and Understanding: On Some Remarkable Connections among the Theory of the Text, Theory of Action, and Theory of History," in *The Philosophy of Paul Ricoeur: An Anthology of His Work,* ed. Charles E. Reagan and David Stewart (Boston, 1978), 165.

47. Ibid., 161, 153–58.

48. Paul Ricoeur, "The Model of the Text: Meaningful Action Considered as a Text," in Rabinow and Sullivan, *Interpretive Social Science,* 83–85, 77–79.

49. Ricoeur, "Narrative Time," 178–79; further references to this work are cited parenthetically in the text.

50. Paul Ricoeur, "Existence and Hermeneutics," in Reagan and Stewart, *The Philosophy of Paul Ricoeur,* 98.

51. Paul Ricoeur, "The Language of Faith," in ibid., 233.

52. Ibid.

53. Ricoeur, "Narrative Time," 178–84.

3. The Politics of Historical Interpretation: Discipline and De-Sublimation

1. I have followed the lead of Max Weber in my construction of the meaning of the phrase "politics of interpretation." In "Politics as a Vocation," Weber wrote that "'politics' means for us striving to share power or striving to influence the distribution of power, either among states or among groups within a state" (*From Max Weber: Essays in Sociology,* ed. H. H. Gerth and C. Wright Mills [New York, 1958], 78). Rather than discuss the age-old problem of the professional interpreter's political responsibilities, a problem already raised and rendered virtually irresolvable by Socrates' insistence that the pursuit of truth must take precedence over political exigencies, that, indeed, the pursuit of truth was the highest political good, I shall consider the politics that is endemic to the pursuit of truth itself — the striving to share power amongst interpreters themselves. The activity of interpreting becomes political when a given interpreter claims authority over rival interpreters. As long as this claim remains unreinforced by appeal to the power of the state to compel conformity of belief or conviction, it is political only in a metaphorical sense. The state is the one institution of society that claims the right to use force to compel conformity to the law. Properly speaking, interpretation becomes political only when its products appear to conduce to the breaking of a law or result in a stand for or against specific laws. Of course, interpretation becomes political when a given point of view or finding is taken as orthodoxy of belief by those holding political power, as in the Soviet Union, Germany under Hitler, or any number of religiously puritanical regimes. But these are the easy cases. It is much more difficult to determine the political nature of interpretive practices that, as in literary criticism or antiquarian scholarship, appear to have no bearing upon political policies or practices.

2. In modern Western culture, the relation between the activity of interpretation and politics has been construed in four ways: Hobbes insisted on the absolute subordination of interpretation to the demands of the state; Kant viewed the interpreter's social function as that of mediator between the people and the sovereign; Nietzsche subordinated politics to interpretation, conceived as the form that the will to power took in its intellectual or artistic manifestation; and Weber held that interpretation and politics occupied different and essentially mutually exclusive domains of culture — science for him was a "vocation" with aims and values quite other than those of "politics" (see Thomas Hobbes, *Leviathan* [Oxford, 1929], pt. 2, chaps. 26, and 29; Immanuel Kant, "The Strife of the Faculties" [pt. 2], trans. Robert E. Anchor, in *Kant on History,* ed. Lewis White Beck [New York, 1963], sec. 8, pp. 148–50; Friedrich Nietzsche, *The Genealogy of Morals,* trans. Francis Golffing [New York, 1956], preface, "First Essay," and "Second Essay," secs. 1–3; and Max Weber, "Science as a Vocation," *From Max Weber,* 145–56).

3. Here I am extending René Girard's notion of "the sacrificial crisis" to include the kinds of crises that arise in situations of radical doubt as to the kind of science that should be used for interpreting social and cultural

phenomena (see Girard's remarks about "impartiality" in *Violence and the Sacred,* trans. Patrick Gregory [Baltimore, 1977], chap. 2).

4. See Michel Foucault, *The Order of Things: An Archaeology of the Human Sciences* (New York, 1910), chap. 10. Cf. Thomas S. Kuhn, *The Structure of Scientific Revolutions,* 2d ed. (Chicago, 1970), a work that, on its appearance in 1962, effectively defined the terms within which the whole question of the difference between "professionalization" in the physical sciences and in the social sciences would be debated for the next twenty years. On the debate itself see Imre Lakatos and Alan Musgrave, eds., *Criticism and the Growth of Knowledge* (Cambridge, 1970); and J. P. Nettl, "Ideas, Intellectuals, and Structures of Dissent," in *On Intellectuals: Theoretical and Case Studies,* ed. Phillip Rieff (New York, 1969), 53–122.

5. This is the neoidealist tradition deriving from Hegel by way of Wilhelm Dilthey and Wilhelm Windelband and any number of "vitalists" and humanists in the twentieth century. On Dilthey see Michael Earmarth, *Wilhelm Dilthey: The Critique of Historical Reason* (Chicago, 1978), esp. 95–108; and for a survey of the modern development of the question of a specifically human science see Lucien Goldmann, *The Human Sciences and Philosophy,* trans. Hayden White and Robert E. Anchor (London, 1969).

6. This is the position represented by Karl R. Popper on the neopositivist side of the question and Hannah Arendt on the more humanistic side. Both thought that pretentions to the scientific in the human and social sciences contributed to the creation of totalitarian political philosophies. For their positions on social and political philosophy in general and their relation to philosophy of history in the "scientistic" vein see Popper, *The Poverty of Historicism* (London, 1957); and Arendt, *Between Past and Future* (London, 1961).

7. On the problem of narration and its relation to historical understanding see Hayden White, "The Value of Narrativity in the Representation of Reality," chap. 1 in this volume; see also Paul Ricoeur, "Narrative Time," *Critical Inquiry* 7, no. 1 (1980): 169–90. For a consideration of recent philosophers' handling of the question see Hayden White, "The Politics of Contemporary Philosophy of History," *Clio* 3, no. 1 (October 1973): 35–53; and idem, "Historicism, History, and the Figurative Imagination," *History and Theory* 14 (1975): 48–67.

8. This kind of division over the political implications of any attempt to transform historical studies into a science is as old as the debate between Edmund Burke and Thomas Paine over the possibilities of a rationalist approach to the study of society. And it appears even within Marxism from time to time (see, for example, Perry Anderson, *Arguments within English Marxism* [London, 1980], 194–207; see also *History and Theory* 17, no. 4 [1978], a special edition on *Historical Consciousness and Political Action*).

9. On historical knowledge as a basis for political realism see Hayden White, *Metahistory: The Historical Imagination in Nineteenth-Century Europe* (Baltimore, 1973), pt. 2.

10. Arendt, *Between Past and Future,* 77.

11. Ibid., 77–78.

12. It seems necessary to register this item of personal belief because the relativism with which I am usually charged is conceived by many theorists to imply the kind of nihilism that invites revolutionary activism of a particularly irresponsible sort. In my view, relativism is the moral equivalent of epistemological skepticism; moreover, I conceive relativism to be the basis of social tolerance, not a license to "do as you please." As for revolution, it always misfires. In any event, political revolution, in advanced industrial states at least, is likely to result in the further consolidation of oppressive powers rather than the dissolution thereof. After all, those who control the military-industrial-economic complex hold all the cards. In such a situation, the socially responsible interpreter can do two things: (1) expose the fictitious nature of any political program based on an appeal to what "history" supposedly teaches and (2) remain adamantly "utopian" in any criticism of political "realism."

13. On the relation between rhetoric and history see Hayden White, with Frank E. Manuel, "Rhetoric and History," in *Theories of History: Papers of the Clark Library Seminar,* ed. Peter Reill (Los Angeles, 1978), 1–25. See also Lionel Gossman, "History and Literature," in *The Writing of History: Literary Form and Historical Understanding,* ed. Robert H. Canary and Henry Kozicki (Madison, Wis., 1978).

14. See Aristotle *Rhetoric* 1.3.

15. Kant, "Strife of the Faculties," 139. Actually, Kant calls the third type of historical conceptualization "Abderitism," after the city of Abdera, where the Atomic School of Philosophy was centered in the ancient world. I have substituted *farce* because, as Beck indicates in a note, *Abderitism* was generally regarded as a synonym for *silliness;* moreover, Kant says: "It is a vain affair to have good so alternate with evil that the whole traffic of our species with itself on this globe would have to be considered as a mere farcical comedy [als ein blosses Possenspiel]" (141). Cr. *Immanuel Kants Werke,* ed. Ernst Cassirer, vol. 7, *Der Streit der Fakultäten* (Berlin, 1916), 395.

16. Paolo Valesio, *Novantiqua: Rhetorics as a Contemporary Theory* (Bloomington, Ind., 1980), 41–60.

17. See Louis O. Mink, "Narrative Form as a Cognitive Instrument," in Canary and Kozicki, *The Writing of History,* 132.

18. This position found its most forceful representation in the work of R. G. Collingwood, *The Idea of History* (Oxford and New York, 1956), pt. 5, secs. 2 and 4. See also Louis O. Mink, *Mind, History, and Dialectic: The Philosophy of R. G. Collingwood* (Bloomington, Ind., 1969), 162ff.

19. No more vexed—and mystifying—notion appears in the theory of historical writing than that of the historian's "style." It is a problem because insofar as the historian's discourse is conceived to have style, it is also conceived to be literary. But insofar as a historian's discourse is literary, it seems to *be* rhetorical, which is anathema for those who wish to claim for historical discourse the status of objective representation. On the whole question see

Roland Barthes, "Historical Discourse," in *Structuralism: A Reader,* ed. Michael Lane (London, 1970), 145–55; Peter Gay, *Style in History* (New York, 1974); and Stephen Bann, "Towards a Critical Historiography: Recent Work in Philosophy of History," *Philosophy* 56 (1981): 365–85.

20. See Thomas Weiskel, *The Romantic Sublime: Studies in the Structure and Psychology of Transcendence* (Baltimore, 1976), 78–103.

21. See Edmund Burke, *A Philosophical Inquiry into the Origin of Our Ideas of the Sublime and Beautiful* (New York, 1909), pt. 1, sec. 8, p. 36 and sec. 10, p. 39. I exclude from this discussion certain rhetoricians who continued to invoke the notion of the sublime to designate a specific style of oratory or poetic mode.

22. "Thus we are affected by strength, which is *natural* power. The power which arises from institution in kings and commanders, has the same connexion with terror. Sovereigns are frequently addressed with the title of *dread majesty*" (ibid., pt. 2, sec. 5, p. 59).

23. Burke dilates on religious awe in a passage immediately following that which describes kingly dread:

> And though a consideration of [God's] other attributes may relieve, in some measure, our apprehensions; yet no conviction of the justice with which it is exercised, nor the mercy with which it is tempered, can wholly remove the terror that naturally arises from a force which nothing can withstand. If we rejoice, we rejoice with trembling; and even whilst we are receiving benefits, we cannot but shudder at a power which can confer benefits of such mighty importance. . . . In the Scripture, wherever God is represented as appearing or speaking, everything terrible in nature is called up to heighten the awe and solemnity of the Divine presence. (ibid., 61)

Later, speaking of a kind of "pain" and "terror" that are "capable of producing delight; . . . a sort of delightful horror . . . which . . . is one of the strongest of all the passions," Burke stipulates as the object of this horror "the sublime." And he adds: "Its highest degree I call *astonishment;* the subordinate degrees are awe, reverence, and respect, which . . . stand distinguished from positive pleasure" (ibid., pt. 4, sec. 8, p. 114).

Then, in his *Reflections on the Revolution in France,* when he turns to a general description of this phenomenon, he writes:

> All circumstances taken together, the French revolution is the most astonishing that has hitherto happened in the world. The most wonderful things are brought about in many instances by means the most absurd and ridiculous; in the most ridiculous modes; and apparently, by the most contemptible instruments. Every thing seems out of nature in this strange chaos of levity and ferocity, and of all sorts of crimes jumbled together with all sorts of follies. In viewing this monstrous tragi-comic scene, the most opposite passions necessarily

succeed, and sometimes mix with each other in the mind; alternate contempt and indignation; alternate laughter and tears; alternate scorn and horror. (Edmund Burke, *Reflections on the Revolution in France,* and Thomas Paine, *The Rights of Man,* together in one volume [New York: 1961], 21–22)

Later, Burke writes that "the very idea of the fabrication of a new government, is enough to fill us with disgust and horror" (ibid., 43).

24. See ibid., 43–47.

25. *Two Essays by Friedrich von Schiller: "Naive and Sentimental Poetry" and "On the Sublime,"* trans. Julius A. Elias (New York, 1966), 205; further references to this work are cited parenthetically in the text.

26. According to Hegel, any merely "objective" view of historical phenomena would suggest that "the most effective springs of human action" are nothing other than "passions, private aims, and the satisfaction of selfish desires." Any "simply truthful combination of the miseries that have overwhelmed the noblest of nations and polities and the finest exemplars of human virtue" forms a "picture of such a horrifying aspect [*furchtbarsten Gemälde*]" that we are inclined to take refuge in fatalism and to withdraw in disgust "into the more agreeable environment of our individual life, the present formed by our private aims and interests" (G. W. F. Hegel, *The Philosophy of History,* trans. J. Sibree [New York, 1956], 20–21).

27. Ibid., 21. I analyze this passage in *Metahistory,* 105–8.

28. See Immanuel Kant, *Critique of Judgment,* trans. J. H. Bernard (New York, 1951), bk. 2, "Analytic of the Sublime": "Now we may see from this that, in general, we express ourselves incorrectly if we call any *object of nature* sublime, although we can quite correctly call many objects of nature beautiful" (83).

29. "Sublimity, therefore, does not reside in anything of nature, but only in our mind, in so far as we can become conscious that we are superior to nature within, and therefore also to nature without us (so far as it influences us)." And again: "Properly speaking, the word [*sublime*] should only be applied to a state of mind, or rather to its foundation in human nature" (ibid., 104, 121).

30. Weiskel, *The Romantic Sublime,* 48.

31. Schiller, "On the Sublime," in Schiller, *Two Essays,* 210.

32. In his essay "On History" Carlyle wrote: "It is not in acted, as it is in written History: actual events are nowise so simply related to each other as parent and offspring are; every single event is an offspring not of one, but of all other events, prior or contemporaneous, and it will in its turn combine with others to give birth to new: it is an ever-living, ever-working Chaos of Being, wherein shape after shape bodies itself forth from innumerable elements" (Thomas Carlyle, "On History," in *A Carlyle Reader: Selections from the Writings of Thomas Carlyle,* ed. G. B. Tennyson [New York, 1969], 59–60; cf. White, *Metahistory,* 144–49. On Michelet see ibid., 149–62).

33. I have in mind such judgments as that of Hugh Trevor-Roper, who

in a recent essay remarks of Carlyle: "Perhaps it is the surest sign of Carlyle's genius that we read him still, and are interested in him still, although his ideas are totally discredited" ("Thomas Carlyle's Historical Philosophy," *Times Literary Supplement* 26 June 1981, 734).

34. On the "revisionist" group of historians of the Holocaust see Lucy S. Dawidowicz, "Lies about the Holocaust," *Commentary* 70, no. 6 (December 1980): 31–37. Dawidowicz surveys the entire literature on the Holocaust in *The Holocaust and the Historians* (Cambridge, Mass., 1981), an invaluable work for anyone interested in the ethics of historical interpretation. Arno J. Mayer summarizes the issues of "revisionism" in "A Note on Vidal-Naquet," his introduction to the English translation of Pierre Vidal-Naquet's "A Paper Eichmann?" *Democracy,* April 1981, 67–95.

35. It is precisely the issue of historical method that I wish to examine in this essay. Vidal-Naquet views this method as the best insurance against the kind of ideological distortion of which the "revisionists" are justly accused (see Vidal-Naquet, "A Paper Eichmann?" 74; further references to this work are cited parenthetically in the text). So, too, Dawidowicz conflates the problem of that "fairness and objectivity" for which historians strive with adherence "to methodological rules concerning the use of historical evidence" (*The Holocaust and the Historians,* 26). She remarks that "in our time, distance in writing the history of the Holocaust can be achieved by an act of will, by the imposition of discipline itself" (130). And she ends her book by citing G. J. Renier's dictum that "the morality of history-writing is exclusively methodological" (146). Yet, in her survey of the work of professional historians who have dealt with the Holocaust since World War II, she finds them all wanting in the kind of "conscientious" approach to history commended by Lord Acton as the sole possible basis of a genuinely "objective history" (144). It does not occur to her, it seems, that her study indicts the very "professionalism" that she prescribes as the necessary precondition of objectivity (133). Indeed, one could conclude from her study that the failure of historians to come to terms with the Holocaust in a morally responsible way is a result of this professionalism.

As for the question of "historical method," one can legitimately and responsibly ask what it consists of. It is a commonplace of current social scientific theory that there is no "method" specific to historical research. Claude Lévi-Strauss is only the most prominent of social theorists holding this view. In "History and Dialectic," his famous conclusion to *The Savage Mind* (London, 1966), he denies that history is either object- or method-specific. The whole issue was debated in a conference organized by Alan Bullock and Raymond Aron, held in Venice in 1971, on the relation between historical, sociological, and anthropological inquiry. Here Peter Wiles pilloried "historical method" by dismissing it as simply "measurement without theory" and stating bluntly: "There is no such thing as a historical explanation." See the account of the proceedings of the conference, *The Historian between the Ethnologist and the Futurologist,* ed. Jerome Dumoulin and Dominique Moisi (Paris and

The Hague, 1973), 89–90 and passim; and my review of this book, "The Historian at the Bridge of Sighs," *Reviews in European History* 1, no. 4 (March 1975): 437–45.

36. A. J. P. Taylor, *The Origins of the Second World War* (New York, 1964). See also William H. Dray, "Concepts of Causation in A. J. P. Taylor's *The Origins of the Second World War*," *History and Theory* 17, no. 2 (1978): 149–74.

37. See Barthes, "Historical Discourse." A new translation with an introduction by Stephen Bann appears in *Comparative Criticism: A Year Book,* vol. 3, ed. E. S. Shaffer (Cambridge, 1981), 3–19.

38. Julia Kristeva, "The Novel as Polylogue," in Kristeva, *Desire in Language: A Semiotic Approach to Literature and Art,* ed. Leon S. Roudiez (New York, 1980), esp. 201–8.

4. Droysen's *Historik:* Historical Writing as a Bourgeois Science

1. Georg G. Iggers and Norman Baker, *New Directions in European Historiography* (Middletown, Conn. 1975), 109.

2. See the essays collected in *Ansichten einer kunftigen Geschichtswissenschaft: Kritik-Theorie-Methode,* ed. Imanuel Geiss and Rainer Tamchina (Munich, 1974), esp. Volker Rittner, "Zur Krise der westdeutschen Historiographie," 75ff.; and F. Engel-Janosi, G. Klingenstein, and H. Lutz, *Denken über Geschichte: Aufsätze zur heutigen Situation des geschichtlichen Bewusstseins und der Geschichtswissenschaft* (Munich, 1974).

3. See, for example, G. P. Gooch, *History and Historians in the Nineteenth Century* (Boston, 1959), 125–31; and Eduard Fueter, *Geschichte der neuren Historiographie* (Munich, 1936), 492–96.

4. Friedrich Meinecke, "Johann Gustav Droysen: Sein Briefwechsel und seine Geschichtsschreibung, 1929/1930," in *Schaffender Speigel: Studien zur deutschen Geschichtsschreibung und Geschichtswissenschaft* (Stuttgart, 1948), 198–210.

5. Hans-Georg Gadamer, "On the Problem of Self-Understanding" [1962], in *Philosophical Hermeneutics,* trans. and ed. David E. Linge (Berkeley and Los Angeles, 1976), 48.

6. Georg G. Iggers, *The German Conception of History: The National Tradition of Historical Thought from Herder to the Present* (Middletown, Conn., 1968), 104–19.

7. Jörn Rüsen, *Begriffene Geschichte: Genesis und Begründung der Geschichtstheorie J. G. Droysens* (Paderborn, 1969); Karl-Heinz Spieler, *Untersuchungen zur Johann Gustav Droysens "Historik"* (Berlin, 1970).

8. Johann Gustav Droysen, *Historik. Band 1: Rekonstruktion der ersten vollständigen Fassung der Vorlesungen (1857); Grundriss der Historik in der ersten handschriftlichen (1857/1858) und in der letzten gedruckten Fassung (1882),* ed. Peter Leyh (Stuttgart, 1977). Since Leyh's first volume contains six works by Droysen, I use the following procedure for citations: when only the

page number is given, the reference is to the *Vorlesungen,* by far the most important of these works and the one most frequently cited. *Grundriss I* and *Grundriss* refer, respectively, to the earliest manuscript version (1857/58) and the last published version (1882/83) of that work.

9. Johann Gustav Droysen, *Historik. Vorlesungen über Enzyklopädie und Methodologie der Geschichte,* ed. Rudolf Hübner (Munich, 1937).

10. Rüsen, *Begriffene Geschichte,* 15, 61–88, 91, 113.

11. Ibid., 29. Droysen, *Vorlesungen,* in *Historik,* ed. Leyh, 258; further references to Leyh's edition of *Historik* are cited parenthetically in the text (see above, n. 8).

12. See Erich Rothacker, "J. G. Droysen's *Historik,*" in *Mensch und Geschichte: Studien zur Anthropologie und Wissenschaftsgeschichte* (Bonn, 1950), 54–58. As always, of course, Arnaldo Monigliano beat the field: see his "Genesi storica e funzione attuale del concetto di Ellenismo," originally published in 1935 and collected in *Contributo alla storia degli studi classici* (Rome, 1955), esp. 181–93.

13. R. G. Collingwood, *The Idea of History* (Oxford, 1956), 165–66; Benedetto Croce, "La Storia ridotta sotto il concetto generale dell'arte," originally published in 1893, now in *Primi saggi,* 3d ed. (Bari, 1951), 3–41.

14. See Louis Althusser, "Marxism and Humanism," in *For Marx,* trans. Ben Brewster (New York, 1969), 232–36; and idem, "Ideology and Ideological State Apparatuses (Notes towards an Investigation)," in *Lenin and Philosophy and Other Essays,* trans. Ben Brewster (New York, 1971), 127–86. On Althusser see Rosalind Coward and John Ellis, *Language and Materialism: Developments in Semiology and the Theory of the Subject* (London, 1977), 71–78. I am especially grateful to Frederic Jameson for his lectures on ideology, which I have heard on many occasions. His recent book *The Political Unconscious: Narrative as a Socially Symbolic Act* (Ithaca, 1981), places the whole subject of ideology on new ground.

15. Coward and Ellis, *Language and Materialism,* 74–78.

16. See Louis Althusser, "Freud and Lacan," in *Lenin and Philosophy,* 189–220.

17. G. G. Gervinus, *Grundzüge der Historik* (Leipzig, 1837), reprinted in *Schriften zur Literatur* (Berlin, 1962), cited in Luther Gall, "Georg Gottfried Gervinus," in *Deutsche Historiker,* vol. 5, ed. H. -U. Wehler (Göttingen, 1972), 25, n. 4.

18. The distinctions between poetry, history, and philosophy are given in Aristotle, *Poetics,* trans. Ingram Bywater, in *Introduction to Aristotle,* ed. Richard McKeon (Chicago, 1973), chap. 9, pp. 681–82.

19. Karl Löwith, *Meaning in History: The Theological Implications of the Philosophy of History* (Chicago, 1949), chap. 3.

20. Georg Lukács, "Narrate or Describe?" in *Writer and Critic and Other Essays,* trans. Arthur D. Kahn (New York, 1971), 110ff.

21. Althusser, "Freud and Lacan," 211–16.

5. Foucault's Discourse: The Historiography of Anti-Humanism

1. The English translator of *The Archeology of Knowledge* translates *énoncé* as "statement" (33). I prefer the technically more specific, or at least philosophically more familiar, "utterance," with its conative connotations, to the more static "statement." I have, accordingly, substituted the former term for the latter in all quotations from the English translation of this work—with apologies to the translator, A. M. Sheridan Smith, who has otherwise done a superb job of Englishing Foucault.

7. The Metaphysics of Narrativity: Time and Symbol in Ricoeur's Philosophy of History

1. This essay is a revised version of an appreciation of Paul Ricoeur's *Temps et récit,* vol. 1 (Paris, 1983), which I was asked to prepare for a conference held at the University of Ottawa in October 1983 to honor Ricoeur on his seventieth birthday. I have used the English translation by Kathleen McLaughlin and David Pellauer, *Time and Narrative,* vol. 1 (Chicago, 1984). When I originally wrote the essay, vol. 2 of *Temps et récit: La configuration dans le récit de fiction* (Paris, 1984) had not yet appeared. In my revision I have made use of this work, now available in an English version by the same translators, *Time and Narrative,* vol. 2 (Chicago, 1985); further references to this work, below and in parentheses in the text, are to the English translations, designated *TN* with the volume indicated.

2. Paul Ricoeur, *The Rule of Metaphor: Multidisciplinary Studies of the Creation of Meaning in Language,* trans. Robert Czerny with Kathleen McLaughlin and John Costello (Toronto, 1981).

3. Paul Ricoeur, "Narrative Time," *Critical Inquiry* 7, no. 1 (1980), 169.

4. By "secondary referentiality" Ricoeur indicates the twofold nature of all symbolic speech, its saying one thing literally and another figuratively (see *TN,* 1:57–58, 77–82). In the case of the historical narrative, its literal referent is the set of events of which it speaks, while its figurative referent is the "structure of temporality" which, following Heidegger, he calls "historicality" (*Geschichtlichkeit*). Two features of "historicality," he writes, are "the extension of time between birth and death, and the displacement of accent from the future to the past" (*Tn,* 1: 61–62).

5. On plot, emplotment, and configuration as a "grasping together" of scattered events in a symbolic mediation see *TN,* 1:41–42. Later on, Ricoeur writes: "This highlighting of the dynamic of emplotment is to me the key to the problem of the relation between time and narrative. . . . my argument in this book consists of constructing the mediation between time and narrative by demonstrating emplotment's mediating role in the mimetic process" (*TN,* 1:53–54).

6. The aporias of time reside in the fact that we cannot *not* think about

our experience of time, and yet we can never think about it both rationally and comprehensively: "The aporetical character of the pure reflection on time is of the utmost importance for all that follows in the present investigation." It is because such reflection is aporetical that the only response to it can be a poetical and specifically narrative response: "A constant thesis of this book will be that speculation on time is an inconclusive rumination to which narrative activity can alone respond. Not that this activity solves the aporias through substitution. If it does resolve them, it is in a poetical and not a theoretical sense of the word. Emplotment . . . replies to the speculative aporia with a poetic making of something capable, certainly, of clarifying the aporia. . . , but not of resolving it theoretically" (TN, 1: 6).

7. "If mimetic activity 'composes' action, it is what establishes what is necessary in composing it. It does not see the universal, it makes it spring forth. What then are its criteria? We have a partial answer in [the expression of Aristotle]: 'it is because as they look at them they have the experience of learning and reasoning out what each thing represents, concluding, for example, that "this figure is so and so"' (48b16–17). This pleasure of recognition, as Dupont Roc and Lallot put it, presupposes, I think, a prospective concept of truth, according to which to invent is to rediscover" (TN, 1: 42).

8. This theme of the historian's task as being twofold a "wording" and a "working," a signifying and an acting, a speaking and a doing, is elaborated by Ricoeur in the introduction to Histoire et verité, 2d ed. (Paris, 1955), 9. This collection of essays introduces many of the problems that will be addressed more systematically in Time and Narrative; see esp. "Objectivité et subjectivité en histoire" and "Travail et parole."

9. See Paul Ricoeur, "The Hermeneutical Function of Distanciation," in Hermeneutics and the Human Sciences: Essays on Language, Action, and Interpretation, ed. and trans. John B. Thompson (Cambridge, 1982), 140–42; cf. TN, 1: 77–80.

10. Compare Ricoeur's discussion of the relation between history and fiction in "The Fictive Experience of Time," chap. 4 of TN, 2, esp. pp. 100–101, with his discussion of historical mimesis in TN, 1: 64.

11. Ricoeur distinguishes three kinds of mimesis in narrative discourse. These are produced by symbolizations that effect mediations between (1) random events and their chronological ordering, which produces the chronicle; (2) chronicle representations of events and the history that can be made out of them by emplotment; and (3) both of these and the figures of deep temporality that serve as the ultimate referent of such modernist fables of time as Woolf's Mrs. Dalloway and Proust's The Remembrance of Things Past. See TN, 2: 30, where chronology and chronography are characterized as "the true contrary of temporality itself," and 2: 62, where "Being-within-time" is viewed as necessitating the impulse to "reckon with time" and "make calculations" of the sort that inform the chronicle form of representing time.

12. On the two basic kinds of myth see Paul Ricoeur, "The Hermeneutics of Symbols and Philosophical Reflection," in The Philosophy of Paul Ricoeur:

An Anthology of His Work, ed. Charles E. Reagan and David Stewart (Boston, 1978), 42.

13. "Without leaving everyday experience, are we not inclined to see in a given sequence of episodes of our lives (as yet) untold stories, stories that demand to be told, stories that offer anchorage points for narrative? . . . The principal consequence of [the] existential analysis of human beings as 'entangled in stories' is that narrating is a secondary process, that of 'the story's becoming known.' . . . Telling, following, understanding stories is simply the 'continuation' of these untold stories. . . . We tell stories because in the last analysis human lives need and merit being narrated" (*TN,* 1: 74–75).

14. Ricoeur, *The Rule of Metaphor,* 72–73.

15. See esp. Paul Ricoeur, "The Language of Faith," in Reagan and Stewart, *The Philosophy of Paul Ricoeur,* 232–33.

16. Ricoeur does not, of course, refer to historical narratives, nor indeed to fictional narratives, as "allegorical" in nature, because this would suggest that their secondary referents, the structures of temporality, were nothing but verbal constructions, rather than realities. He uses the term *allegory* to designate the "level of statements" in a symbolic discourse, in contrast to *metaphor,* which designates the level of "figures of speech." Symbolic discourse can then be seen to use the technique of "allegorization" at the level of statement to speak about its double referent — events or actions, on the one side, and structures of temporality, on the other (see Ricoeur, *The Rule of Metaphor,* 171–72). But this means, it seems to me, that we can distinguish a proper and an improper use of allegorization in those forms of symbolic discourse that, like historical narratives, seek to "speak otherwise" about real events, especially when it is a matter of speaking about them in their diachronic, as against their synchronic, aspects.

17. "The question that I shall continue to pursue until the end of this work is whether the paradigm of order, characteristic of tragedy, is capable of extension and transformation to the point where it can be applied to the whole narrative field. . . . the tragic muthos is set up as the poetic solution to the speculative paradox of time" (*TN,* 1: 38).

18. Charles D. Singleton, *Commedia: Elements of Structure* (Cambridge, 1965), 14.

19. Ibid., 15–16.

20. Referring to Heidegger's idea of "deep temporality" (*Zeitlichkeit*), Ricoeur says that it is "the most originary form and the most authentic experience of time, that is, the dialectic of coming to be, having been, and making present. In this dialectic, time is entirely desubstantialized. The words 'future,' 'past,' and 'present' disappear, and time itself figures as the exploded unity of the three temporal extases" (*TN,* 1: 61).

21. Ricoeur, "The Hermeneutics of Symbols," 46.

8. The Context in the Text: Method and Ideology in Intellectual History

1. For a general survey of modern theories of the sign see Roland Barthes, *Elements of Semiology*, trans. Annette Lavers and Colin Smith (New York, 1968), chap. 3; Oswald Ducrot and Tzvetan Todorov, *Encyclopedic Dictionary of the Sciences of Language*, trans. Catherine Porter (Baltimore and London, 1979), 84–90; and Paul Henle, ed., *Language, Thought, and Culture* (Ann Arbor, 1972), chap. 7.

2. See now the comprehensive survey of modern theories of ideology by Fredric Jameson, *The Political Unconscious: Narrative as a Socially Symbolic Act* (Ithaca, 1981), chap. 1.

3. Paolo Valesio, *The Practice of Literary Semiotics: A Theoretical Proposal*, Centro Internazionale di Semiotica e di Linguistica, Università di Urbino, no. 71, series D (Urbino, 1978), 1–23. For a more comprehensive theoretical statement and application, see idem, *Novantiqua: Rhetorics as a Contemporary Theory* (Bloomington, Ind., 1980), chaps. 1, 3.

4. The formulation is, of course, that of Louis Althusser, "Ideology and Ideological State Apparatuses (Notes towards an Investigation)," in *Lenin and Philosophy and Other Essays*, trans. Ben Brewster (New York, 1971), 127–86.

5. The standard edition is *The Education of Henry Adams: An Autobiography*, ed. Ernest Samuels (Boston, 1973), with indispensable notes. For reasons that are obvious I have used the earlier edition, with an introduction by D. W. Brogan (Boston, 1961).

6. See Roland Barthes, *S/Z*, trans. Richard Miller (New York, 1974), 16–21; and John Sturrock, ed., *Structuralism and Since* (Oxford, 1979), 52–80.

7. John Carlos Rowe, *Henry James and Henry Adams* (Ithaca, 1977), 242.

Index

238

INDEX

Chronicle (cont'd)
compared with history, 17, 22,
45; ending of, 18; as form of historical representation, 17, 19; as
historical truth, 45; and morality,
19; and narrative, 17–18, 42, 48;
nature of, 20–21; Richerus of
Rheims, as example of, 17; subject of, 17, 20
Chronology: in annals form, 15; and
chronicle, 17; as code, 42; and
historical representation, 20; and
history, Lévi-Strauss on, 34; as
organizing principle of historical
narrative, 16
Classics, historiographical, 180–81
Closure: in historical narrative, 19,
21, 24; Kermode on, 22–23
Codes, narrative: in annals, 8; and
tropes, 47
Communication: and narrative form,
40; theory of, and narrative, 41
Compagni, Dino, *Cronaca* of, as example of chronicle form, 22
Composition, historical, and the
imaginary, 67
Configuration, as understanding,
Ricoeur on, 50
Consciousness, historical: and authority, 16; and desire, 20–21; Hegel
on, 12; and historical reality, 20;
and humanism, 34–35; and law,
13, 15; and morality, 12–15, 23–
24; Nietzsche on, 37; and politics, Hegel on, 12; and storytelling, 14
Context, historical, and text, 186
Croce, Benedetto, on historical narrative, 5, 28, 86
Culture, historical and nonhistorical,
55–56

Dante, on allegory, 182–83
Danto, Arthur, 40
Derrida, Jacques, 201
Description, historical, and tropes, 47
Desire: and historical consciousness,
20; and historical representation,
21; in narrative, 10, 12, 19

Discipline, historical: and ideology,
60; and interpretation, 59; and
political values, 63; Ranke as
model of, 71; and repression, 62;
and rhetoric, 65; and style, 68
Discourse, historical: Barthes on, 35;
and intellectual history, 185;
meaning in, 42; and narrative, 3,
41, 53; nineteenth-century, 101;
performance model of, 42; and
reality, 20
Discourse, poetic, and logic, 39
Discourse, prose, genres of, 43
Discourse, scientific, and narrative, 26
Discourse, symbolic, Ricoeur on, 52
Discourse, theory of, x; Jakobson's,
39–40; Structuralist, 33, 36
Droysen, Johann Gustav: achievement
of, 88, 99; against Aristotle, 94;
as bourgeois ideologue, 97; compared with Marx and Nietzsche,
99; compared with Ranke, 100;
on content of history, 97; on
ethical interpretation of history,
93; his historics, 89–90; on his-
torical dialectic, 96–97; on his-
torical experience, 92; on histori-
cal interpretation, 92–93; on his-
torical objectivity, 95; on histori-
cal representation, 93–96; on his-
torical truth, 96; on historical
understanding, 89, 92; on history
and science, 93; ideology of, 88;
Methodik, 80; originality of,
102–3; on the past, 89; realism
of, 98; on referent of historical
discourse, 90–91; reputation of,
83–86; *Systematik,* 90

Education of Henry Adams: authorial
persona of, 207; D. W. Brogan
on, 194–96; codes in, 202–4;
ideology of, 204; narrative mode
of, 208; prefaces of, 197–99;
style of, 199–200
Elton, Geoffrey, 31
Emplotment: as configuration, Ricoeur on, 52; and historical
meaning, 44; and historical

Idealism, 49
Ideology: and alienation, 87; Althusser on, 86–87, 154; Arendt on, 62; bourgeois, 81; and discipline, 60; and historical knowledge, 80–81; and historical representation, 23, 30, 87–88; and historical understanding, 80–81; and history, 36, 72, 79–80, 87, 90–91, 102; and myth, x; and narrative, x, 30, 57
Iggers, Georg, 83
Imagination: and historical composition, 67; and history, 66–67; and reason, 67
Information, historical, and narration, 42
Intellectual history: and classic text, 211; and economic history, 210; and hermeneutics, 193; and ideology, 190–91; methods of, 209–10; and semiology, 208, 210–12; text and context in, 209, 212; and theory of language, 191
Interpretation: conflicts of, 58–59; in history, 28, 78; and narrative, 60; nature of, 58–59; and politics, 58–59; and taste, 78; as translation, 49
Irony, in historical thought, 104

Jakobson, Roman, 15, 139–40
Jameson, Fredric: and Auerbach's figuralism, 150–51; on Benjamin, 168; on Conrad as proto-modernist, 152, 160; on contradiction, 157–58; on dialectical criticism, 166–67; on ethical criticism, 164; on form-content relation, 153–54; and Frye, 144–45; on historical causation, 146, 149–51; on historical epochs, 156; historical theory of, 146–47; on historicism and Marxism, 155; on history and narrative, 148; on history and politics, 167–68; on history and textuality, 147; on ideology, 148, 154, 163; on ideology of form, 145–

46; on interpretation, 144, 146; on Lord Jim, 159–60; on Marxism as science and myth, 155; on Marxist criticism, 145–46; on Marxist vision of history, 156, 165; on Marx's master narrative, 148, 151, 166–67; on modernism, 152, 161–63; on modes of production, 156–57; on myth and historical vision, 154–55; on narrative and cultural identity, 149, 157–58; on narrative as socially symbolic act, 144, 148; on nineteenth-century novel, 160–61, on plot in Conrad, 160; on plot in historical representation, 158; on plot in history, 148, 150; on plot of Romance, 152; on political unconscious, 145; on referent of history, 147; on relation of Romanticism and modernism, 152, 154, 161–62; and Sartre, 147–48, 167; on text as symbolization, 146; use of Althusser's theory of causation, 147, 154; use of Greimas by, 158–60; use of Hjelmslev, 152–54; on Utopian moment in Marxism, 155, 166

Kant, Immanuel: on farcical view of history, 65; on historical knowledge, 65, 70; on knowledge, 73; on the sublime, 70
Kermode, Frank, 15, 22–23
Knowledge, historical: and ideology, 80–81; Kant on, 65, 70, 73; in Marxism, 73; and visionary politics, 72

Lacan, Jacques, 20, 36
Language: Hegelian theory of, 189; Marxist theory of, 189; Saussure's theory of, 190
Latouche, Robert, 18
Law, and historical consciousness, 13, 15
Lévi-Strauss, Claude, 33–34, 142
Literature: and history, 44, 120; and

Hayden White is professor of the history of consciousness and Presidential Professor of Historical Studies at the University of California at Santa Cruz. He is the author of *Metahistory: The Historical Imagination in Nineteenth-Century Europe* and *Tropics of Discourse: Essays in Cultural Criticism*, both available from Johns Hopkins.

THE CONTENT OF THE FORM

Designed by Martha Farlow.

Composed by A. W. Bennett, Inc., in Sabon.

Printed by the Maple Press on S. D. Warren's 50-lb. Sebago Eggshell Cream Offset and bound in Arrestox A cloth with Linweave Textra endsheets.